FROM THE HEART OF MY BOTTOM

by

William (Bill) Blevins

PROLOGUE

This account of my life and times is not meant to be a literary masterpiece. It is merely a collection of memories, anecdotes and observations, of a life lived from one point in time, to another point in time. I have written it with satirical humour because that is the way I am inclined to observe life in general, (with exceptions of course). I promise you 'the reader' that it is a true and factual narrative of my life. There will be times when it may seem farcical or even fanciful but I swear that it is none the less true.

First names will be correct as will surnames when I can recall them, unless I think that discretion is required to save someone from any embarrassment.

I hope that you find this account of my early life and formative years interesting I know that I have enjoyed recalling it for you. If on the other hand it fails to meet with your critical acclaim, it only leaves me to apologise,

'FROM THE HEART OF MY BOTTOM'.

✶✶✶✶✶✶✶

This book is dedicated to my wonderful parents.

Hilda May Blevins *(Nee Clarkson) and* Archie Blevins.

Bless you for your Genes.

CONTENTS

CHAPTER 1

The beginning

I don't know if Adolf Hitler had a personal grudge against me or what but I have been told that the German air force were dropping bombs on my home town while I was being born. It may have just been a coincidence I would have thought that I was a bit young to have offended him at that time. Unless he had thought that I had the potential to become a nuisance to him in the future. I have to admit that I have been told often enough that I can be a bit irritating, so he was possibly correct if this was his assumption.

Yes, I was born in 'The Green' maternity hospital in the town of Wallsend on Tyne, Northumberland, England, on the 27 of January 1941. This is long before the evil Margaret Thatcher (Hoick spit) changed the boundaries of the counties to fiddle the voting in her favour. She changed my part of Northumberland on the north bank of the River Tyne into 'Tyne and Wear'. Not a name to evoke romantic poetry is it. Still, I am a born Northumbrian as is my wife and three children, so, 'up yours Thatcher'.

My future wife and soul mate, Margaret Rose Magee, was born in the same maternity ward in The Green hospital, only five days earlier than me on the 22 of January 1941 the fairest of them all. My mother, Hilda May Blevins, without doubt the kindest, warmest most loving and patient woman I have ever known, had been neighbours with Margaret's mother, Mary Ann Magee for years but they had moved apart and lost touch.

The story goes, that my eldest sister Joan took me to the new Magee home to visit her friend Connie, Margaret's sister. While there, I was laid down on a couch next to the lovely Margaret and I defecated (shit to the less cultured) into her little bonnet. This story has been popular in both of our families for many years, so I thought it was worth a mention. (Our eyes met over a steaming bonnet), there must be a romantic poem in there somewhere.

My parents were Archibald (Archie) Blevins and Hilda May Blevins (nee Clarkson). When they met, my dad was a boilermaker in the shipyards of the river Tyne, although he was serving in the Royal Engineers with the British army at the time. It was during the Great War, world war one 1914-1918 and he had joined up as soon as hostilities started. My mam was a cook, in service to a posh family in a big country house, Catherine Cookson books stuff you could say. Archie was home on leave from fighting in France, he was seven years older than mam and in uniform, so it's not surprising that she fell for him. (I feel that I must point out, that although it can be a burden at times, the men in my family are all without exception, devastatingly handsome and charming).

My mother had six children, three girls and then three boys, with me being the youngest. My sisters have always referred to me as the bairn right up to the present time. My sister Joan is the eldest and is sixteen years my senior. She had a hard life, at least early on. Not long after I was born, she suffered from rheumatic fever leaving her blind due to the formation of cataracts on both of her eyes. She could tell night from day but could not see shapes at all. In those days there were no operations to remove them and in fact she remained blind until she was in her mid forties. At this point in time they decided to operate on one eye to see how successful it would be, having obtained a suitable donor cornea. The first cornea graft operations were pretty rough going because they did not have laser technology then and they had to stitch the donated cornea onto Joan's eye after first removing the cataract. This had to be done while Joan was still awake for some reason. Her head was fastened in a vice like clamp and she had to lie on her back for many days without moving before they could remove the stitches and take her head out of the clamp. It sounds like some sort of medieval torture to me. The upside of course, is that it was a success and she was able to see her own four children for the first time since they had been born. It was a very emotional time as you can imagine. Several cornea grafts later to both eyes and she is still going strong at the age of eighty five as I write this, God bless her.

My sister Hilda was a bit of a tomboy, always coming home injured after climbing trees, walls, fences etc! She once jumped a stream in the local burn and landed on some broken glass, gouging a lump out of her inner thigh. Now aged eighty three, she is still happy to lift her skirt and show the dreadful scar to anybody who is interested. She was a Tailor/dressmaker by trade and has made the wedding dresses etc., for most of the extended family. Although a very talented and skilled lady, she is as daft as a brush. She once asked my dad why the old wireless set was making a crackling sound and he told her that it was atmospherics. Later, her boyfriend came in and asked her the same question. "Oh!" she replied, "It must be that miss Ferricks again, I don't know what she's doing". I swear that this is true she always interprets things in her own innocent and usually hilarious way. I told her a joke recently "Is a sack of cackie (shit) the name of a Japanese motorbike?" I said this with reference to a 'Kawasaki'. She had a good laugh and said she would tell her husband when he came in. Later, her husband came in and she said to him, "Is a bag of shit a Japanese motorbike?" I almost fell off my chair laughing at her change of words it was funnier than the original. Apparently, she had not understood the joke and didn't know what a Kawasaki was but thought it sounded funny and just told it the way she could remember it. Priceless stuff or what?

My sister Alma, was always the drama queen of the family. I remember her having tantrum's, screaming and shouting and slamming doors, right up until she got married and left home. What I didn't know of course being a child was that she was the victim of long and painful menstrual cycles, during which she suffered greatly and had huge mood swings. (Woman troubles, Tch!). I thought a menstrual cycle was an exercise bike. (Male ignorance, Tch!) I could never understand how my loving and sweet sister could turn into a Banshee at the drop of a hat. She suffered this monthly ordeal for most of her early life, until she was given a Hysterectomy after the birth of her son Ian. Alma has a lovely singing voice and used to sing Italian opera arias for me. Joan has a lovely singing voice too and used to sing the popular ballads of the time to me, (Cultured upbringing or what?) Hilda on the other hand, sings like she's got her nipples caught in the wringer, (An old clothes drying device that squeezes the water out between two rollers) I think you get my drift. Alma has always been verbally eloquent when it comes to telling someone off for something. I've often wished that I could string my words together the way she can when I'm having an argument. She's eighty two year old as I write this and still arguing. All three of my sisters live in the same sheltered accommodation, 'Iona court' Wallsend and they take turns at falling over, when they are not driving in convoy on their electric three wheel scooters terrorising the pedestrians.

My brother Alan is probably the biggest influence on my sense of humour. While my brother Bob was always great at remembering and telling jokes, Alan has always had a unique and surreal quality to his outlook on life. All three of us boys slept in the one bed together until Alan and then Bob left home to join the army. Alan would tell us stories that he would make up as he went along. They were vulgar, sectarian, violent, anti-social, often humanly impossible but always absolutely hilarious. Bob and I would often piddle ourselves laughing and tears would roll down our cheeks. The hero in all of his stories was a lad called Eeportetie and he was the scourge of Adolf Hitler and the Nazi party. He sometimes had to chastise the Japanese too if he wasn't too busy with Adolf and his cronies. Eeportetie was only about fourteen years old and was too young to enlist in the British armed forces but he always managed to stow away on a war ship, or a Lancaster bomber. His weapons always had something to do with human excrement, urine, vomit or snots. All good boyish type humour, guaranteed to have adolescents (of all ages) falling about with laughter, it still works with me. My dad was forever at the bottom of the stairs, shouting for us to settle down and go to sleep. I asked Alan recently where he got the name for his hero from because I was never sure if it was Teety with an exclamation, as in, ee! poor Teety. Alan said no, it was just a name that he had invented. I asked him to spell it for me but he didn't know how because he had never written it down before. So, the spelling was created for 'Eeportetie' and he is now immortalised in print. Alan is seventy five years old as I write this and he is still a unique individual.

My brother Bob was considered the black sheep of the family, not because he was a bad lad or a villain but because he was a typical boy of the 'Just William' books type. He was the one that the neighbours would complain about, nothing serious, just general boyish mischief. He was always smaller than the other kids his age but he was as hard as nails. He thought of himself as a Robin Hood figure and was always getting into fights defending someone who was being bullied. (He always won too). I think because of these things, he was always our mam and dads favourite and he went on to endear himself to everyone he met in later life. While he was in the army, stationed in Germany, he became the welterweight boxing champion, three years in a row. At some point in the 1980's, he became the northern areas Judo champion, like I said, hard as nails. You may have noticed that I am using the past tense when I'm writing about Bob this is because he is the first of my siblings to have died. It has been eighteen months now and I am still trying to come to terms with the fact that he is no longer here. This is probably the reason why I decided to start this potted history of my life.

✶✶✶✶✶✶✶

CHAPTER 2

Earliest memories

The earliest memory is of my dad, standing in the back yard of our house in 'Union.St'. Wallsend. (I will describe the house later). He was holding me up to see the search lights sweeping the night sky looking for German bombers whose mission was to try and destroy the shipyards and engineering factories on Tyneside. When one of the searchlights located an enemy plane, other searchlights would focus their attention on it too. Then, the ack ack (anti- aircraft) guns along the river would endeavour to shoot them down. The tracer shells arcing across the night sky must have been a lovely sight to a child, though not to a German pilot I would surmise. When dad judged that they were getting too close, he ushered us all into the pantry located under the staircase. We never used the air raid shelters that were in every back lane between the old terraced houses. Dad reckoned that we were safer under the stairs because every bombed house he had ever seen still had the staircase intact. A lot of people had been crushed by the collapse of the concrete roofs of the shelters when the walls had been blown in by near misses.

Our house had been hit earlier in the war by an incendiary bomb designed to burst into flame and set whatever it hit ablaze, luckily it was a dud and didn't go off. It crashed through the roof, through the back bedroom ceiling, on through the bedroom floor into the kitchen below. It came to a stop when it hit the solid concrete floor of the kitchen. Instead of spewing out its evil phosphorus innards, it just lay there in abject shame for failing

Adolf and the fatherland. Every household was obliged to have a bucket of sand on the premises on the off chance that these devices could be smothered before they could go off. On this occasion the sand wasn't required and the fire wardens removed it before it could do anymore damage. The patches in the kitchen and bedroom ceilings were still there to be seen right up until I left the house in 1961 when I was twenty years old. When we were all under the stairs we would put our gasmasks on. Mine was green with a blurty thing on the front that was supposed to amuse me I assume. As I breathed, it made a loud farting noise, a laugh a minute I'm sure. I'm willing to bet that the hilarity of it wore a bit thin during the duration of the air raid.

Once we were all under the stairs, my dad would go off to his job as a volunteer ambulance driver for the rest of the night. He had been mustard gassed during his time in the Royal engineers during world war one and his lungs were too damaged for him to get into the army again for this, world war two. Still he was doing his bit by driving the ambulance during air raids.

The lung damage that he had sustained made it impossible for him to work at his trade as a boilermaker because it was really heavy work. There was no such thing as an army pension in those days and he had to take any job that he could get, driving a charabanc, (an old fashioned, single decked, open topped bus) night watchman, gate keeper, labourer. It did nothing for his self esteem that my mam had to go out to work too, to make ends meet, she was a post woman while she was pregnant with me. I didn't have the Kaiser or Adolf to contend with when I grew to be a man thank God. My 'nemesis' was the evil Margaret Thatcher (hoick, Spit). Yes, she managed to destroy the shipyards, mining and engineering on Tyneside without the use of explosives and that's more than the German air force could do.

✶✶✶✶✶✶

My next memory is of going into the scullery to get a drink of water, I was about three or four at the time. As I returned,

I tripped over the step and fell onto the concrete floor of the kitchen, the cup broke and I fell onto it gashing my nose. I was rushed up to see doctor Hacket our GP, who needed to put four stitches in it. I was left with a scar on my poor little hooter that is still there today. Luckily it doesn't detract from my innate good looks perhaps it enhances them with a touch of ruggedness. To be honest, I'm too modest to have noticed. Around the same time period, my dad took me up to the Newcastle quayside Sunday market while my mam prepared the Sunday lunch for us all. I loved going to the quayside market, because there was a stall that sold family pets such as rabbits, puppies, kittens, tortoises etc! To my young eyes, it was like a mini-zoo. The man who ran the stall would let you handle the animals if you wanted to, which of course I always did.

The stalls in those days were much more varied than they are now. With home made pies, cakes and sweets, with no refrigeration or even covers to keep the flies off but they all smelled lovely. A butcher's stall would have meat hanging everywhere and being sold at knockdown prices. There were men with accents that were strange to me, probably Yorkshire or Cockney, selling crockery or bed linen and making the crowds laugh with their sales patter. There were magicians and jugglers but best of all there was an escape artiste and I loved watching him the most. He always performed in the same spot every Sunday and his act fascinated me. He would ask someone from the crowd to fasten him into a straight jacket, wrap him in chains fastened with big padlocks. Then he would step into a large canvas bag and have the top tied with rope through eyelets. Everyone would watch him, struggling on the ground trying to free him self as they shouted encouragement. After awhile the crowd would get bored and drift away laughing, leaving my dad and me to do it alone. Dad would coax me away with the promise of a treat of some kind, after he had became bored too. I went to the quayside market for many years and I swear that I never once saw him get out of the sack. I can only assume that he had someone who rescued him every Sunday. He always got some money in his hat from the crowd though, for the amusement value I suppose.

My treat from my dad on this day was a Union Jack flag on a stick that I wanted. I was over the moon and waved it out of the trolley bus window on the way home. When we arrived, I rushed into the scullery to show my mam my lovely new flag. She was making the gravy in a large roasting tin at the time and in my excitement, I dropped the flag in the gravy. Needless to say, my flag was ruined, dripping with a mixture of meat juices, gravy salt, fat and flour. I remember being distraught when it was thrown into the bin. This is more than likely the reason why this particular trip to the quayside has stuck in my mind.

Another early memory is of a little adventure I had in about the same time period. I had been to Newcastle with my mam and dad and on our way home I spotted two horses in a field out of the upstairs window of the trolley bus. The next day, I decided to go back and find them. So without telling my mam, I got some bread out of the pantry and went to the bus stop. Trolley busses had an open platform at the back for passengers to get on and off, so when the bus came I just climbed on and went straight upstairs, sitting myself at the front so that I could see where I was going.

Being just a toddler, I couldn't be seen from the stairs at the back, so the bus conductor would not have been able to see me if he came up. When I came to the field, the horses were still there to my delight. I went downstairs and got off the bus without anyone even noticing me. I had to crossover City road, which was always busy, being a main road into Newcastle but to be honest, I can't remember how I did it.

I spent hours with the horses, following them around the field. The bread didn't last very long when I fed it to the horses but I enjoyed watching them eat the grass. When I got hungry myself, I decided to make my way home and headed back to the bus stop. Thank God I didn't have to make my way across City road again for the return journey. When I climbed onto the bus this time, the conductor spotted me and said, "Where do you think you're going little lad". I told him that I had been to see the horses and that I wanted to go home now. He asked me where home was and I reeled off, 'Union street', Wallsend, just like my mam had taught me. He must have been a parent himself and he believed my story. "Just sit here, where I can keep an eye on you", he said. When I recognised my home turf I called to him, "this is my stop mister". He asked if I was sure and a couple of passengers confirmed that Union Street was just around the corner. He let me off the bus and said, "Go straight home, do you hear". I nodded and set off around the corner to my house. When I reached it, there was a congregation of our neighbours comforting my weeping mother. When she saw me, she grabbed me and hugged me until I thought I was going to be crushed. I couldn't understand why she was so distressed and crying and threatening me with violence between hugs and kisses. I knew that the threats of violence were rubbish of course because my mam never so much as smacked my hand in her entire life, though I know that I must have deserved a good smack now and then, soft or what?

ARCHIE BLEVINS

HILDA MAY CLARKSON

HILDA MAY CLARKSON
IN SERVICE AS A COOK

MY PARENTS

11

JOAN, HILDA + ALMA

FIRST THREE

'ME' BOB + ALAN. 1956

SECOND THREE

MY MAM THE 'POSTIE'
PREGNANT WITH 'ME'
1940

MY MOTHER WITH 'ME'
HER YOUNGEST. 1941.

FIRST CLASS DELIVERY

12

CHAPTER 3

Starting school

The day that they start school is likely to be a memorable time for any child and my first day certainly was, in fact, it turned out to be a bit of a farce. Both of my parents were at work and it was left to my eldest sister Joan to get me there. Remember that Joan was blind by then and she had to rely on her memory of the area to find her way to the school. The Carville Infants school was only a few streets away from our house and she was used to finding her way to the local shops and to her boyfriends house. She was always very self-assured and confident and convinced my mam that she could do it. I've just realised that I never saw her with a white stick, perhaps they didn't give them to blind people in those days, or more likely she just wouldn't use one. Anyway, Joan duly delivered me to the school gates, gave me a kiss and sent me in.

I immediately turned around and walked past her, knowing that she couldn't see me and made my way back home. When she arrived, I was sitting on the back door step waiting for her. This scenario played itself out again the second time she took me, so she eventually had to take me inside and find my classroom. I wasn't very happy to be left there and turned into a spoiled (which I was), whining little brat (which I wasn't normally). Luckily, my first teacher, Miss Pinkerton was a lovely young woman and I remember her as having long wavy blonde hair, being tall and slim and smelling like flowers. Yes, this was the start of my first crush.

I was quite happy after that but it wasn't to be the end of the farce for me, or my sister. When the mid-morning break came, known to us as playtime, I thought that I was finished for the day and went home. Once more Joan had to take me back to school, although this time there were no tantrums, in fact I could hardly wait to get back and see the lovely Miss Pinkerton again. It was patently obvious even at this tender age that I was wired up properly.

I enjoyed my time in the infant's school, playing with plasticine, drawing with coloured crayons, learning to count with the help of littlie red and blue counters. I used to hand out the little wooden blackboards and white chalk for the class to practice the alphabet letters on. I soon learned to keep a nice new matt finished one for myself because the chalk used to skid on the old shiny ones, making it hard to write on. I was of course 'teachers pet' by now, having honed my inherent charm on the fragrant Miss Pinkerton and she also made me the milk monitor. With this lofty position, I was in charge of the distribution of the small bottles of free milk to the children. Stopped by the evil Margaret Thatcher. (Hoick, Spit). Any spare bottles were mine.

The bottles had little round cardboard inserts in the neck to retain the milk. In the centre of these inserts was a small push through hole to accommodate the drinking straw. The girls would save these cardboard caps and string them like a necklace, wearing them for days until they became too rancid with sour milk to tolerate. The infant school was the only time that I was with girls or even female teachers during my education. Once I moved up to the middle school, it was an all male environment, even when I left school and went to night classes. I made the most of my time with the fair sex I suppose, I used to drop my chalk on the floor, so that I could look up the girls skirts and see their knickers. (I didn't know why, just that it was naughty). In those days all of the girls wore navy blue gym knickers, or so it seemed to me at the time. They appeared to be about half an inch thick, with elastic in the legs that was tight enough to stop the flow of water in a fireman's hose. I never tried to look up Miss Pinkerton's skirt, due to (abject cowardice) (total respect), one of these answers is true and the other is pure conjecture. At least my memories of this lovely young woman are pure and unsullied.

The only other teacher I remember in the infant's school was the headmistress, Mrs Caruthers.

CHAPTER 4

Junior school

The Carville School was divided into three sections, mixed infants, junior/senior girls, junior/senior boys. Each section had its own schoolyard separated by a wall six feet high and no fraternising was allowed between the boys and girls except in the infants school. My move to the junior school hit me hard because I was expected to work and it was a shock to my system. My natural charm had no affect on the all male teaching staff and I have to admit that I am not the most academic person you could meet, then or now. My spelling and my maths are pitiful even to this day. In my defence, I truly believe that I may have a touch of dyslexia. It wasn't recognised back then, so I have just had to make the best of my shortcomings, rechecking everything I do, making corrections that sort of thing. I was always a good and ardent reader and I was usually the one picked to read a story out loud to the class. It must have frustrated the English teachers to hear me reading faultlessly and then having to mark my atrocious written work. I was always either top or bottom of the class in all of the subjects and I never averaged out in the middle.

I had this pointed out to me in the senior school by one my teachers, Mr Fred Airy. (Yes, the name on his door plaque was, F.AIRY). His parents must have been either completely insensitive or they had a sense of humour not too dissimilar to mine. He told me that I had what is known as a lazy brain and that if I liked a subject I would excel at it but if I didn't like a subject my brain would simply close itself down. Over the years he has been proved correct, I can actually feel myself developing tunnel vision if something doesn't grab my interest. I even tried going to a hypnotist when I was younger but it didn't help, perhaps he failed to grab my interest also.

I remember in middle school that I just couldn't grasp long division, or long multiplication sums for the life of me. One day, my usual maths teacher was off sick and the headmaster Mr Watson took over the class. Apparently he was one of the top mathematicians in the country. (He was pretty good in the towns too. Ha!Ha! Sorry). He taught me how to do long division and long multiplications in one lesson. This proves that it all depends on who is teaching you a lot of the time.

I did get to be a dinner monitor while I was in junior school, because at least I could charm the dinner ladies. This meant that I sat at the head of my table with eight other lads, four each side, I felt like a baron or something. I had to get a trolley that had been loaded by the dinner ladies and distribute the dinners and puddings to the rest of my table. "A bit menial", I hear you say, "Not a bit of it", I reply. I got any spare dinners or puddings that were left over to share with my mates you couldn't hope to get more kudos than that.

Just before I left the infants to go to the middle school, I caught measles. Nothing too serious about that but I developed pneumonia at the same time. I was a very sick little lad and at one point the doctor told my mam and dad that I may not make it through the night. These days, I would have been sent straight to hospital but I was in a makeshift bed in the living room. Mam and dad just had to sit and watch me wheezing throughout the night. I must have regained consciousness a couple of times because I can remember the room and my mams tearful face bending over me. Well I obviously survived I am still here writing this, so no cliff hanging here then. The reason I backtracked to the infants, was to point out how prone I was to childhood maladies if it was going around, I caught it. I blame it on the fact that I was not breast fed and was fed on national powdered milk because there was a war on and my mam had to go to work. This meant that I missed out on the inherited immunities I would have naturally assimilated.

The best plague by far that I caught while in the junior school was 'ringworm'. I had to have my head shaved and painted with some purple stuff. Not very attractive as you can imagine but I had a woolly commando hat that I wore to hide it. I say it was the best plague, because it didn't cause any discomfort and it wasn't debilitating. It was however contagious, which required you to stop off school for a couple of weeks. Even better, you could play outside without fear of being captured by the school board man. In those days, the school board man would come to your house if you did not turn up at school to make sure that you weren't playing truant. He took his job very seriously and I can remember him climbing over the eight feet high backyard wall and looking through the kitchen window while I was hiding under the table. I think it would be classed as trespass these days but he seemed to have certain powers of authority and people were fined for not assuring school attendance for their children. I was reminded of him when I saw the character of 'The Child Catcher' in the film 'Chitty Chitty Bang-Bang' written by 'Ian Flemming'. He was very tall and thin and always wore a long Trench coat, winter and summer. His bicycle was the biggest one that I've ever seen. Very handy for standing on, while scaling high walls no doubt. As I said, you didn't have to worry about him if you were afflicted with 'ringworm' you just took your hat off and showed him your purple baldy head. I reckon that if I'd had alopecia and a purple crayon, I might never have been educated.

The worst malady that I managed to catch was 'whooping cough', (what a sickly child I was). Whooping cough made you have prolonged coughing fits that left you almost unconscious with the lack of oxygen. Between the bouts of coughing, you had to suck in as much air as you could, which made the characteristic whooping sound. It was distressing to have and dreadful for others to listen to. I have a high pain threshold, which has been a blessing to me over the years but the thought of not being able to breathe still scares the excrement out of me since that time. I watched my uncle Willie die slowly of suffocation due to 'Emphysema' and it was a living nightmare.

My two angelic older brothers, Alan and Bob found a way to solve the noise problem if I had a coughing fit in bed. They simply pushed me under the covers and kept pushing with their feet until I reached the bottom, thus, the blankets muffled the annoying din that I was making. The boys were ahead of their time when it came to innovative thinking. I still don't know how I didn't expire though. During the winter, this technique was utilised with me becoming their hot water bottle, it's true that I'm always very hot in bed even to this day. To be fair, I had more say in the proceedings this time. It would depend on who was in my favour at the time as to which of them could put their feet on me. I suppose that it was bullying and that I should have been traumatised by it but to be honest, I never gave it a second thought. It wasn't done out of malice, it was just a solution to a problem to them, the pecking order thing.

The fact is, I could not have wished for two better big brothers. Alan used to make me wooden swords, daggers, catapults, bows and arrows on request. Bob used to stick up for me and fought many a fight on my behalf. He also showed me how to build a bogie, a wooden cart fitted with old pram wheels, with the large wheels on the back axle under the box seating section and the small wheels on the pivoted front axle for steering. You could steer by sitting with one foot on either side of the pivoted axle, pushing with the right foot to turn left and the left foot to turn right. Or if you sat with your feet on the centre floorboard you could steer by using the pulling rope attached to each end of the pivoted axle, like the reins on a horse. I preferred steering with my feet because it gave me better access to the crude handbrake. This preference was to cause me a lot of frustration in later years when I was learning to fly a glider. The rudder pedals on a glider require the exact opposite procedure and I kept turning the wrong way. Perhaps the bloke that designed gliders never had a home built bogie, what a shame. So, taking everything into account, I can see why my big brothers were always my heroes. Alan was seven years older and Bob was five years older than me.

★★*★*★*★*★*★

The six weeks summer holidays from school seemed to last forever and it was always sunny. Of course this is highly unlikely but that is how I always remember it. It was just one long adventure for my pals and me. I would get up in the morning, have a cup of tea and some jam or condensed milk on bread and then I was off out of the door. I wouldn't return home until about 5 o-clock for my tea, absolutely filthy, with scraped knees or whatever. When I said it was one long adventure, I should have said misadventure. My parents would have had a severe melt down if they had known the things that I got up to, both with my pals and sometimes on my own if I was bored.

One of our favourite places to go was the 'Howden staithes'. This was a gap in between 'Cooksons lead works' and 'Northumberland dock' on the river Tyne. It was the only place that we could reach the waters edge, with a scruffy beach about one hundred yards long. It was filthy, because in those days all of the sewers fed straight into the Tyne. Thankfully the river Tyne is the cleanest and best salmon-river in the country now. Apart from human waste, there were always lots of used condoms washed up on the shore. One of my pals told me that he had been reliably informed by his older brother, that they were what Scotsmen wore under their kilts to keep their willies warm, I believed this little fable for many years, how innocent was that. We devised a charming little game in which we each got a stick, hooked one of these river-bloated sheaths and threw them at each other. Many were the times that I had one of these latex missiles squelch around my legs or neck, hours of fun I can tell you. You don't see kids improvising like that these days do you. In a way, you could say it was a sort of re-cycling couldn't you.

CHAPTER 4

Another game we played at the staithes was a bit perilous to say the least. There were always ships tied up at the dock wharf and the bow or aft lines were tied to huge iron rings set into concrete on the staithes beach. The Tyne was a busy river then, with ships going up and down laden with exports from our area, coal, machinery, flour from our huge flourmill. This is apart from the ships that we built and repaired on both sides of the river. Not now of course, since the curse of the evil Margaret Thatcher. (Hoick, Spit). This river traffic caused bow waves to sweep up both sides of the river in watery chevrons, carrying flotsam and jetsam up the beach and causing the ships that were moored alongside the wharf to move in and out. The mooring cable would go slack when the ship was against the wharf and then it would tighten as the ship moved away from its moorings again.

The game was to grab the cable when it was slack and hold onto it as the ship moved outwards lifting us like washing on a clothesline up to about sixty feet. We would dangle there precariously until another set of waves pushed the ship back against the wharf lowering us as it did. Sometimes there would be a lull in the river traffic and we would be aloft for a longer period than was comfortable. When this happened, we would reach up with our legs and wrap them over the cable, then just hang on for the duration. One day, there was a wind blowing from the north while I was on a solo flight. The ship was being pushed away from the moorings by the strong gusts. It needed the bow waves from a large vessel to push it back but none seemed imminent. After what seemed hours but was more likely to be about ten minutes I was getting tired hanging there. Luckily I had the sense not to panic and worked my way down the cable until I was close enough to the ground to drop off, missing the rocks, old oil drums, excreta etc! We wisely gave up this game, at least for that day anyway.

We found a dead dog among the rocks one day and it held a macabre fascination for us. You couldn't tell what breed it was because it was bloated out of recognition. It could have been a Labrador from its colouration and length but it had been in the river for a long time and looked more like a maggoty pig. At someone's suggestion we decided to poke it with pointed sticks to see if we could deflate it. It proved to be a harder job than we thought and we were all getting more forceful with our thrusts. Eventually the poor distended canine burst, enveloping us in a putrid stench that defies description. Needless to say, we all regurgitated our breakfasts with projectile vomiting but at least our natural boyish curiosity had been satisfied. We now knew the unforgettable smell of decomposition, isn't science wonderful.

There was a lumber- yard close to the staithes, with huge logs piled up on top of each other and covering an area of about the size of a football pitch. There must have been thousands of these three and four feet diameter tree trunks piled in heaps like wooden mountains. Apparently they were left there to weather for many years before they were cut into timber. To us, this place was an adventure playground and we would climb the wire fence and play for hours. It was usually hide and seek or cowboys and Indians but a more adventurous pastime, was to find a gap between four of these stacked logs. It had to be just wide enough to shuffle into lying flat on our stomachs. Then we would dare each other to snake our way through the gap to the other end of the pile, about thirty feet or so. Not a game that I would recommend to those with claustrophobia, it was a bit scary at times. We would do this until the watchman spotted us and chased us out.

Also down at the staithes there was a small pit heap. There were many small coalmines in Wallsend over the years and of course many small pit heaps. We used to get bits of sheet tin or cardboard and slide down the side of the heap. It consisted of slate, rock and coal dust, which made us take on the appearance of a coalminer after a hard shift down the pit. The strange thing is, my mam never gave me a hard time when I came home absolutely scruffy. She was always smiling and happy just to know that I had been enjoying myself with my pals. She wouldn't have been able to sleep, had she known the half of it. She worked full time at 'George Angus & co., ltd.,' an oil seal manufacturer and then had to come home to do all of her housework. My sisters were all married and living elsewhere and my brothers were working. Although I did not know it, my dad was seriously ill with cancer, so the last thing that mam needed was a disaster zone of a young son to contend with.

I will describe the sort of housework that women had to cope with in those days and the facilities my mother had at her disposal. The house had one large bedroom and one small bedroom upstairs. On the ground floor we had a large front room, looking out onto a tiny garden. This room had a really lovely marble fireplace with a cast iron grate and beautiful ceramic tiles, typical of the Victorian period that the house was built in. The back of the house had the original old kitchen with a stone floor and a cast iron cooking range complete with an oven on one side and a small boiler on the other. The large fire grate had a deep shelf at the back to store coal on, so that you could just rake some of it forward onto the fire when it was getting low. This meant that you didn't have to keep going to the coalhouse all night on a winters evening. The trouble with this idea was that the little stockpile of coal could sometimes catch fire and in turn, set the soot in the chimney ablaze. This could become an inferno and the fire engines would have to be called. I've seen a couple of our neighbours houses with flames shooting out of their chimneys like rockets, very spectacular. If you swept your chimney regularly it didn't occur and dad had his own set of brushes so we never had a problem. My mam had to keep the old range black and gleaming by polishing it with black lead, (Hard work, I've tried it). Dad would get some wire wool and burnish the hinges and knob on the oven door and the tap and lid on the boiler until they looked like chrome. He had made the brass fender surround and mam would polish it with 'Brasso' or 'Meppo' till it shone like gold.

We had a wooden lean-to shed in the back yard that ran from

the original back door of the kitchen to the coalhouse. It had a fixed window to the yard and an opening skylight. We called this outbuilding our scullery. It housed a Belfast sink with a cold-water tap, a wooden workbench under the window between the sink and the door into the yard. On the other side of the scullery we had a gas oven with four gas rings. There was a small table, (The one on which my mam was making the gravy that I dropped my flag in). The beauty of having the scullery was the fact that you didn't get wet going for coal in the rain. The same couldn't be said for going to the lavatory, which was at the bottom of the yard next to the back gate. In the winter, we had to dress like Eskimos to go for a dump. We left a hurricane lamp burning to keep the water pipes from freezing up. There was no nice quilted lanolin infused toilet paper back then, so my dad would cut old newspapers into six-inch squares and hang them on a piece of string from a nail. I swear to you, on damp mornings I would go to school with yesterday's news headlines on my backside in printers ink. In the back yard we had a full-length zinc coated tin bathtub hanging on the wall. On bath nights, my mam had to boil water in pans on the gas stove and in the little boiler in the kitchen cooking range. She would put some cold water in the tin bath standing in the middle of the back yard and then pour in the hot until it was just right. Alan and Bob would get in together for their bath and when they were done I would get in for mine because it wasn't big enough for all three of us. By now, the water was a bit murky but mam would replenish it with freshly boiled water from the pans and the carbolic soap wasn't deterred by a little muck. I have no idea what my sisters did with regards to their ablutions.

During the winter we were lucky because my Granny Clarkson, the only grandparent that I knew, had a proper bath with hot and cold running water. We couldn't use it in the summer because she didn't have the fire on and it was a back boiler behind the living room fire that supplied the hot water. I loved having my bath around at my Granny's house because you could stay in for ages just topping it up with hot water from the tap now and then. She had no electricity supply and the house was lit with gas lamps in the main rooms. The bathroom was just a wooden cordoned off bit at the end of the kitchen and it didn't even have a window. This made it even better to me because you had to have candles. I was always a bit of a daydreamer and I would watch the reflections of the candles dancing off the water onto the walls and ceiling in a trance, until my mam had to almost drag me out.

Our house didn't have electricity either when we first moved into it but my dad got the electricity board to run a cable from a pole outside of the house and connect it to a coin meter and fuse box in the front room next to the gas meter. He then wired lights in every room including the lean-to scullery. He also fitted a two- hole socket onto the wall next to the window in the kitchen. I don't think that anything was earthed at all but there didn't seem to be any hard and fast regulations with regards to health and safety in those days. If you were capable, you just went ahead and did things and my dad was certainly capable. He used to fix clocks, bicycles, wireless sets, gramophone's and burst water pipes for our neighbours when he wasn't cobbling their shoes. He never got paid for any of these jobs because our neighbours were as poor as us, so they all just helped each other out as best as they could. I lived in that house for twenty years and we never had any problems with the electrics, apart from the fuse blowing now and then and even that was a rarity. Right up until I left, there was still only the one two- holed socket in the entire house. If you wanted to use any appliance such as a hairdryer, you had to plug it into a ceiling light fitting via a special adapter. Some of these adaptors had three outlets, so that you could have three appliances hanging off the same ceiling fitting, scary or what.

Having electricity in the house meant that my mam could buy a second hand washing machine. It was really only a boiler with a hand operated agitating device on the inside. You had to turn a crank backward and forward on the lid of the boiler to activate the agitator and wash the laundry. I could do this for about five minutes before I was completely exhausted, my mam would do it for half an hour changing arms between each load of washing. On top of the 'washer' was a hand operated 'wringer', two parallel rollers, turning in opposite directions when you turned the handle. You fed the wet clothes or sheets between the rollers and it squeezed the water out of them. (Remember my sister Hilda's singing, 'wringer nipples'). I was never strong enough to take over this task for my mam.

The washing was then hung on clothes lines strung across the back lane between the terraced houses if it was a nice day. If it was a wet day, it was hung on lines in the kitchen and scullery. I hated wet days because it was like living in a maze and an obstacle course all in one. All of the women did their washing on the same day, so that the back lane was only inaccessible for one day a week. This meant that they could inspect each other's washing and make critical comments, so it kept them all on their toes so to speak. Another thing that women were fanatical about was their back and front door step. These had to be scrubbed and donkey stoned regularly. Donkey stone was a block of yellow hard packed chalky substance that you dipped into water and rubbed onto your step. It left behind a smooth yellow deposit that dried like a skin on the stone step. They all used the same pattern, leaving a clear eighteen inches in the middle of the step to walk on. This left a yellow band on both outer edges and down the front of the step and I must say that it looked lovely when the whole street had been freshly donkey stoned. Another job was taking out the clippie mats, hanging them over the clothesline in the back lane and beating them with a carpet beater to get the dirt out of them. Carpet beaters were shaped like tennis rackets made from interwoven bamboo and quite ornate. Some women did in fact use tennis-rackets for the job but we had a proper one. The women usually did this on the same day too and it was like a dust storm in the 'Sahara' when they were all out bashing their mats.

My mam had her own clippie-mat making frame and I used to love helping her to make them. She would fasten hessian (sackcloth) onto the frame and lay it across two chairs so that the hessian presented a tight flat surface. We would have saved old clothes and rags for months before which the entire family would then cut into strips of what I would guess to be about four inches by half an inch. Then they would be sorted into the various colours and separated into shoeboxes. Mam would take her progger and thread the strips through the hessian. There would be a loop on one side and two tails on the other eventually forming the desired pattern. You could buy patterns for clippie mats but she had made so many over the years that she just improvised her own designs. They were really just crude versions of Indian or Turkish rugs but they were colourful and hardwearing. We had them in every room in the house in various sizes, shapes and designs. It's an arts and crafts course in some adult education colleges now.

On top of all of this, there was the ironing of the washing, which was quite a daunting task with eight people in the house. Mam would stand at the kitchen table with a sheet folded on it to act as an ironing board until late at night and sometimes through the night. The old fashioned flat iron would be on the coal fire to get hot and mam would pick it up now and then, holding it with a piece of rag, and spit on it. Depending on how much it sizzled would determine if it was the correct temperature for the type of clothes she was ironing, this was the prototype for the thermostat. My dad was given a broken electric iron off someone and he fixed it for her. This was a great help because she could just plug it into the two hole socket beside the window next to the table. She had to keep unplugging it when it got too hot because it didn't have a safety cut off. So she still had to do the spit and sizzle thing. I am almost sure that it was a 'Pifco' iron.

✝✝✝✝✝✝

Anyway I digress, I believe that I was recalling some of my misadventures. Perhaps I should introduce my pals from this period. My first two pals were, 'Jimmy Sutherland' and 'Micky Mulligan', they both lived in the next street to us 'Carville Gardens'. This meant that all of our backdoors were in the same back lane and because everyone in those days used the backdoors for entry and exit we naturally palled up from an early age. The front doors were for visits from the rent man or the doctor. The backdoors were never locked, even when everyone was out, I would like to say that this was because everyone was honest back then. More likely, if not as romantic, it was just that nobody had anything worth pinching. Jimmy Sutherland was a smashing lad whose family were all good Salvation Army goers, which was handy because the Salty bacon army (as we always called it) had their hall just across the lane from their backdoor. We were best friends until his family were given a council house a few miles away when we were about fourteen years old. We still saw each other now and then but with us going to different schools it became less and less often. Sadly Jimmy died from kidney failure when he was only twenty one and Micky and I didn't hear about his death until after his funeral. We both went to see his mam and dad and talked for ages about the wonderful times Jimmy, Micky and I had had together from being toddlers in the lane. Jimmy's mam had been over the moon that we had came to see them and talk about our wonderful friendship but his dad had to excuse himself and go upstairs to be alone. Jimmy was from Scottish stock as you can tell from his surname and you could see it. He looked like a more handsome version of 'OOR WULLIE' the cartoon character from the Scottish newspaper 'The Post'. Blonde curly hair, cheeky grin and always full of fun and mischief. I don't have a single negative thought with regards to Jimmy and I'm not just saying that because he died young.

Micky Mulligan, as you can also tell from the name, was from Irish stock and you could see that too. He was like a happy faced little leprechaun. He was a good lad too but a bit excitable at times. If he was happy or scared, he used to shake his hands wildly in front of his chest, it was very bazaar but it was Micky's own thing. He did this right up until our teens, he may still do it for all I know. We were best pals until I started work in the shipyards and he started in the coalmines and then as often happens we just saw less and less of each other. We still bump into each other now and then in Wallsend and he still has the leprechaun look about him.

Then there were my pals from school. John Moulden and John Bartlay were my pals right from the first class in the infants and stayed that way until we left school at fifteen years old to start work. We all knocked about together when we first left school and then once again drifted apart as often happens with school pals. I saw John Moulden in later years when I was working in the shipyards as an engineering fitter and John was a welder. Sadly though, I never saw John Bartlay ever again after I was sixteen. I know that he was an apprentice butcher at the time. I hope he has been happy he was a smashing lad. We all had a great childhood together, getting ourselves into some scrapes and dodgy situations and I wouldn't change it for the world. We became quite a gang in the end, not the hoodlum type gang, just a crowd of typical kids of the time.

Apart from Jimmy, Micky and the two Johns, there were, Robert Gray, Keneth Ion, Alan Oliver, Walter Meakle, Brian Ewan, Walter Duffy and Raymond Knox. There were many others who came and went but this is all getting too boring and I will only refer to any of them by their first names most of the time. Raymond Knox was an outsider, because he didn't go to a local school and he didn't live near any of us. His acceptance into our crowd was because he visited his granny on our patch. Walter Duffy was a couple of years younger than the rest of us but he lived at the top of our lane, so we let him tag along. The girls on the fringe of our gang were, Eunace Weatherstone, Winnie Howe, Marian Morgan, Gloria King and Winnie Cox.

Winnie Cox was my first girlfriend at the age of about six

but I binned her when she told me that she had kissed Billy Adams, a part time member of the gang, the flighty little tart. When my wife read this traumatic little anecdote, she laughed and said that she had fancied Billy too when she was little. I can't understand it he was a stunted little runt, whose head was too big for his body. (Pathetic isn't it, still bitter after more than sixty years). When I was about seven or eight, I got engaged to Gloria king. I bought her a little lead ring shaped like a heart at the local shop to make it official but she went back to the shop and changed it for one with a shield emblem. So I binned her as well, the insensitive little ingrate. To my satisfaction, I can tell you that her finger turned green due to the lead after a while, (there is justice in the world).

Most of our adventures were innocent but we did stray into the, shall we say, risqué at times. One day, Jimmy Sutherland and I were underneath a parked articulated lorry, inspecting the wheels and brake pipes of the huge trailer just like any boy of eight would do. Then along came one of the girls about the same age as us. I am not going to name this young lady to save any embarrassment, although I still know her and I know that she would be amused at this recollection. She couldn't find any of her female friends and wanted to play with us. We were obliged to refuse her request, explaining that it was too perilous for girls to venture beneath parked trucks and that it was a boy's job (budding chauvinists). She conceded her inferior female status and came up with an alternative pursuit for us to consider. She said, "have you ever seen a girls bare chest, because I'll show you mine if you want (The little minx). She was onto a good thing with this ploy because both Jimmy and I had seen the underside of lorries before but neither of us had seen a girl's bare chest. Being a Salvationist didn't mean that Jimmy should miss out on a free biology lesson and I was easily led. She led us to the green bus depot on Buddle Street and behind the sheds (perhaps she had made this pilgrimage before, methinks). She then undid her white blouse and lifted up her vest, displaying her boyish undeveloped chest. Jimmy and I must have looked a bit disappointed after our close inspection of her pre-pubescent upper torso, so she then made this indelible vow to us. "When I grow up and have breasts I'll show you my bare chest again", (you can't be fairer than that).

We were both gob-smacked, not because of her magnanimous offer but because she had said 'breasts'. We only knew words like that by eavesdropping adult conversations.

I still know this more than generous lady to this day and sometimes bump into her when I'm out shopping with my wife Margaret. She never did show me her bare chest again after that time. I think it was just a dangled carrot so to speak, in case she had trouble finding her pals again (I feel used). She moved away from the area with her family when she was about twelve and I didn't meet her again until I went to work in a factory. She was the union shop steward for the people in her department and a very good one at that. I can certainly vouch for her ability to negotiate from a very early age. Sadly, she is crippled with arthritis now and has trouble walking but she is still a highly intelligent and lovely warm person.

✸✸✸✸✸✸

The most perilous thing that I got up to at this age, involved an airshaft for the 'Rising Sun' coalmine in Wallsend. I have to say that I still get cold shivers up my spine when I think about what I did. The airshaft was in a field and looked like a giant well. It was a concrete circle of about fifteen feet in diameter, standing about ten feet high with a wall thickness of about two feet. We would get a large fallen tree branch, stand it against the wall to climb up and sit on the shaft rim. We always had a pocket full of stones to drop down into the black abyss and wait for the faint sound of the splash of water. I remember that I could count eight seconds before I heard a splash, so without doing the maths, lets just conclude that it was scarily deep. We would shout and listen to the echo reverberating softly in the hellish blackness, it was indeed spooky.

Now I will tell you why I said that it was perilous. Around the rim of the shaft were steel bars set into the concrete and pointing at a shallow angle inwards towards the centre. The bars were two feet long and had three holes drilled in each of them through which was threaded barbed wire. This was meant to discourage entry into the shaft obviously. The barbed wire had mostly rusted away, leaving a couple of the bars just sticking out over the black void. I can't remember whose idea it was but a new game was hatched that involved grabbing the steel bar and allowing yourself to dangle into the gaping hole, to see how long you could hang there before getting tired. The group of us on that day were, as far as I can remember, John Moulden, Robert Gray, John Bartlay and myself. Being a born leader, (correction) the daftest among the ensemble, I went for it first dangling there for I don't know how long, probably only a minute or two but it seemed like an age to me. Then John Bartlay took his turn, due to the fact that he was almost as daft as me. After a while he got tired and tried to climb back up to the rim but he just couldn't manage. I got hold of his arm and helped him to haul himself back up to safety. I remember the look of fear on his face as he hung over the echoing, hungry blackness and as we stared into each other's eyes, I have no doubt that he could see the fear in mine. The other two lads wisely declined the opportunity to give it a try and I resolved silently never to play this game again. Oh, we still climbed up to the rim now and then to drop stones and listen to the echoes but the other game was never referred to.

✶✶✶✶✶✶

A safer pastime we enjoyed (at least less horrific) was taking our bikes up to the top of the Powder Monkey hill and racing down one or other of the several tracks that we had created. The hill, we had been informed was ballast from the old sailing ships that had traded from the river Tyne for hundreds of years. The ships would fill their holds with soil from abroad rather than sail home empty, this would stabilise them and make them more seaworthy in bad weather. The story is true about the ships carrying ballast and there were several ballast hills on both sides of the river when I was young. In this case though I have my doubts because the hill was a couple of miles north of the Tyne and it doesn't seem logical to carry the ballast so far when all of the other hills were along the banks of the river. It is more likely to have been some of the excavations from the 'Rising Sun' coalmine. Come to think about it, it was right beside the airshaft that I was just telling you about. The hill was known as 'the red hill' by the kids from Newcastle because it was entirely red, the soil, dust, grit and boulders. I don't know anywhere else in the area that was so completely red, so I suppose that is why it was assumed it was brought from afar. I don't imagine any of the sailing ships ever reached Mars, do you?

We had a great time zooming down the hill just missing boulders (or not at times) and each of the tracks had a different gradient and skill level. When I was about twelve years old, I got a job on Saturday mornings with a local butchers shop. I loved this job because I had a proper delivery bike, with a small wheel on the front and a large wheel on the back. Above the front wheel was a square tubular frame, holding a large wicker basket for carrying the parcels of meat products to the butcher's customers around Wallsend. I was popular with my pals after I had delivered all of my meat because I would take them for rides in the basket. I don't know how they explained the bloodstained trousers to their mothers. One day, my first delivery was in High Farm estate, not far from the Powder Monkey hill and the temptation was too much for me to resist. It took a lot of hard work to push the heavily laden delivery bike up to the top but I thought it would be worth it. True enough, the extra weight gave me unimagined velocity but sadly the ancient mechanical steel pull-rod brakes didn't live up to the job and were virtually non-existing. I managed to navigate this cumbersome, carcass carrying, projectile all of the way to the bottom of the hill but while avoiding a large red boulder my small front wheel found an identically proportioned hole in which to take up residence. As I came in to land, I remember seeing the parcels of meat on the same trajectory. They were unwrapping themselves in slow motion and distributing their colourful animal parts like confetti at a cannibal wedding. I suffered the usual scraped knees, elbows and nose but worse than that, there were sausages, chops, liver, kidneys and various joints of meat scattered all over and covered in red dust. I gathered all of the wrapping paper and sorted out the sheets with an address on them but I still had no idea which customer got what when it came to the meat orders. I wiped as much of the red dust from the meat as I could, then I made up little parcels, sharing it all out evenly between the addresses. I then delivered them around Wallsend, making hasty exits before any customer could open up their parcel. I don't know how I got away with it but I swear to you, not a single customer complained about their order. I worked for the butcher for about a year and it was never mentioned.

✦✦✦✦✦✦

By far my favourite haunt (haunt being the operative word) was an old house that we knew as 'Doctor Aitchesons'. It was a small mansion, standing in its own walled and fenced grounds on the corner of 'High street west' and 'The Avenue' in Wallsend. It had been empty since at least before World War Two because I found out that the home guard had been billeted there during the hostilities. I have no idea why it had been abandoned for so long, it was a lovely looking structure and the building seemed to be in good repair. It had two large stable blocks, running parallel to each other away from the east wall of the house, separated from the house by a cobbled path that ran the length of the east wing. The path continued around the rear of the building and stopped at a paved terrace in front of some French doors. This was our means of entry into the house, although I hasten to add, that we didn't break in. The doors were unlocked and undamaged so I assume that some careless home guard 'squadie' had forgotten to lock up after the war.

In my memory the façade was Georgian. You entered the grounds through large ornate wrought iron gates past a cottage sized stone gatehouse. There was a large red gravel turning space for horse drawn coaches or later I suppose motorcars. The gravel continued up the side of the house to the stables before it turned to cobbles. The southern stable block had a large weather vain shaped like a headless horseman on the roof which we all thought was very spooky, it even creaked as it turned in the wind just as you would imagine it doing. The grounds to the east of the house were full of apple and pear trees, they were very tall and of the crab variety. Although we did risk life and limb to get them from time to time, they were always hard and tasteless and gave us cramps. Among the trees were many shrubs, so it was ideal for playing jungle warfare, or as we called it, 'Jap's and English'. This was politically incorrect of us on two counts. Firstly calling our Oriental brothers 'Japs' instead of Japanese and secondly for not acknowledging the assistance of the Scots, Irish, Welsh, Commonwealth and American forces in our struggle. Yes, it was very remiss of us it could be said and all I can say in our defence is, that we were war babies, it was our game anyway and last of all, even if we had heard of political correctness, we probably wouldn't have given a shit.

At the back of the house beyond the terrace, a small field stretched to the southern fence in which we had removed a plank as an escape route. It circled around and up the west side of the house, stopping at the front wall on The High Street. In the field was a concrete air-raid shelter with earth ramparts up the walls almost to the top. It must have been for the use of the home guard lads when the bombing got too close. With its ramparts, it looked like a medieval castle to us, and we would split into two groups, one group on the top defending and the other attacking. The lads on the top would stock up with old lumps of wood, cardboard boxes, discarded Christmas trees, in fact anything that could be hurled down on the invaders. Then when the missiles had been used up, we resorted to our trusty home made wooden swords. I was always the leader, due to the fact that I always had the best sword and dagger among the lads. They were carved for me by my eldest brother Alan and I am not exaggerating when I tell you that they were works of art. There were no plastic swords like they have today and my pals would just have a plain piece of timber, with a wooden hilt tied on. Mine on the other hand were made to look like the real thing with a shaped hilt and handgrip with a jewel shaped pommel. Sometimes Alan would wrap the handgrip with string to give me a better grip and also make me a matching dagger to go with the sword, they were truly beautiful. Even better than all of this, if I broke my sword he would just make me a new one without complaint, he must have inherited my dad's patience. The other lads just accepted without question, that if you had weaponry like mine, you had to be the leader. So I was always, 'Robin Hood', or 'Zorro', anyone in fact who was a heroic swordsman on the Saturday morning picture shows. Perhaps they were awe inspired by my weapons, or I could have just had a latent talent with a sword. All I know is, that I became the best swordsman in the gang and could rout any of them with ease, using either my right or left hand due to being a bit ambidextrous like my dad.

Now for the inside of the house, that we gained entry to via the French windows off the terrace you will recall. On gaining entry, you came into what I suppose was either a ballroom or a large dining room. With the light coming in through the gaps in the several boarded up 'Georgian' windows and the French doors, it was quite easy to see when your eyes became accustomed. From the doors, it was a bit spooky looking down the long rectangular room into the comparative darkness only vague shapes and outlines could be seen. There were no pieces of furniture with white sheets over them like you would expect in a ghost story, just empty wooden boxes and layers of dust on everything. At first, we would dare each other to walk to the far end of the room and back. Then we got braver and we would all go to the end and through the door on the right hand side. This portal led us into the large entrance hall that was less gloomy because of the sunlight streaming down the lovely staircase from the large window above the front door on the stair landing. It looked very inviting to us and it wasn't long before we ventured upstairs for a scout about in the upper floor rooms. Strangely, I can't remember the layout of the upstairs rooms at all, apart from the fact that we found a dumb waiter in one of the large bedrooms at the front of the house. You know the kind of thing, a small pulley operated lift device between floor's for the conveyance of food and drink etc. On further investigation, we discovered that it was linked to the dining/ ballroom downstairs.

On one occasion I was visiting the house with Micky Mulligan, Jimmy Sutherland and Walter Duffy. With Walter being a couple of years younger and quite a lot smaller than us, it was very easy for us to talk him into getting into the box of the dumb waiter to go for a ride. O K, it was probably my idea and me that talked him into it but I can promise that there would have been no coercion used, it's not my style. I have always relied on my powers of persuasion, with considerable success I have to say. (On reading that sentence back, it sounds a bit insidious doesn't it?). The upshot is, Walter was persuaded and climbed into the little box with his knees pulled up to his chin and looking apprehensive. We then pulled the rope of the pulley and he slowly disappeared into the blackness between floors and there we left him while we went outside to play. He must have been up there in the total dark for an hour before we remembered to retrieve him. As you can imagine, he was distraught and sobbing when he emerged from the box and it took us ages to comfort him. I still can't believe that I could have been so cruel and thoughtless. Walter is a retired postman now and doesn't seem to be traumatised by his nightmarish ordeal in the dumb waiter. I hope he didn't develop claustrophobia in later years, come to think about it, he did take on a job that would keep him in the open air. Children can be cruel without trying to be because they don't consider the consequences of their actions.

This has just reminded me of a remarkably stupid stunt that my brother Alan played on me when I was about five years old. He and my brother Bob had been told by my dad never to poke anything into the holes on the two-pin electric wall socket because it was very dangerous. This of course made Alan curious as to what would happen if you did. So he and Bob sat me on the kitchen table, gave me a pair of scissors and told me to poke them into the socket. I can remember a loud bang and being thrown backwards off the table and hitting the living room door. I was sitting on the floor half stunned, still holding the scissors with the tips of the blades burnt off. Smoke was pouring from the 'Bakolite' socket on the wall and the main fuse had blown leaving us with no electricity until dad could fix it. Needless to say, Alan went to bed with a very sore backside that night and I went with a burnt thumb and finger. I don't think that Alan was trying to murder me, he was just curious and Bob wasn't daft enough to comply with his wishes, so it was just the pecking order thing again.

One day when I was ten years old, we were in the old house messing about in the gloom, putting things into the dumb waiter at the far end of the ballroom to transfer upstairs. Someone yelled that they could hear footsteps coming down the stairs, so what else could it be but a ghost. This caused us all to go into escape mode and we ran for the door, this was a regular event when we played inside the spooky old place. The French windows had been closed without any of us noticing, more than likely by the same person who had yelled 'ghost'. In my headlong flight towards this rectangle of light and sanctuary, I failed to notice this unfortunate fact. I crashed through them headfirst and fell onto the terrace dazed. There was wood and glass all around me and I could feel blood pouring down my face in a cascade. I think that it was Robert Gray who took me home and I told him to say that I had tripped and hit my head on a garden wall at the top of 'The Avenue'. The reason for this subterfuge was because I wasn't supposed to play in Doctor Aitchesons house or grounds as it was still private property. My brother Bob was the only one at home and he had the sense to wrap my head in a towel, put me on the cross bar of his pushbike and take me to the accident department at 'The Green' hospital. My scalp had been lifted in a semi-circle when I had hit the wooden cross member in the French window, so that I had a flap of scalp and you could see my skull. Bob sat with me while the doctor put forty stitches in it, so I had no choice but to be brave and not cry in front of him. When they had finished stitching my scalp began to swell up like a balloon. The nurse wrapped some cotton wool around a circular bottle and used it like a rolling pin on my head. The blood gushed out like a tidal wave between the stitches and down my face and neck. I must have looked like Sissy Spacek in the film adaptation of the Steven King story 'Carrie'. We were brought home in an ambulance and the driver let Bob bring his bike in the back with us, I don't think they would do that these days. On the way home I asked Bob not to tell my dad about the bits of glass and wood that they had removed from my scalp because it would have given my story about hitting my head on a garden wall less credence. He never told, bless him.

I still played in the grounds but I never went back into the house after that. It wasn't because I was afraid to, in fact I really liked the old place but I felt guilty about destroying the French doors. I still don't know why it stood empty for all of those years it would have made a beautiful home for someone with a few quid to spend on it. I think today, it would have been at least a grade-two listed building. Unfortunately it was completely demolished along with the gatehouse and stables. The trees and shrubs, perimeter fence and wall were also taken away, leaving a large square empty plot, as though it had never existed, very sad. It was like that for many years, until they eventually built a residential home for old people on the site. It now has lawns with flowerbeds, plus a few small trees and looks very nice in its own way. I don't think that it is very likely that it will evoke wonderful and indelible memories of fun and adventure in future generations though, do you?

The last time I walked through the grounds of this magical old house, was when I was about fifteen and it was yet another adventure for me. I was on my way home late on a winters evening after being to a cinema in Newcastle to see a horror film. It was an old black and white one, 'The Beast With Five Fingers' starring 'Peter Lori'. It would have been tame stuff, compared to the blood and gore films of that genre today but it scared the crap out of me I can tell you. I got off the bus at The Avenue just across the High Street from Doctor Aitchesons, leaving my pal John Bartlay to continue to the next stop, nearer his home. It was a cold night, with the full Moon shining through fleeting clouds and sparkling on the frost covered trees. I resolved that I would test my bravery by walking right through the grounds on my own in the dark. I started out quite confidently past the gatehouse, down the drive to the left of the house leading to the stables. I remember the cobbles being slippery after the gravel of the drive and I had to tread carefully to keep my footing. The Moon went behind a cloud and I stood still in the dark waiting eagerly for its return. All I could do was listen to the thud of my heart and the squeaking of the headless horseman on the stable roof swaying in the light breeze. I couldn't stop myself looking up at him silhouetted against the moody sky. When the Moon made its welcome return and cast its lovely silver light for me, I continued my intrepid journey at a steady pace. I left the cobbles and began walking on grass, past the air raid shelter towards the gap in the fence that I knew was still there about one hundred yards in front of me. It was then that I realised that I could hear a rustling in the grass a few feet behind me. Every time I stopped, the rustling would stop a second later and when I resumed walking the rustling would begin again after a second. I looked over my shoulder with not inconsiderable reluctance, only to find no one there. The house was a mixture of dark shadows and silver, with the Moonlight glistening on the roof and un-boarded upstairs windows. The rustling that I had distinctly heard had only been a few feet behind me, so nobody could have hidden them selves that quickly. My legs needed no coaxing as I went into escape velocity in the direction of the gap in the fence. Happily the gap was still there otherwise the fence would have suffered the same fate as the French windows. It wasn't until a while later when I was crossing some frosty grass that I noticed the same rustling sound behind me. I realised that it was the frozen grass springing back up after I had trodden on it, nothing spooky. OR WAS IT. ? My new dilemma was, could I consider myself brave after this odyssey or was I just a big girls blouse for legging it for the last hundred yards. I decided in my favour due to the fact that I had made it all of the way through without actually messing in my pants.

As I have mentioned earlier, I used to follow my brother Bob around a lot in those days, not at his invitation I must add. My mam used to make him take me with him sometimes, the poor lad. It must have been a bit of a drag for him meeting his mates with his snotty nosed little brother in tow. I always returned home hurt in some way, so I think my mam stopped insisting that he should take me in the end. One time, Bob and his mates had leaned an old door against the side of the air raid shelter at the top of our back lane on 'Roman Wall'. The idea was to climb onto the roof of the shelter, which was about eight feet high and then jump off, grabbing the gas-lamp post next to it and slide down. This process would be repeated until everybody was too tired or got bored with the game. I was about six at the time and a bit scared of being on the shelter roof, so I got hold of Bob's woollen jersey for security. Bob hadn't noticed and made his jump for the post with me still hanging on. I was a skinny little thing and probably fluttered down like an autumn leaf. I landed on my chin, giving me a nasty little gash that bled profusely. Bob took me home, telling me that I should say that I had tripped over the kerb. That is how I gained the invaluable art of having a good alibi when one was required. I also gained another four stitches from Doctor Hacket.

Another jolly day out with Bob and has mates, took me to the local cricket field, opposite the Carville school on The Avenue. They had dug a shallow hole and filled it with pieces of 'Tarry-Toot' to make a fire. Tarry-Toot was a roofing material covered with tar, a bit like the roofing-felt they use today but less sophisticated and stickier. There was plenty of this stuff lying about the field because they were building American prefabricated temporary housing. This was to be a stopgap to house people who had been bombed out of their homes during the war. These temporary homes were still there into the nineteen eighties. I have to admit, that they certainly were a splendid house including central heating, bathroom with hot and cold water, built in refrigerator and wardrobes. All of these things were considered to be absolute luxury at the time, no one had a fridge and central heating was unheard of, even in the middle classes. Eventually they had to be carefully demolished because they were constructed from compressed asbestos and the new health and safety laws wouldn't allow them to be used as dwellings. Most of the occupants were still reluctant to move out and some had to be compelled I believe. Anyway, back to the Tarry-Toot burning cooking facility they had created. They planned to roast potatoes in the acrid conflagration, (sounds tasty). I would guess that I was about seven or eight at the time and I managed to fall face first into the fire. I was pulled out very quickly (they may have thought I was attempting to purloin one of their spuds) but I had hot tar on my face and I was in agony. Once again, Bob had to take me home, trying in vain to think of a plausible reason for roasting his little brothers head. On our way home with me understandably crying we crossed the path of a local bully. He wanted to know why I was crying like a big baby and pulled my hand off my face presumably to see for himself. The pain of this made me cry even louder, which was like a red flag to a bull to my brother Bob. The lad was at least a foot taller than Bob and heavy built but he got the tanning of his life that day, he must have thought he was surrounded Bob was hitting him so hard and fast. I was sitting on a garden wall and shouting, "hit him again Bob go on, hit him again". It was great being avenged and I stopped crying. When the bully started crying himself, Bob made him say 'sorry' to me. (What a hero).

When we eventually arrived home with the bully suitably chastised, my sister Joan was the only one in the house. She took charge straight away and told us that before she went blind, she had read an article somewhere that a tealeaf compress was a good way to treat burns. She went to the teapot and scooped a handful of the warm tealeaves from breakfast time and put them on my face. I held them there while Bob took me see Dr Hacket yet again. The Doctor told Bob that Joan had done the right thing because the 'tannin' in the tea had beneficial properties. On a really cold day you can still see the faint scar left by the burn. I always seemed to be doing harmful stuff to my face and head perhaps I had a subliminal guilt complex about being so damned handsome. I have no idea why I have remained so incredibly attractive for seven decades it must be in the genes I suppose. (I know you are sneering and shaking your head you philistine, can't an old man cling on to his lifelong delusions). None of these mishaps was in any way Bob's fault I have always been more than capable of getting into trouble on my own.

✶✶✶✶✶✶✶

Another of the pastimes my pals and I pursued involved climbing over the wall onto the railway tracks. There were two tracks that ran through Wallsend, the bottom line was mainly to carry shipyard workers between Newcastle and Tynemouth along the riverside. This left the top line to carry commuters in a large circle from Newcastle down to the coast and back around to Newcastle. We knew that the raised lines that ran between the two sets of rail tracks carried the electricity to power the trains. They were twice as high as the tracks that the wheels ran on. We would dare each other to jump on and off the raised track because we had been told that if you had both feet on the track at once, you would not be electrocuted. I think what saved us from certain death was the fact that the electric current only came on in short sections, just in front of the train and then off again after the train had past. My pal John Moulden had a little brother who was about three or four years old, he was somehow able to squeeze through the railings onto the top line that ran along the head of the street where they lived, 'Sharp Road'. He climbed the embankment and began crossing the tracks. He managed the rail tracks but his little legs were not long enough to get over the raised power line. He must have put one foot onto it or took hold of it I don't know but there was a flash and the poor little lad was killed instantly. The whole incident was witnessed by a man looking out of his upstairs flat window unable to stop the unfolding tragedy, how horrific is that for someone to have as an indelible memory.

This was my first introduction into the concept of death and grieving and I remember seeing how distraught Mrs., Moulden was and how vulnerable I felt witnessing such raw emotions.

A less dangerous game that we played on the railway lines was to place a half-penny piece on the rail track and then sit and wait for the train to come and run over it. The thrill was in not moving away from the track as the train thundered past us a couple of feet away from where we sat. After it was past, we would retrieve the coin from the rail and it would be the size of a penny. Strangely, it always stayed on the rail and we soon learned that you had to leave it for a while to cool down. So in effect, it was a science lesson for us, although I certainly wouldn't recommend that it becomes part of the school curriculum. There was a man who lived near to the bottom line who lifted electrocuted people off the 'live' rail on a couple of occasions with his wooden clothes-prop. He must have felt like the 'Grim Reaper'.

✚✚✚✚✚✚✚

ALAN AGED
19 YEARS

BOB AGED
17 YEARS

MY TWO BROTHERS.

'ME' AGED
14 YEARS

MY SISTER 'HILDA'.

MY MAM & SISTER
'JOAN' WITH MY
GRANNY CLARKSON
AND MY NIECE 'ANN'.

MY DAD AND MY
SISTER 'ALMA'.

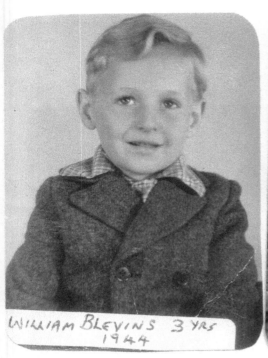

WILLIAM BLEVINS 3 YRS
1944

'ME'
AGED
8 YRS.

MY BEST PAL
JIMMY SUTHERLAND
AND 'ME' AGED 10 + 11

O.K.
ADMIT IT
I WAS A BONNY
LAD.

ALAN, BOB, 'ME,'
JOAN, HILDA, ALMA,
AS WE WERE IN 1980

HILDA AND ARCHIE BLEVINS' FAMILY

GENETIC ENGINEERING AT IT'S BEST.

48

On Neptune bank at the west end of Buddle Street in Wallsend, there is a scientific glass-making factory. It was called the 'Thermal Syndicate' but I think that it is now called 'Heraeus'. It produced glass apparatus for laboratories such as tubes, bottles and flasks, like the sort of stuff you would see bubbling away in films about mad scientists. We used to climb over the fence from the railway embankment into an enclosed yard at the rear of the factory to raid the scrap bins for glass tubes. These tubes were ideal for use as peashooters and came in opaque glass or clear glass. We also had a choice of length, the longer the tube the more accurate you could be but the shorter ones were easier to conceal if you wanted to take them into the cinema with you and be a nuisance to everyone.

One day, I had broken my peashooter and decided to get a new one to take to the pictures that night. It was raining and none of my pals wanted to join me in clambering over walls and fences to look through the bins. I resolved to go on my own, telling them that I would have more choice without them in the feeble hope that this would stir one of them to join me. It didn't, so I had to bite the bullet and go off on my own, the mutinous dogs. While I was climbing over into the yard, my foot slipped on the rain soaked railings and I fell astride the pointed steel spikes. The pain was terrible because apart from landing on my nuts, I had speared myself in the groin. I hung there for ages shouting for help but no one came. It was the rear of the factory and away from the main road so there were no passers by to hear my plaintive bleating and it was unlikely that the workers would be out to the bins in the rain. Eventually I summoned the strength to lift myself off the spike and fall back onto the railway embankment. I limped home and stuffed some of my mams clippie mat rags down my short trousers and kept them there until I stopped bleeding. I never told anyone about it because as usual I shouldn't have been there in the first place. Luckily, I did not get blood poisoning and I made sure that I didn't limp if anyone could see me till was it healed. Years later, I had to have my pubic hair shaved off for an operation and found a nasty scar in my groin. I had completely forgotten my impalement but at least it wasn't my face for a change.

✦✦✦✦✦✦

When I was nine, my maternal grandmother Sarah Ann Clarkson died, she had been a big part of my life until then. Granny Clarkson was the only grandparent that I ever knew. She was tiny, about four feet eight and she was a little firebrand in the defence of her family. If any of us had problems at school or with neighbours she was the one who would sort it out. I was given corporal punishment at school one day, which consisted of getting the flat of your hand belted with a leather strap. A teacher called Mr, Borchel was the executioner so to speak. I probably deserved it and I never complained when I got the belt, which was often I have to say. I wasn't a bad kid but my sense of fun and my already sardonic wit must have been a bit tedious for the teachers. This time I was going to my granny's for my lunch and she noticed the big red weal on the inside of my right wrist. Mr Borchel would get you to face him with your hand straight out in front of you with the palm up. Other teachers would have you standing sideways to them to give you the belt. His way meant that the leather strap made contact with more flesh, going straight up your arm as well as your hand. My granny went ballistic when she saw the ugly raised mark on my arm and took me straight back to the school. Her house was only a couple of hundred yards from the Carville School on Denham Terrace. The other kids were sitting in the hall having their school lunch when this little demonic granny entered, demanding in a loud voice, "BORCHEL, I want to see BORCHEL, NOW." I was mortified to hear her shouting Borchel instead of 'Mr', Borchel like we were expected to do to show respect but granny wasn't interested in the niceties at that moment in time. He came out of the staff room with the headmaster Mr Watson, he was looking very sheepish to say the least. Granny went through him like a dose of salts in front of the children and the headmaster I thought she was going to physically assault him. Mr Watson eventually got her calmed down and we went into the staff room. He examined my arm and then tore a strip off Mr Borchel for his obvious abuse of corporal punishment in front of the other teachers. My granny was appeased by this but left Mr Borchel knowing exactly what would happen to him if she ever had to come back to see him. She was well known at the Carville School with having three grandsons to defend. (She was a wonderful little woman my Gran).

I can still see her in my mind, standing on her cracket (a small wooden stool) possing her washing in a wooden tub of soapy water. The wooden poss stick was about the same height as she was and probably almost as heavy. She would then feed the wet washing through a huge cast iron mangle with adjustable fat wooden rollers. I loved to help her turn the big ornate cast iron wheel on the side and watch the clothes fall into her wicker wash basket. She loved cowboy films and I used to dread it when one of the local cinemas showed films featuring 'Gene Autry' or 'Roy Rogers' and more so if it was 'Hopalong Cassidy'. Although 'Hoppy' was my favourite, I couldn't really enjoy the film because my granny used to get too involved in the story. She would get excited with the action on the screen and would stand up and shout things like "HE'S BEHIND THE DOOR HOPPY". It was a bit embarrassing for a boy of nine with most of his pals in the audience.

I went to see her just before she died and she looked like a little doll lying there in her white night hood and her shawl around her shoulders. Everyone in the room spoke in hushed voices and I could hear the soft hiss of the flame in the gas mantle, which was turned down lower than normal. My visual memory of my granny Clarkson is of a petit Victorian woman with silver hair, who always wore ankle length dark clothing, lace up boots and a long pinny. She was strict with me but never stern and it would seem by all accounts that she had mellowed a lot by the time she got me to look after from time to time.

✦✦✦✦✦✦

We had seven cinemas in Wallsend when I was a youngster, five in the town itself, the 'Ritz', the 'Tyne', the 'Boro' the 'Royal' and the 'Queens'. The other two were on the outskirts of the town, the 'Lyric and the 'Pearl'. It had to be a picture that I was desperate to see for me to go to the Lyric and I never ever went to the Pearl because it was too much bother to get to. I was a member of the A.B.C. minors club at the Ritz and every Saturday morning the cinema would be heaving with hundreds of kids. My pals and I would always go upstairs to the balcony so that we could throw our empty cardboard ice cream cups onto the kids downstairs in the stalls. You always got a short black and white comedy film with someone like 'Charlie Chase' or my favourites 'The Three Stooges'. Then there would a cartoon, such as 'Donald Duck' or 'Tom and Jerry'. Then what we had all been waiting for, the serial, 'Flash Gordon' with 'Buster Crabbe' or 'Captain Marvel' or 'Superman'. The episode would always end in a cliff-hanger situation with Flash or his girlfriend falling into a pit of snakes or the likes. You would see them fall at the end of the episode and the following week it would begin with them staggering away from the edge before they could fall. Young as I was, I realised that there was something amiss with the continuity but it was all good fun regardless. After the serial came the main feature film, it was usually something swashbuckling like, 'Zorro. With 'Tyrone Power' or 'Robin Hood' with 'Errol Flynn' and it would have us sword fencing with pretend swords all of the way home.

There was no television or computer games then, so the cinema was a place of magic to us. I remember seeing 'The thief of Baghdad' with 'Sabu' and I was transfixed by it. I don't know how many times I have seen it on the television but I still love it, even though the special effects are crude by modern standards it is still mesmerising. Money was a scarcity to us, so we had to improvise by inventing ways of sneaking into the cinemas for free. The most daring of these scams was our means of getting into the 'Ritz'. It involved one of us (we took turns) climbing up a drainpipe that went up the back wall of the cinema past the upstairs men's toilet window, which was about forty feet high. The window was always left open, presumably to allow fresh air into the toilets. I don't know why it was but there was always an emergency fire exit next to the gentleman's toilet in all of the cinemas. Whoever climbed the drainpipe would listen at the window to make sure that the coast was clear then climb through into the toilet. They would then come down the emergency stairway and open the fire exit door. The rest of us would then close the doors behind us and go up to the toilets. We would leave one by one at intervals so as not to attract attention and finding a seat. The easier way was to club any money that we had together and one of us would pay to get in then follow the same procedure with the fire doors. This method caused arguments because we didn't all have the same coppers to put into the kitty. Also of course, it wasn't as fiscally attractive or as daring as climbing the pipe. My big brothers had a better plan, involving the exploitation of me, naturally. My job was to stand on Wallsend high street and pretend to be crying. Alan told me that I wasn't to approach anyone because it would look too contrived. I was to just stand there and look really sorry for myself until someone approached me. (He was a true scam artist). Someone would always ask me if I was alright and I was to say that I lived in 'Byker' and that I had lost my bus fare home and would be late getting back for my tea. They would give me the coppers to get home and tell me not to cry, (Most people are nice). It was one shilling (five new ence) to get into the 'Royal', so when I had collected two shillings worth of charitable donations Bob and Alan would go to the pictures. They never waited until I had amassed three shillings so that I could go in with them, they would just say, "see you inside". I never bothered trying to get my own ticket money I just made my way home. Now that conjures up a pitiful little scenario does it not? I bet you have tears in your eyes.

Another clever stratagem that we used to get into the 'Royal' was to find a discarded half ticket for the balcony that someone had dropped on the way out. The patrons from upstairs were obliged to come downstairs to use the toilet facilities. This entailed them having to exit the theatre on the High Street and walk around the corner onto Chestnut Street where the ticket booth was situated. Then having been shown their halved balcony ticket, the cashier would then wave them through the doors into the stalls. We would just walk up to the ticket booth show the lady our found half ticket and she would wave us through. Once in the theatre, the usherette would check that it was a balcony half ticket and we would go to the toilet only to exit again and find ourselves a seat. The ticket lady and the usherette would only give the ticket a cursory glance so it always worked. The fly in the ointment was the manager, who every now and again would decide to check the tickets of any young people without adult company. He was equipped with a list of the serial numbers on the tickets for that showing of the film and he could tell at a glance if your ticket wasn't in his block of numbers. I have been dragged by my ear and ejected from the 'Royal' on more than one occasion I must admit.

Comics were another big part of our lives and I used to get the 'Dandy' and the 'Beano' every week. One was delivered on Tuesday and the other on Thursday and I loved the anticipation of looking for them in the short passage between the front door and the stained glass passage door. One of my pals would get the 'Rover' and the 'Hotspur', not my favourites I have to say and some would get 'Film Fun' and 'Radio Fun'. The best comic of all, or should I say the 'Rolls Royce' of the comic world was 'The Eagle'. This comic featured 'Dan Dare' a heroic spaceman and his arch-enemy, 'The Mikon'. Dan was undoubtedly the catalyst of my lifelong love of science fiction stories. It was out of my price range at sixpence (two and a half new pence) but there was a thriving swap meet every couple of weeks and I could get an 'Eagle' for a couple of 'Dandy's and 'Beano's', depending on the competition. As we got older, about nine or ten, we progressed to American comics such as 'Superman', 'Batman' or 'Captain

Marvel'. Then when we were about twelve or thirteen we would buy horror comics like, 'Erie' or 'Weird' or 'Tales from the Crypt'. I have to say that these comics lived up to their titles and they were horrific in the extreme even by today's standards. The artwork in these publications although obscenely explicit was superbly executed, with the word executed being quite apt a lot of the time, I can see why some comic illustrators have become iconic in the art world. I must admit to having some bad dreams due to reading these comics in bed to the light of my torch.

✦✦✦✦✦✦✦

I have just thought of another of my brother Alan's solutions to a problem that seems with hindsight to be too daft to be true. My mam and dad had gone out for a rare treat to the pictures, leaving the next door neighbours teenage daughter Joan Thompson to look after us. (Poor lass). I don't know why Alan was on the kitchen table, he was probably dancing or singing for us but he managed to knock my dads prized pendulum clock off the wall. It landed bottom first, smashing the base and the glass of the pendulum case. Alan brought his planet-sized brain into action removing the broken glass and pushing the mahogany case back together as best he could. The nail hole had crumbled a bit and the nail wouldn't hold the weight of the clock. Not to be beaten, Alan went to dad's toolbox and came back with a six-inch screw. He hammered it into the nail hole until it took hold and then hung the clock back up. I have no idea why we all thought that dad wouldn't notice. The clock was hanging three inches away from the wall and had no glass in the door but I for one was impressed with Alan's ingenuity. Alan, as you may have guessed, retired to his bed that night with a sore rear once again. Even in this he was surreal, he would come up to bed wailing like he had been lashed with a cat-o-nine-tails and then the wails would turn into an Irish ditty and he would sing merrily for Bob and me. What a weird kid he was but never boring. Dad cut the box section off the clock, leaving the pendulum swinging in the open and we had it for years.

One day, close to 'Guy Fawkes' night, we went up to bed as usual and Alan produced a large impressive firework that he had hidden under the bed. He said that it was called a 'Mount Vesuvius' and as the name implies, it was shaped like a volcano and about six inches high. He had brought matches to light it, so we were all ready for a pyrotechnic extravaganza. He stood it in the middle of the bedroom and lit the blue touch paper as we all sat around it in anticipation. It was indeed a spectacular sight I must say, gushing sparks and smoke and frothing like a shaken bottle of beer. The bedroom quickly filled with the acrid smoke until we couldn't see the volcano or the sparks, although we could still hear the crackling and frothing. It seemed to go on forever and Alan was starting to panic a bit. We held our breath as he opened the two windows in the room. It smelled like the gun decks on 'H M S Victory' after the 'Battle of Trafalgar'. After the smoke had cleared a bit we all got blankets and wafted the stench of gunpowder towards the windows as best we could and Alan threw the still smouldering firework out into the garden. On closer inspection of the volcanic epicentre, we discovered that it had burned a hole through the linoleum floor covering and charred the floorboards. Alan simply moved the clippie mat over the offending crater and we then retired to our beds, having had our entertainment for the evening. Obviously it must have been discovered quite quickly but I have no memory of when, or the subsequent consequences. In my mind, it is just another of my big brothers amazing slapstick shows and imaginative but ludicrous cover-ups.

'Guy Fawkes' night and the lead up to it was always an exciting time gathering wood for our 'Bon Fire'. We would go to the local tip at the foot of 'Neptune Bank' next to the bottom railway line, to get any discarded furniture. We went around the houses asking if anyone had something they wanted rid of that would burn. Most people kept stuff just to give us at this time of year, rather than dump it themselves. Then there was

'Howdon staithes' where we would collect driftwood from the beach. We knew that if it was really heavy for its size, it was waterlogged and no good for burning. This collecting went on for weeks before the fifth of November and all of our back yards were full of wooden rubbish. Our parents must have been amazingly tolerant to put up with the mess, I don't think that it would happen today. When it was close to the big day, we would start building the bonfire. Ours was always on what we called 'The Square' which was a gap between the terraced houses along 'Neptune Road' at the bottom of 'Carville Gardens'. Other gangs would try to plunder our wood, just as we were trying to plunder theirs. This meant that a guard had to be stationed close to your unlit fire. We did shifts, depending on who was allowed to stop out the latest on these dark nights.

'Rawden Road' and 'Kitchener Terrace' were our biggest rivals and I have to admit that their Bonfires were always considerably bigger than ours. It didn't matter too much to me because I had pals in 'Kitchener Terrace' and my sister Joan's in-laws lived in 'Rawdon Road'. This meant that I could go between the three fires with impunity.

Fireworks were a great source of fun and experiment for me. My favourite by far was 'The Little Demon', which was a simple banger and cost one (old) penny. I would buy them at every opportunity on the run up to Guy Fawkes night. They were amazingly powerful and I used to place one under a steel dustbin lid in the back lane and watch it blow the lid eight feet into the air. We used to throw them at each other like hand grenades when we played soldiers and there were always reports in the papers about kids having their fingers blown off after holding them too long. My parents wisely forbid me to purchase these dangerous miniature sticks of Dynamite and because I was a considerate child, I felt obliged to make sure that I always kept my lethal hoard well concealed from them. Another of my experiments was to go down to the cross Tyne ferry-landing at the bottom of 'Benton Way' between 'Swan Hunters' shipbuilding yard and 'Wallsend dry dock'. I would take some empty milk bottles and some stones the idea was to put enough stones in the bottle to make it sink. I would then light the touch paper and drop in a 'Little Demon' stuffing newspaper into the neck of the bottle to make it semi-watertight. I would then drop it off the ferry landing into the river and we would watch the little trail of bubbles moving with the flow of the tide as it sank. Then Woomph! it would explode like a depth charge from a Naval Destroyer, the yellow/green murky water would erupt on the surface. My mates thought I was a genius when I did this for the first time, they may not have done, had the bottle exploded in my face.

My second favourite firework was the 'Roman Candle' and one day I found a piece of steel tubing that was just the right bore to allow a Roman Candle to be slid into it, like a cartridge into a shotgun. I realised that if I did this, I would be able to aim the little coloured balls of fire as they exploded out of the tube. I was playing in Jimmy Sutherlands back yard at the time and through the backdoor we could see Eunace, Marion and Winnie playing skippies on 'Roman Wall' at the top of my street. I lit the Roman Candle and shoved it into the breach of my gun, (OK pipe if you like). I guessed the trajectory and the first ball fell short of the girls, so I raised the pipe to compensate and the next five balls were nearer their target. The girls were screaming and making their escape when Jimmy's dad came out of the house having witnessed this stupid stunt through the window. He went mad at us, shouting how dangerous the whole thing was. I think that if he had not been a good 'Salvation Army' goer, he would have given us both a good hiding, luckily for me, he didn't tell my dad.

I was the victim of a firework accident myself when I was seven or eight, when a 'Catherine Wheel' came of its nail and started whizzing about wildly. It flew past my face (yes my face again) and fired sparks across my eyes, burning off my eyelashes and my eyebrows. Luckily I had closed my eyes but the lids were scorched and I couldn't see. This meant another trip to 'The

Green' hospital, where my eyes were bathed, drops put in and my eyelids covered in some sort of ointment. My brother Bob had promised to take me to see a feature length 'Walt Disney' cartoon that night and I still pestered him to take me. The cartoon was called 'The Three Caballeros' with 'Donald Duck' and two other characters that I don't remember. He took me to cheer me up and I enjoyed it, even though I can only remember seeing blurred coloured images. This is probably why 'Donald' is the only one that I can remember due to his distinctive voice.

A lad that I knew from 'Kitchener Terrace' had a 'Little Demon' dropped down his Wellington boot and was badly burned. This is why I never let my own children go out on 'Guy Fawkes' night or have any fireworks unsupervised, hypocritical I know. I knew that all three of them had inherited the 'Barmy' gene from me because they had all demonstrated their eccentricities from time to time. It was therefore inevitable that given free access to explosives they could have wreaked havoc on the community and themselves. I don't know what they got up to when they were out of our sight and I suspect that it's probably better that way. I certainly know that it was better that way for my parents, without a doubt.

✻✻✻✻✻✻

I didn't mention earlier that our house in Union Street was haunted did I, you may well laugh scornfully but it was, I can assure you. Things would go missing and then turn up in weird places, strange things happened on a daily basis like smelling pipe tobacco smoke in an upstairs bedroom when nobody had been in the house all day. You could be sitting on your own in the house listening to the wireless in the kitchen when the living room door would open and then close, then the door to the scullery would open then close again. It was as though someone had passed through the room. There was a cooling of the air when this happened. This phenomenon happened regularly as did hearing the sound of footsteps on the stairs and when I was old enough to talk I would say, "That Was Charlie' every time that it occurred. This puzzled my mam and dad because they couldn't think where I could have heard the name. There were no Charlies in our family and none of their friends or neighbours had the name for that matter. Then one day, a neighbour told my mam and dad that the previous tenant of our house had committed suicide in the small bedroom at the back. He had gassed himself, using the wall light fixing by sealing the door and window, turning on the gas and not lighting the mantle. Mam asked the name of this poor sad person and the neighbour said that it was 'Charlie Donelly'. Both of my parents told me in later years that it had sent a cold shiver down their backs, knowing that I had been calling our 'presence' 'Charlie' long before they had heard the story.

The gas pipe for the wall light fitting was still sticking out of the wall where my dad had plugged it while converting us to electricity. It was still there twenty years later when I left the house for the last time. The house didn't feel possessed or anything, in fact it was a nice house as far as I was concerned. I have to admit that I didn't feel happy going through the front living room if it was dark and I was alone in the house. It was the closet to the right of the fireplace that disturbed me. This closet housed the gas meter and if the door was the least bit open I would have to go and close it before I could cross the room to go upstairs. To make matters worse, the light switch for the room was at the far side next to the door to the stairs.

Once I had closed the closet door, my anxiety would disappear at once. I feel that perhaps this was the place where Charlie had finally made up his mind to take his own life. He would have fed coins into the gas meter and went upstairs to play out his final tragic act, so sad. The rest of the house felt perfectly normal to me, even the small bedroom. Charlie's comings and goings and mischievous acts became part of our everyday life. When we heard footfalls on the stairs or witnessed doors opening and shutting, we would just say 'hello Charlie'.

Having him with us was a great source of fun for Alan, Bob and me as you can imagine. One night when we went up to bed, Alan stayed in the hall at the bottom of the stairs and hid behind my dad's overcoat hanging on the wall coat rack. He must have stood there for thirty minutes (time means nothing to an artiste) waiting for our sister Alma to come to bed. The hall, stairs and upstairs landing had no lighting, so it was completely dark. At last, his patience was rewarded and as Alma came to the foot of the stairs, Alan reached out and put his hand on her shoulder. She moaned loudly and passed out, collapsing onto the stairs. My parents, on hearing the muffled cry, rushed through to investigate switching on the living room light as they came. Alma was lying on the stairs with eyes like organ stops gibbering about the blameless Charlie. Dad gave Alan a good telling off and sent him up to bed, while mam pacified Alma, telling her that it was only her daft brother. Bob and I were crying with laughter at Alan's account of the events. According to him, she was convulsing and frothing at the mouth with her eyes rolling like pinwheels. A gross exaggeration no doubt but it was graphically funny to us. I told you that Alma was a drama queen but I think under the same circumstances, I would have kacked my pants before I passed out.

Another ridiculous scenario also involved Alan, Alma and Charlie. My brothers had been pinching apples from a nearby orchard as boys do but when they got home mam and dad were in so they hid them in the front garden. That night when we were in bed, Bob said that he could just fancy one of the apples before we went to sleep. Alan said that he would sneak out of the front door and retrieve the stash for us. So clad only in his shirt, no pants or even underpants he went on his mission. While he was collecting the apples and holding them in his shirtfront, Alma and her boyfriend 'Jimmy Ducker' came into the little passage behind the front door to say their goodnights. Alan could hear them and knew that they would be there for ages, so he decided to go around to the back of the house. He knew that he could gain entry through the upstairs landing window from the roof of the scullery. We used to use this way of exit and entry quite often, if we had clandestine, none parentally approved tasks to perform. It was lucky that it was dark, with him holding up his apple filled shirtfront and not wearing any skiddies. He had to scuttle in his bare feet down the street, around the bottom and up the back lane to our back door. The back door was open so he was able to enter and save the blushes of any passing females. He then had to hold his shirt in his teeth while he climbed up the back door to the scullery roof. His next task was to get through the landing window, using the same teeth holding method. Half way through, he lost his toothy grip on his shirtfront and it slipped from his mouth, allowing the apples to make a break for freedom. Onto the landing they tumbled and down the stairs like the feet of an angry mob out for blood. Finally they pounded on the passage door as though they were in a frenzy to gain access to those inside. Alma went hysterical, thinking that 'Charlie' had come to get her again, you couldn't have planned it could you. (Well, perhaps Alan could have). Dad came upstairs demanding to know what was going on, we were all pretending to be asleep. At first Alan denied all knowledge of the incident but he eventually realized that it was a bit too obvious even to him. He confessed the whole farcical story, from pinching the apples to his semi-nude nocturnal odyssey but he swore that he hadn't meant to almost put his big sister into a cataleptic state. My dad gave him a telling off but he could hardly keep a straight face. Mam told us in later years, that when he got back down stairs and told her the comical chain of events, they were both in tears laughing for the rest of the night.

****

Talking about farcical stories has reminded me of the time I was in the 'Western School' playing field with my pals. There was a large horse tied to a post and happily grazing. We were wondering if it was tame enough to let us ride it, so my pal John Moulden volunteered to go up and feed it some grass to make friends with it. He gathered some lush grass and clover and approached it slowly, holding out his gift. The horse seemed pleased with his offering and started eating out of his hand, a good start we all thought. Then it took a fancy to his green woollen jumper and reached past his hand to take a bite of his belly and lift him off his feet. It didn't let go and he was just dangling from its mouth and screaming, it was like the equestrian version of the film 'Jaws'. The horse eventually decided that it didn't like the taste of wool and dropped him. Although I am sure that sheep everywhere would have been relieved to hear this news, it didn't relieve the pain that John was in at that time. When we lifted his jumper, we were glad to see that it hadn't drawn blood but he had a huge bite mark on his belly. I'm sure that a 'Vet' would have been able to tell us how old the horse was by counting the teeth marks.

Another story involving a painful episode in John's childhood involves us climbing a tree in 'Doctor Aitchesons' grounds. The branches of this beautiful old tree drooped to reach the ground and we used to climb the tree via its branches rather than its main trunk like we would normally have done. This day it had been raining earlier and the branches were slippery. I was half way up my branch when I heard John yell, he was sliding down the outside of the branch next to mine, having lost his grip on the wet bark. As I watched his rapid decent, he suddenly stopped and toppled over backwards leaving him hanging upside down. His screams were heart-rending to hear, he had hooked his scrotum on a small branch and was hanging by his testicles. It must have seemed like an eternity for poor John as he waited for us to stop laughing long enough to un-snag his nuts. I am happy to tell you, that this trauma to his tackle did not impede him in later years and he went on to procreate quite efficiently with his future wife Elizabeth.

Going to the swimming baths was another favourite pastime of mine, Wallsend baths mostly but I also visited Walker, Byker,

Newcastle and Tynemouth pools quite often. I started going at the suggestion of 'Doctor Hacket' after my bronchial period, whooping cough, pneumonia etc! He told my mam that it would be good for me to get the exercise and work my lungs. My sister Hilda's future husband Val Borthwick was a member of the Wallsend swimming club and a champion diver, so he took me under his wing. The first time that I went to Wallsend baths Val told me to ignore the low end and go straight up onto the top diving board at the deep end and jump off. I know that this journal may have given the reader reason to believe that I was a bit sparing in the common sense department but on this occasion even I was a bit dubious. Val assured me that the moment I jumped he would be diving from the side of the pool to bring me out safely when I surfaced. The clincher to this deal was when he told me that he would give me a 'half crown' (twelve and a half new pence) if I did it. This was a fortune to me and if he had wanted me to tie a house brick around my neck first it would have still seemed like a good idea to me. I climbed up to the high board and looked over the edge, it seemed like a mile down to the water but in fact it was only about ten feet. I looked over at Val and he was smiling and cheering me on. I don't think I hesitated too long before I jumped and true to his word Val was there when I surfaced. He put one of his arms around me and conveyed me to the stairs I was truly exhilarated by the whole experience. I couldn't wait to do it again and did so several times with Val waiting to rescue me. That is until the last time when I came up to find that Val wasn't there. I looked towards the side of the pool and he was standing talking to somebody while I was floundering. I shouted but I knew that he couldn't hear me for the clamour of noise and echoing in the enclosed swimming pool. I splashed and spluttered my way towards the side in a crude dog paddle style and then Val just reached down pulling me out of the water saying, "There you go, now you can swim". He was right, I had learned to swim in one easy lesson and I was half a crown richer into the bargain. Val went on to teach me how to swim in a more orthodox way but he had allayed any fears I may have had about water and being out of my depth.

The Wallsend swimming pool was another place of adventure and drama for me. I could swim like a fish and could do the length of the pool under the water, which proved that Doctor Hacket was correct about it being good for my lungs. My sense of fun may seem a bit strange to you but you have probably gathered by now that it's a family trait, here are a couple of examples. As I have said, I could hold my breath for a long time and well in excess of any of my pals. Like any boy, I would challenge them to see who could stay under water the longest, knowing that this was something that I was good at. I was playing this game with John Moulden one day and he asked me how I could hold my breath for so long. This stupid idea for a joke came into my head and John was to be a victim of it. I told him that it was a trick that someone had shown me, that if you took tiny little breaths very quickly, you could breathe under water for a short time. I demonstrated the technique of closing my lips and breathing rapidly through a small gap but not using my nose, it sounded technical and John was impressed. We were in the low end of the pool so John kneeled down with his head under the water. He was like this for a few seconds and then his arms shot up grabbing me, his eyes were staring into mine, he was choking to death in front of me. I bashed him on the back several times and he eventually coughed out water and started to breathe wheezily. I got a fright but not as big as the one that john got. I told him not to try it again because he didn't have the right sort of lips or something just as ludicrous. It never occurred to him that it was one of my daft jokes thank God or it may have put a strain on our friendship. Another stunt that I pulled, involved the bathing hat of one of my sisters. The idea was that I pulled the rubber bathing-hat up over my chin and mouth, trapping air in the hat as I did. This would act as a reserve air supply when I needed it. I would just hold my breath for as long as I could then breathe out through my nose. Then I would nip my nose and breathe in the air from the bathing hat giving me a couple of minutes more. (Try it I swear to you that it works).

We planned our joke so that the pool lifeguard was on the opposite side of the pool at the low end. Then one of my pals waited until I had taken a deep breath, fitted the bathing hat over my chin and mouth and swam under the wooden steps at the side of the deep end. Then he ran around the pool shouting to the lifeguard to help me because I had been trapped under the steps for ages. The guard must have been thinking that I was a gonner as he ran the full length of the pool and around the diving boards. When he reached the steps on the opposite side of the pool with my pal, minutes must have past. He dived in and swam down and under the steps only to find me sitting waving at him in my makeshift aqualung. He looked stunned and gestured for me to follow him to the surface. I innocently explained my innovative breathing device but he was still furious with me for giving him a scare. His relief at finding me still alive won the day though and he eventually calmed down and promptly banned me from having a bathing hat. I think it would have been a different story if he had known that the whole incident was supposed to be a joke. Still, you have to admit that it was a brilliant invention for an eight year old to think of.

I remember watching a group of people being taught to swim by a proper instructor who was throwing a rubber brick into the water for them to retrieve from the bottom of the pool. This intrigued me because it conjured up images of diving for pearls or treasure in the southern seas. I resolved to bring something from home that I could dive for on my next visit to the baths. I searched the house for a suitable object and eventually decided on a block of steel measuring twelve inches long and two inches square. It was what my dad used as an anvil when he needed to hammer things into shapes, like the mugs he made us out of condensed milk tins to save my mothers best china cups for special occasions. I wrapped it in a towel with my bathing trunks and set off, at ten years old it took me all my time to carry it.

I got changed into my trunks in one of the little cubicles that ran up both sides of the pool and went down to the waters edge to commence my new game. Fortunately for me, the lifeguard spotted me struggling to carry the block down the big steps to the pool and blew his whistle before I could heave it into the water. He went berserk, telling me how much damage I could have done to the tiles on the bottom of the pool and how much it would have cost to fix it. The outcome of this sorry episode was that I was thrown out and banned from the baths for a month. I managed to talk him into letting me have my dad's anvil back, so it wasn't a total disaster. I wasn't really banned for a month as it happens I just went to walker baths for a couple of weeks to let the dust settle. When I chanced going back into Wallsend baths I tried to keep a low profile but the lifeguard eventually spotted me. He just looked at me and scowled, then he pointed to his eyes and then at me, I got the message.

I wasn't always doing daft things at the swimming baths I actually managed to save the lives of two people. The first turned out to be a lad that I knew from school called 'Billy Roper' although I didn't realise it at the time. I was walking down the side of the pool near the deep end, when I saw a shape lying on the bottom. It was hard to make out what it was because of the overhead lights glinting on the rippling water. I remember thinking that someone must have thrown some clothes into the water. I decided to dive in and investigate the phenomenon out of curiosity. I recognised Billy at once lying on his back, perfectly still, with his eyes closed. So I shook him, hoping to get some response from him but he didn't stir. I managed to get my arms under him and lifted him off the bottom, he was a big lad and it was a struggle to reach the surface. I swam to the side, keeping his head above the water the way that Val had taught me to do in life saving. Holding on to the spit trough with one hand, I started shouting for help. The lifeguard heard me and rushed to pull Billy up out of the water, lying him face down with his arms at his sides. He began the old-fashioned artificial respiration technique of pulling the arms back by the elbows till they met in the middle of Billy's back. He looked like he was using an old village pump and not having much success. Mouth to mouth resuscitation had not been discovered yet and Billy wasn't responding to the lifeguard's best efforts. Luckily the fire station was next door in the same municipal building as the swimming baths and someone had called them for assistance. After the fireman had worked on him with proper resuscitation equipment, Billy began breathing again but was still unconscious, so he was taken to hospital. I'm happy to say that he made a full recovery.

The second person that I saved was none other than 'Raymond Knox', who you may remember was a part time member of our gang because his granny lived near us. The scenario was exactly the same, I saw him at the bottom of the pool lying face down near to the large drain hole grating for the water circulation. I didn't think anything was amiss at first because we all used to swim down to the drain hole to feel the suction through the iron grid. I soon realised that he had been down too long and dived in to see if he was OK. Like before, his eyes were closed and he didn't respond to my shaking him. So, I performed the same procedure as I had with Billy and got him to the side of the pool, calling for help. This time, the lifeguard was able to get Raymond breathing after about five minutes arm pumping, before the firemen got there.

This may seem hard to believe but I never got any sort of recognition for my part in either of these rescues. I had to make a statement on both occasions and yet no one thanked me, not even the parents of the lads concerned. It was talked about at school assembly, telling the pupils to be more careful when they were at the swimming baths. And yet my name was never mentioned in regards to the incidents. I never gave it a second thought at the time and I can't even remember if I told my parents about the rescues but thinking about it now as I relate this is a bit rankling. I would have been given some sort of award on television these days for saving the lives of two of my friends.

There is a heart-warming end to this story though I'm happy to say. I had completely forgotten my heroic past deeds until, I was fifty years old and working in 'Swan Hunters' shipbuilding yard in Wallsend. I was sitting in the canteen with some of my workmates when Billy Roper came and sat at the same table to have his lunch. I had seen Billy now and then in Wallsend over the years but hadn't had any conversation with him. He proceeded to tell the lads all about me saving his life when we were young and got quite emotional when he said that he was now a grandfather thanks to me. I was taken aback to say the least, having forgotten the incident until this moment. Putting it into perspective, having Billy sitting there with a wife, children and grandchildren is enough reward for anybody isn't it?

It wasn't until I was about sixty years old that my wife Margaret and I were having our lunch in 'The Heighley Gate' garden centre near 'Morpeth'. On the next table to us sat non other than 'Raymond Knox' with his wife 'Ann' and his brother-in-law 'Fred Weldon' a mutual friend of ours. Ray immediately began telling them that he would not be sitting there with them if I had not saved him from drowning as a young lad. I have to say that I enjoyed this belated recognition, especially in front of my lovely Margaret, I felt so proud of myself that I thought I would burst. Ray had grown up to become a policeman, so he may have saved a few lives himself over the years, what more could I ask as a lasting legacy for my heroic deeds.

✶✶✶✶✶✶

When I was eleven years old, an incident unfolded that would have a profound influence on me for the rest of my life. I had been up to the high street with my dad and we were walking slowly home, I didn't realise at the time how ill my dad was. Like any eleven year old, my thoughts were mostly about me. As I have told you earlier, dad's lungs had been damaged by mustard gas during the First World War and smoking cigarettes hadn't helped the situation. No one had been warned about the damage that smoking does to your body in those days. He had chronic Angina and what I didn't know, was that he had lung cancer as well. I volunteered to hurry on ahead of him and put the kettle on for a cup of tea when he got home. I was halfway along 'Denham Terrace' just passing the bottom of 'Rawdon Road' (rival faction territory) when a member of the local gang spotted me. Normally I was safe in this area because of my brother-in-law 'Alby Ashburner' living in Rawdon Road. Today however, I was on my own and so was the lad in question. I new him vaguely, I think his name was Terry. He was two or three years older than me but not much taller, I was quite tall for my age. He seemed quite intimidating to me due to him being older. He grabbed me by my jersey front and told me that he was going to beat me up for being near his street and that it was his job to defend his area (what a moron). At this point, my dad turned the corner from 'Carville Road' onto 'Denham Terrace' and was about one hundred yards away. I pointed this out to Terry who immediately pushed me away and retreated, shouting over his shoulder what he would do to me if I ever trespassed again. I was mortified to think that my dad might have seen me being manhandled in this way and hurried home, hoping that he had missed the whole sorry scene.

He hadn't missed a thing he had witnessed me cringing while being dragged about by my jersey as soon as he had turned the corner. He had given me rudimentary boxing lessons a couple of times using my brother Bobs boxing gloves. I had even knocked a pal of mine 'Stan' out for the count during one such lesson. The trouble was, I'm not my brother Bob and I don't have the natural aptitude for fighting. Dad wanted to know why I had let a lad the same size as me push me about and then point out that my dad was coming to make my escape. Yes, he had missed nothing just as I had feared. I explained that Terry was a couple of years older than I was but it sounded like a lame excuse even to me. I could see the disappointment in his eyes and I wanted the ground to swallow me up. I suppose that if you know you are dying of cancer, you are going to want to know that you're youngest son can take care of himself. I went to my bedroom and cried with shame and I was almost too afraid to come down and face him again. When I did eventually come back down, dad had obviously realised that I was only eleven and deeply embarrassed by the situation. He was apologetic about how he had been and said that he would give me some advice on how to deal with the same situation should it arise again.

He sat me down beside him and gave me advice that has stayed with me all of my life. He told that there was nothing to be ashamed of in being scared and that he got scared him self in some situations. The way that you handle yourself and the decisions that you make are what is important in the long run. If you are faced with a situation where a fight is going to ensue and you think that your chances of victory are slim and escape unlikely, his advice was this. If it is one to one, hit the other person first as hard as you can, in the middle of a sentence is usually good. If you have more than one assailant, the same tactics apply. You hit the ringleader first and by surprise and then just allow yourself to go berserk until it's over one way or the other. He stressed that you may not win the fight but it is easier to live with yourself, than knowing that you had been pleading and begging with them when the outcome was inevitable. I know that this may not be everybody's idea of good fatherly advice but it has stood the test of time as far as I am concerned. I would like to give this little supplementary bit of advice of my own if I may. I have unfortunately been in this type of situation from time to time and I have found that allowing my-self to look a bit deranged is a great help. It can often dissuade someone with violent intent from proceeding through lack of nerve due to the look in your eyes. I hope you don't ever need to try it but I can assure you that it has worked for me.

I have to say, I was taken aback by my dad advising me to take someone by surprise and smack him in the middle of a conversation because of his love of boxing. I told him this and he said that street fighting wasn't boxing and your own personal interests were more important than the 'Queensbury Rules'. Dad did go on to tell me that avoiding trouble and confrontation was still the best way to live. He told me never to resort to violence unless it was unavoidable in my own defence and that I should never become a bully myself. This is the most indelible memory of my childhood, possibly because in my eyes I never got the chance to redeem myself to my dad. I still feel uncomfortable recalling these events even though I know that it is irrational after all this time. The thing that I hate the most in life is any form of bullying, whether it is physical or mental, institutional or by individuals. I despise myself if I realise that I have been a bully in some way, which sadly does happen and I try my best not to be.

CHAPTER 5

Moving to the senior school

When the pupils in the junior school reached the age of eleven, they were obliged to take the 'Eleven Plus' examination. This was supposed to sort the 'wheat from the chaff' as far as brains went. The fact that children develop at different rates had not been given any credence at that time. The ones who passed were sent to the 'Wallsend Grammar' school until they were eighteen and enjoyed better facilities and theoretically better teachers. Needless to say, I was one of the 'chaff' among the pupils and destined to leave school at fifteen to find work. There was only one of my classmates who passed the exam, I hope he made the best of his opportunity he was a nice lad. The entity that was known as Margaret Thatcher (Hoick, Spit) was always prattling on about being an ex-grammar school pupil. I can only assume that Adolf Hitler and Mussolini were exchange students in her school. The pupils that failed the eleven plus exam would normally have just remained at the 'Carville' school until they left at fifteen. The education system was going through one of its metamorphose stages at this time and was to be called the 'Secondary Modern' system. The new plan involved making the 'Carville' into the infants and juniors only and we as seniors were to be transferred to the 'Western School' on 'West Street'.

Just before we were transferred to the 'Western', I got into my first ever fight and it had to be the daftest reason ever for having a fight. A classmate of mine called 'Alan Oliver' was showing a group of us how hairy his arms were and claiming that this meant that he must be the toughest. I disputed this theory on the grounds that I had the same amount of hairs on my arms as him but they were harder to see because I had fair hair and he had black hair. The argument soon became heated because my scientific observation had cast doubts on our eleven year-old rights of passage into adulthood, virility and prowess. Not that we knew anything of these concepts, it was just a case of, 'are black-haired people tougher than fair-haired people'. Someone in the class suggested that we should have a fight in the playground to prove it one-way or the other. We both agreed to this Gladiatorial confrontation, me possibly less enthusiastically than Alan due to my barely contained urge to renege. Remembering the shame I had felt in front of my dad previously was enough to spur me on. It began with the usual pushing and pulling then it progressed to rolling about on the schoolyard until I found myself on top punching him whenever and wherever I could get a dig in, It was then that the teacher on yard duty pulled us apart. It was the consensus of opinion among the other lads that I had won the fight and Alan graciously conceded defeat in the hairy arm debate.

Shortly after this we transferred into the 'Western' school and took our place in the classroom before the teacher 'Mr Whitehill' arrived. The lads from the 'Carville' sat together on one side of the classroom and the original pupils of the 'Western' sat on the other. Obviously we were the interlopers and were viewed with mistrust by the indigenous lads. One of them, whose name I later learned was 'Alan' stood up and announced that he was the best fighter from his side. (I must say that he looked it). He had a face like a welder's apron due I can only guess to chickenpox, or some other such affliction and he wanted to know who the best fighter was on our side. To a man and also to my horror, my mates all pointed straight at me, basing this perception on my recent victorious defence of fair-haired arms against Alan Oliver. So, the second Alan, or perhaps I will refer to him as 'Pocky Alan', now proclaimed that he was going to 'get me' at playtime and I assumed that he was going to try and make me as ugly as he was. This was a great deal for him to aspire to, considering how pig ugly he was. Thinking that I was going to be humiliated on my first day in a new school filled me with dread and almost filled my pants with something else. The playtime bell sounded, too early for my liking and all of the pupils were obliged to make their way into the schoolyard. I resolved to secrete myself somewhere in the yard and hope that the whole nightmare would just blow over (If only life could be as simple as that). There were two adjacent exits into the schoolyard, both with double doors that opened into a small covered recess with three steps down into the yard. Only one of the doors was used and the other one was always kept closed. So I left by the open door and then doubled back and hid at the top of the steps in the recess of the closed door. I could see most of the yard and the kids playing but it was hard for anyone to see me lurking in the shadows. I spotted Pocky Alan approaching John Bartlay, knowing that he was one of my pals and punching him in the face. He then roamed around the yard with his entourage until he came across my other pal John Moulden and he smacked him in the mouth too. I witnessed these events while skulking in the shadows of the exit recess and trying to be invisible, not my finest hour it shames me to admit. Eventually Pocky Alan got his eye on me and swaggered over, telling me to come down so that he could give me a smacking. I remembered what my dad had told me and took one of the steps down to meet him and saying that I didn't want any trouble. On the word 'Trouble', I punched him as hard as I could right on his pocky nose. He catapulted backwards into his crowd of mates and landed on his back on the yard with blood pouring from his nose and onto his jersey. I leapt from the second step and landed astride him with my arms going like pistons as I tried to flatten his nose even further. This time, it was two of the older lads who pulled me off, they were wearing Prefect's badges and were on yard duty in place of a teacher. Pocky Alan's nose was bleeding profusely and I had scraped my knuckles quite badly when the sneaky swine had moved his head and I punched the concrete of the yard instead of his nose.

The prefects took us to the toilets in the schoolyard and told us to get ourselves cleaned up before we went back to class. We washed in silence until Alan said, "That was a good fight so we'll call it a draw and be pals". I said OK! And we shook hands but it was only so that he could save face with his pals, we both knew who the victor was. I wasn't the one with a nose like an Aubergine and he hadn't landed a punch on me.

We were never destined to be pals but we did manage to stay civil to each other until we left school. Pocky Alan had two quite amusing party tricks that he loved to perform for the class. Sadly, after the tenth enactment even the dimmest of us could find no more mirth in the performances. Our apathy did not put Alan off, he just continued with the same two tricks every week for four years, what a showman. His first trick was to drink the ink out of the little inkwell in his desk and go around all day with a blue mouth. His second trick was during the art classes when he would paint his penis red, white and blue and display it like a small rolled up 'Union Jack'.

Very patriotic I admit but he never changed the design or colour scheme and it got a bit boring. A few polka dots or something wouldn't have gone amiss but I think he had reached his peak as far as his artistic leanings went.

✛✛✛✛✛✛

I have not related these last two personal confrontations to you to enhance my 'macho' image but as an appendage to the story about the advice of my father on self-defence. Sadly I never told him about my two victorious fights because I thought that I would get told off for fighting in school. Of course I wish that I had now because he died a few weeks later on the 24th of July 1953, the day that the school closed for the summer holidays. So, I blew my chance to shine in my dad's eyes, at least that was how I felt at that time and I carry the mental scars to this day. I don't mean that the memory has been at the forefront of my mind since then but I have to confess that writing this down did make me sad. I still wish that he had known that his youngest son could take care of himself and that his timely advice had worked for me then and on several other occasions since.

It was late afternoon and we were all sitting in the classroom full of anticipation, our teacher Mr Whitehill was telling us all to enjoy our six-week summer break from school. A knock came to the door and I was summoned to the head master's study. When I arrived, my sister Joan was sitting with the head 'Mr Johnson' and crying into her handkerchief. She told me that she had to take me up to her house at the top of West Street because something very sad had happened. I was shocked to see Joan crying in front of the head master and asked her what was wrong. She told me as gently as she could between sobs, that my dad had died and gone to heaven. It took a while for it to sink in but I knew what death was because of my granny dying a year earlier. Then I realised that I would never see him again and the gravity of what she was saying hit me. I broke down and sobbed my heart out with Joan holding me to her. We left the school and Joan gave me the key to her house so that I could run on ahead of her and let myself in.

As I have said, I didn't even realise that my dad had been ill, even though I remember wondering why he walked so slow now when I used to have trouble keeping up with him. I was too busy in my eleven year olds life, cocooned in security and love to notice anything else. Dad had been taken into 'Shotley Bridge' hospital in Durham a few days before his death and I am relieved to remember that I had kissed him goodbye before he left. I say relieved because like most boys of eleven I was at the stage where kissing grown-ups seemed a bit soft.

Dad's coffin was brought home and put into the small bedroom at the back on the day before his funeral. This was so that people could come and pay their last respects to him and there were more people in our house on that day than I could have imagined. I feel that it's a great pity that this custom of coming home in your coffin for a day seems to be dying out. They just stop the hearse at your door and then proceed with the funeral from the street. It's probably because the funeral directors are likely to charge hundreds for bringing you home and picking you up again, it's a lucrative business death. My pal has just arranged his own funeral and asked for a cardboard coffin to keep the price down a bit. He was told that the cardboard ones were considerably more costly than a wooden one. When he asked how this could be possible, the undertaker told him that he thought it was because you were being given the privilege of being ecologically friendly while you were being cremated. How is that for a lucrative scam?

While my dad was lying upstairs, my aunt 'Ethel Poxton' (mam's sister) asked me if I wanted to see my dad for the last time. I was apprehensive but felt that I should. I don't remember being afraid at all, it was just the finality of it and as young as I was I knew that it was the end of an era. I went over to the open coffin and looked at my dad, or should I say what seemed to be a caricature of my dad. The distinctive nose and forehead were there but he was grotesquely thin and he was wearing makeup. I fled the bedroom crying and went into the front bedroom to lie on the bed and compose myself before I went back downstairs to be with my mam. I've realised since then that when the spark of life leaves someone with cancer, they suddenly seem so much more skeletal than they were in life. A bad undertaker can overdo the makeup in an attempt to compensate for this. When he died, my dad was still six feet and one inch tall and his weight was only seven stone.

I didn't go to my dad's funeral, my mam had arranged for me to go camping with an older lad 'Billy Cockburn' who lived at the bottom of our lane. She thought that it would be better for me to have a little holiday than to go through the sadness of a funeral. I had got to know Billy when I had ring worm a year or so earlier because he had it too and we were off school together. With no one else to play with during the day, we just gravitated together as children do. He and a couple of his pals were going camping at 'Ryton Willows' further up the river. They were a couple of years older than me but didn't seem to mind me tagging along. I suppose that they knew my circumstances and were happy to oblige my mam. We went on the bus to Ryton, a nice little village on the south bank of the river Tyne and then carried our camping gear down to the Willows, a grassy stretch of land leading down to the river. This was a far cry from the murky effluent filled river that I knew in Wallsend. The Tyne this far upstream was a lovely tree lined meandering river like you would expect to see in a 'John Constable' painting. We were all in an old army surplus ridge tent, with our blankets, torches and comics. There were no such things as sleeping bags back then but we were cosy that night with our 'Cocoa' and 'Jam and Bread'. We had plenty of tinned food and Cocoa and we bought bread and milk at the little shop near by. I can't remember where we got water from, probably the river.

On the first night, when the laughing and talking had died away and I could tell that everyone had gone to sleep by their steady breathing, I was alone with my thoughts. It occurred to me that my dad would not be there when I got home in a few days time and that he would never be there ever again. I buried my head in the blankets and cried myself to sleep as quietly as I could so that the other lads wouldn't hear me. I must have cried myself out completely because I'm ashamed to say that I can't remember thinking about my dad for the rest of the week that we were there. We spent our time playing cricket or football and swimming in the river or just scouting the area. Every day, one of the cross-Tyne ferries would come up from Wallsend with a bunch of kids and their mothers on a day trip. There were three ferries that ran between, 'Hebburn' on the south side of the river and 'Wallsend' and 'Walker' on the north. There was always one of them not in service for cross Tyne commuting, so during the school holidays it would be utilised as a pleasure boat for these trips up to Ryton. Their names were the 'Tyne Queen' the 'Tyne Princess' and the 'Tyne Duchess'. One of them features in the original film version of 'Get Carter' starring 'Michael Cain'. He is in a gunfight with some gangsters from Newcastle and the ferry gets one of it's windows shot out at Wallsend ferry landing. The same ferry landing I may add, that I used to drop my home made 'Little Demon' depth charges off. (That is almost fame, surely).

While we were camping at the Willows, I saw my very first real black people a man and I assume his little boy of about six. I know that this is hard to believe but there were no ethnic minorities of any kind in our area up to this point in time. This is before Indian, Chinese or even Italian restaurants had established themselves. In fact, I had never even heard of 'Pizza' or 'Spaghetti' and to me, 'Macaroni' was a milk pudding that my mam used to make. The only black people that I had seen were in 'Tarzan' films or the newsreels at the cinema and they were always poor and hungry. This man and boy were walking along the river path, so I gathered some of my comics and took them to give to the little black lad. In my mind, I thought that he would be too poor to buy comics of his own. The boy smiled and reached out to take them but his father wouldn't allow it, dragging him away along the path without speaking. He was probably a doctor or something and felt that they were being patronized because they were black. I think that his reaction although understandable, was a bit ungracious towards a boy of eleven who thought he was making a kind gesture.

Talking about doctors, I had cause to visit the local doctor while we were camping at the Willows. I have a bit of a phobia about 'Earwigs' or forkytails as we used to call them. Someone had told me that they would crawl into your ear while you slept to lay their eggs, which would subsequently hatch out and eat your brain. So, before I went to sleep in the tent I would stuff my ears with cotton wool so tightly that it must have met in the middle of my head. One morning, it was impossible to remove so

I was stone deaf all day much to the amusement of the other lads. After tea, Billy Cockburn decided to take me to the local doctor's surgery. After he explained my plight to the receptionist she took me through to see the doctor. I told him my fear of having my brains eaten by baby earwigs and he had a good laugh. It only took seconds for him to extract the cotton wool and restore my hearing to normal. He then explained that earwigs were given that name because they have ear shaped wings when they open them (which is not very often) and that it was just an old wives tale about them crawling into your ears. I was greatly relieved to hear these indisputable facts from a professional and I only packed my ears half as tightly that night.

When we were due to go home, I went to the local shop to buy a present for my mam. I had seen a little 'Welsh' doll in the window and the old lady who owned the shop told me that the dolls apron changed colour if it was going to rain. It cost me two shillings (ten new pence) and I had saved it from the pocket money I had been given. When I gave it to her on our return, she burst into tears and told me that it was lovely as she hugged me to her. I thought that she was crying because it was such a good present but of course she was grieving for my dad and for quite a while it didn't take much to make her cry. The little Welsh doll stood on the windowsill for as long as mam was alive and its apron did change colour when it was going to rain, just like the old shopkeeper had told me.

My mam received the princely sum of ten Shillings (fifty new pence) per week widows pension nothing else, so she had to carry on working full time at 'George Angus & co. ltd. My sisters were all married by now and living their own lives. My brother Alan was in the army and my brother Bob worked as a waiter in a restaurant in Newcastle earning peanuts and relying on tips. Mam volunteered to work nightshift on alternative weeks for the extra money and did so for the rest of her life. Remember that the normal working week was fifty-two hours at this time and you will realise how hard things were for her. On the day shift weeks she always worked three extra half shifts overtime, which meant that she had to get to work and clock on at 7-30am. Then after working until 8-30pm she would be lucky to get home by 9pm in the evening, God bless her.

✴ ✴ ✴ ✴ ✴ ✴

What image do I have in my head when I think about my dad? He was bald, except for over his ears and a narrow band at the back of his head. Because he lost his hair early in life he always blamed wearing his helmet during world war one for his baldness (Nothing to do with heredity). What hair he did have on his head was ginger but cropped short. Strangely from his neck down, his body was covered in thick ginger curly hair apart from his abdomen that was only sparsely covered. He looked like a tall wiry but muscular Orang Utan. I remember that I could often see ginger curls sticking out over his starched shirt collar. Just like an Orang Utan, he too was immensely strong and could twist horseshoes until their 'U' shape had one leg pointing the opposite way to the other. He was always smartly dressed when he left the house with his shoes polished to a mirror like shine. He would sit for hours snipping the frayed bits off the collars and cuffs of his white shirt. His shirts always had separate collars that were attached front and back with collar studs. It was always a laugh watching him struggle to fasten them when they were freshly starched until my mam came to his aide. He kept his old three-piece suit brushed and clean at all times and always wore a tie and a Trilby hat. His waistcoat pocket contained his cheap but reliable 'Smiths Empire' pocket watch. The watch may have been cheap but the chain that it was attached to was beautiful. It was solid silver with each of the large links hallmarked individually and a charming silver shield with a filigree border hanging from it, I believe they are called 'Albert's'. This watch and chain were dads pride and joy and I wonder now where or how he acquired it. He may have inherited the chain from his father, I just don't know. I do know that I inherited it from him after his death.

Sadly, I loaned it to my brother Alan when he was a bus driver because his watch was broken and he couldn't afford another. He needed a watch to follow his timetable while driving his route. A long time later, after he had left the bus-driving job, I asked him for my dads watch back and he quite casually told me that he had been a bit pushed for money so he had sold it. I was devastated at this news but you would have to know my brother Alan to realise that in his world this was a normal solution to a problem and guilt or remorse would never have occurred to him.

I can still see the chain with the 'T' bar through one the buttonholes on dad's waistcoat and looped across the front of his chest with the silver shield hanging at the bottom of the loop. He always looked handsome and distinguished to me as I ran along at his side, holding his hand and trying to keep pace with his long strides. Then when I couldn't keep up, he would scoop me up onto his shoulders as though I was weightless. I used to love this because I was so far off the ground, I felt as though I was flying. He had a great sense of humour and always had my mam laughing, even when she was annoyed with him about something. I can remember one such occasion when he just smiled at her and said, "Hilda, you're about as ferocious as a hen". She began to smile and then started laughing, the tension gone.

One day, my granny was going to throw an old wardrobe out and my mam told dad that she would like the mirror off the back of the door. We were all standing in granny's back yard watching him as he carefully took the retaining clips off the mirror. Granny called to him, "Be careful that you don't break the mirror Archie, or you will have seven years bad luck". Dad started to laugh, picked up a hammer and smashed the mirror saying, "I just want to see how it could get any worse". Mam wasn't too pleased at this but I thought it was highly amusing at the time. I look back on the incident now and I realise how much pent up frustration there must have been in him to give in to this childish compulsion. He may have already known that he was dying of cancer, I don't know. Another time that I remember his unusual sense of humour was when my mam asked him to make a little shelf for the scullery wall. He told her that by the time she returned from the High street after doing some shopping, her new shelf would be on the wall. True to his word, she returned to find a beautifully crafted Mahogany shelf on the scullery wall where she had indicated. She was over the moon and showered dad with kisses. She had only asked for a shelf, she didn't expect this Mahogany masterpiece. What she didn't know was, he had cut the wood for the shelf out of the lid that covered the keyboard on his old 'Harmonium' a small portable organ. It used to stand in the bedroom and dad could play it beautifully as he pumped the bellows with the foot pedals. She couldn't believe that he would do that to his beloved Harmonium. He just laughed and said that she now had her shelf, and he could still play the organ with a hole in the lid. The lid had the shelf shaped hole in it for months until he removed it altogether to utilise for some other project. This behaviour is considered normal in my family.

One day, dad built a hutch in the back yard and I thought we were going to get a rabbit. When I asked him he just smiled and said that I would have to wait until the weekend to find out, making it a long week of anticipation for me. He went out on Saturday and returned with a lovely speckled red chicken. I was euphoric, lots of my pals had rabbits but nobody I knew had a chicken for a pet. I named her 'Clara Cluck' and when she wasn't in her pen she had the run of the house. We had a black and white cat called 'Felix' at that time and they became firm friends. You would find them upstairs sleeping on one of the beds together and they would both drink the milk from Felix's bowl and share his biscuits. She laid her first egg on the same day that my niece 'Valerie' was born to my sister Hilda and her husband Val and continued to lay one every day after that. I don't know how long she kept laying her eggs but to me it seemed like ages and I loved going out every morning and finding them. Then one day she just stopped laying eggs and dad told me that she was missing all of the other chickens and he thought it would be best if he took her back to the farm. I was devastated to see her go but I wanted her to be happy and see all of her friends (what a good kid I was).

We will jump twenty years into my 'then' future for the heartrending finale to this sad tale. I was in my thirties, married with children and visiting my sister Joan's house. While I was telling my brother Bob's wife Mary about my pet chicken I noticed that Joan and Bob were both smirking. When I got to the part where my dad had said that he would take Clara Cluck back to the farm, they were sniggering behind their hands. Naively, I asked them what was so funny and they almost wet themselves laughing. Eventually, Bob composed himself enough to tell me. "I can't believe that you still thought that story was true", he said, "Clara got broody and stopped laying eggs, she just became too expensive to feed because times were hard". I still couldn't see what they were laughing at, whatever the reason was that she went. This brought on more laughter and Bob had to explain to me that we had all eaten Clara for Sunday lunch. I was stunned and horrified, I had eaten my pet and it had taken me more than twenty years to find out. I can understand the economics that were involved, my dad had a family to feed after all and at least he had made up the lovely story about the farm to spare my feelings at the time. I can even see the funny side now but part of me still wishes that I had never found out.

If dad got a tin of paint from somewhere, it would take possession of him and he would have to paint things until the tin was empty. He would start with the backyard gate, then the lavatory door in the yard then every door in the house. If it were a big tin, he would paint the table and chairs in the kitchen, then the bench in the scullery. It didn't seem to matter what colour the paint was, everything would be the same. We didn't usually have to wait too long if our colour schemes were a bit garish. This was because he always seemed to be coming in with tins of paint that he had been given in exchange for the use of one or other of his many talents. I suppose it is fare to say that he was a bit eccentric. He built a hand-cranked generator with a pair of copper handgrips attached to it with electrical cable. He would get us to hold the handgrips while he turned the crank on the generator. There would be a tingling in your fingers and a bulb on the machine would glow a little. He explained that the tingling feeling was electricity and it was also making the bulb glow. He then turned the crank faster and as the bulb got brighter we involuntarily gripped tighter on the copper handles. It was even more amazing when he told us to try and leave go of the handles. Try as we might it was impossible to let go and as he turned the handle faster or slower our arms would twist in and out of their own volition. It felt really weird, a bit like muscle cramp but it didn't hurt. Dad told us that this was the difference between direct current (DC) that we were experiencing and alternating current (AC) that was used for domestic purposes. Direct was dangerous because it took over your muscles and you couldn't let go but alternating although still dangerous threw you off. It's likely that he made this generator to teach us the difference between AC & DC after the incident when Alan got me to stick the scissors in the socket. Our mam hated the machine but we all loved it and were always asking for another try.

Dad gave me a lot of good advice in the short time that we had together as well as the self-defence thing. We were walking down the road one day when a car coming towards us indicated that he was turning left into a side street in front of us. This was before winking indicators back and front had been invented. The state of the art modern alternative to hand signals was a little arrow shaped arm that lifted out of the door pillar on either side of the car. My dad pointed this out and told me never to take any notice of these mechanical devices and only believe a driver giving hand signals (a lost art). When I asked him why, he explained that a driver could forget that he was still signalling from a previous corner (they weren't self-cancelling) and drive straight ahead. If you believed the signal, you could step out into the road or drive out from the junction and be hit by the car. I remember thinking how astute he was to have spotted this possibility. This advice has probably saved my life a few times, especially on my motorbikes because it happens every day and of course nobody gives hand signals any more.

He also told me that I would have to face many problems in my life and how I dealt with them would determine how hard or easy my life would be. He said that if there was a solution to any problem that I may encounter, I should do my utmost to resolve it. On the other hand, if I was to be faced with a problem that I knew for a fact could not be resolved I should dismiss it and move on. He said that this wasn't easy to do but that pursuing something that is unattainable would only lead to sadness or bitterness. This advice has been proven to be true for me over the years. He also told me that whatever I said or did would always have consequences and I would be wise to try and think of the possible consequences before proceeding. The world would be a better place if we all heeded that bit of advice. On dealing with other people his advice was that I should talk to them about any problems that we may have with each other and listen to what they have to say. He pointed out that I may not always like what I hear but at least I would be in a better position to try and resolve things.

This may all seem a bit heavy for an eleven year old to take on board but I think my dad knew that it would be his last chance to influence the way that I would grow up. So! Possibly because he died soon after these fatherly talks, his advice is stuck in my head forever. I have passed it all on to my own three children more than once over the years but without the catalyst of me dying young its indelibility is quite frankly debatable.

One of the things that I am most grateful to my dad for is with regards to how I feel towards organised religion. His father, my grandfather 'Absalom Blevins' came over from 'Ireland' and was a staunch 'Orangeman' (Irish Protestant). He was a heavy drinker and every Orange-mans day he would get drunk and fight with

Catholics. Sometimes he came home victorious and sometimes he was carried home badly beaten up. My dad realised at a very early age how stupid this mindless bigotry between Protestants and Catholics was and vowed that he would never be part of it. My grandfather Absalom died in 1913 from alcohol induced liver failure. Although we were all baptised in the Church-of-England (Protestant), dad would encourage us to go to churches of different denominations from week to week. He reckoned that we would have a better informed and less biased point of view when we were adults. That was pretty enlightened, especially for the times. Oddly, for all of his open minded thinking, he always asked any boyfriends of my three sisters what their religion was at the first meeting, he may have just wanted to protect the girls from potential future bigotry, who knows?

One week I would go to the C of E or Catholic churches or the Methodist or Presbyterian chapels and finally the Salvation Army at the top of our street. The Catholic service was the most boring because it was all conducted in Latin in those days. My favourite was the Salvation Army, not because I was more impressed with their doctrine but that their interpretation of the Bible was more upbeat and the congregation always seemed happier. It was more on the lines of Negro spiritualist gatherings with less of the 'Hell and Damnation' and more of the 'love your neighbour'. On top of this, the Salvation Army always got involved with the community to a greater extent than the other denominations and I still have a soft spot for the 'Salty bacon Army'.

Due to my dads enlightened approach to religion, I now feel content in my beliefs. Having taken an interest in all religions I have come to the conclusion that all organised religion is a man made creation woven around some historical events. The purpose I believe was to police the masses by having the possibility of divine retribution for any perceived transgression. The people who create religions old and new always consider themselves 'The Hand of God' and administer their own versions of retribution. This is not in itself a bad concept after all we have laws that are designed to do the same thing. The trouble is, when you get extremist factions in any religion that believe they alone are right, (which of course they can't all be) you are bound to have conflict. They all preach that there is one God and overlook the fact that it must therefore be the same God. Their interpretations of the same stories are the true issue and it is their own egos that breed the confrontation. I am sure the God of love will be able to differentiate between devotion and dementia during the slaughter. (I was on my high horse for a moment there).

All of the above does not mean that I don't believe in anything, I just don't buy into organised religion. I know right from wrong, I know there is evil in the world and yet I have been touched with the kindness of people all of my life. My church is in my head and I don't need a man or woman in strange attire and carrying an ornate shepherds crook, or a smoking, dinging, or water dribbling stick to tell me if I have erred in some way. The fact is that unless we are psychotic we all know when we have done something bad. It is how we deal with this realisation that defines whether we are a good or bad person. Many people think that every thing is random and chaotic in the world and the universe but it has been proved by science that everything has order. From the smallest microbes and the evolution of life to the formation of the constellations there is always a pattern. It may take seconds or millions of years to achieve this order but it would seem that it is pre-ordained to do so.

When it comes to us humans, I can understand instinct being necessary for survival but why have we been given emotions. Guilt, compassion, love, hate, selflessness, envy, these are things that make life more difficult and yet more worthwhile. There are intelligent people who still refuse to accept the idea of evolution and cling to the story of the Garden of Eden and Adam and Eve. That is exactly what it was a simply written story about how God made us perfect and because of the symbolic picking of the forbidden fruit, evil was introduced into the world. I have always thought that the evolution of man is more rational and beautiful with us evolving from the first spark of life in the ocean to the incredible creatures that we are today. Instead of having perfection snatched away from us in a mythical garden we have been allowed to strive towards perfection. Yes I know that we have a long way to go but I believe that we have been given free will so it's up to us all to make the effort. I find it hard to believe that this brief burst of consciousness that we call life is all that there is and I look forward to the next part of the adventure. (A long way forward I hasten to add).

If anyone, of any religion who reads this, Hindu, Muslim, Buddhist, Jewish or Christian would like to say a prayer for me I will be very grateful. It really is the same God after all is said and done. HERE ENDETH MY LESSON FOR TODAY.

⁑⁑⁑⁑⁑⁑⁑

It was at about this time or shortly after that I had another shall we say risqué encounter. I could have said sexual encounter but I don't remember having any sexual thoughts at all about it, I just knew that it was a bit naughty. I was playing with Stan Fee and John Moulden when we were joined by a few of the girls who lived beside Stan. I won't give their surnames for gentlemanly reasons. The girls, Gloria, Mabel, and I think Marjory wanted to play 'catchy kiss'. We had to give chase to them and having made a capture we were allowed to have a kiss. We played this innocent game for a while until the older sister of one of the girls joined us. Her name was Betty and she was about fourteen years of age with a mop of ginger hair. She decided to amend the rules and play 'catchy pully (pull your) knickers down'. She explained that when a girl was caught she would go into the outside toilet in the backyard of Betty's house with the boy who had caught her. Once there she would stand on the toilet seat, lift her skirt and pull her knickers down for the boy's perusal. I was all in favour of this because as with Winnies chest I had never made the acquaintance of a girl's lower torso. John and Stan also nodded their acceptance of the amendment on scientific grounds I'm sure.

So, the game began and one by one the girls were caught and as with Winnie, it was a bit of a let down. I don't know what I was expecting but it seemed that girls just didn't have anything at all down their pants. Then I caught Betty and this was a different story entirely. She climbed onto the toilet seat, pulled down her knickers and showed me hers. At first I just didn't know what it was, I had never even heard of pubic hair and Betty had a mass of ginger curls. At first I thought, "What a strange place to keep your mittens", then I realised that it was hair and I was almost catatonic, it was apparent to me that girls became Werewolves as they got older. I was scared to move in case it bit my neck out. It wasn't knickers she needed it was a muzzle, there was no chance that she would ever get frost bite down there, she should have changed her name from Betty to 'Yeti'. (OK, that's enough of the one-liners I think you've got the picture). Anyway when my flabber became less gasted I made some excuse like, "I think it's time to go for my tea", or something just as lame and backed out of the toilet traumatised. After that I just stuck to catchy kiss, it seemed less perilous.

When I was about sixty years old, I was on the bus on my way to Wallsend when the woman sitting beside me said, "I know you, you're Billy Blevins from Union street aren't you". I looked at her and recognised her immediately, it was Betty and she still had a mop of ginger hair. We got chatting about old times and I said, "The last time I saw you, you were standing on a toilet seat with your knickers down to your knees". She was silent for a moment and then she burst out laughing, "I wondered if you remembered that", she said. "It is indelibly printed on my mind", I told her," I was afraid to leave the house for a week". We laughed all the way to Wallsend talking about it. Thinking about her unruly mop of ginger hair now prompts me to speculate what would happen if she was ever strip searched at an airport.

They would think that she was trying to smuggle an Orang Utan down her pants.

I have to say that all of that catchy kiss stuff stood me in good stead because I became highly proficient in the art of face sucking. I went to the house of Marion Morgan at the top of my street and on entering her backyard I could hear girlie laughter and talking and my name was mentioned. I crept to the kitchen window and eavesdropped on what they were saying about me. The little group consisted of Marion, Winnie Cox, Eunace Weatherstone and Winnie Howe. They were discussing who they considered to be the best kisser out of all the lads in the gang and with a unanimous vote, Billy Blevins came out on top. I left the yard bursting with pride at this accolade from the girls. All of that practice on the mirror and the back of my hand had not been wasted. In later years, my wife Margaret also told me that I was the best kisser ever but that could have been expedience on her part (Very wise). This incident boosted my ego a great deal and although I've always had a shy side to my character I've always been confident in the company of women. 'Thank you girls'.

✦✦✦✦✦✦

CHAPTER 6

Short detour

Well, I have not written anything in this journal for nine months so I will explain the reason and then I will resume where I left off.

In October last year 2009, I developed pneumonia and was taken to North Tyneside General Hospital in North Shields. It turned out that I had pneumonia in both lungs and pleurisy. I was put in a private room under quarantine because my symptoms were similar to Swine Flu which was a bit of an epidemic at the time.

During the night my condition worsened and I began to shake from head to toe and have hallucinations. The shaking became more violent and in one of my more lucid moments I realised that I should tell somebody. I looked around for the bell push to summon for help and found that it had fallen onto the floor. The door to my room was shut and I couldn't get enough air into my lungs to shout for help. I kept lapsing into a dream like state that I must admit was very pleasant. Then I would become aware of the fact that I was shaking as though I was using a pneumatic road drill and could hardly breathe. I had no option but to get out of bed to retrieve the bell push. To my dismay the bell push was on the opposite side of the bed to the stand that held the drip that was piped into my left arm. I slowly made my way around the bottom of the bed pulling the drip stand along behind me. I picked up the bell push and summoned for help as I made my tortuous way back. The nurse arrived before I could get back into bed and was just about to berate me for being up when she saw the state that I was in. She called for the doctor and helped me back into bed.

It was all in blurred slow motion after that as I slipped in and out of lucidity. They took my temperature and I remember the look on the doctor's face he wasn't happy, which in turn ruined the moment for me too. My temperature was dangerously high and he instructed the nurse to strip me of my hospital gown and remove the blankets from the bed. I didn't feel hot at all and in fact I thought I was shivering because I was cold. They kept taking my temperature and it wasn't coming down. The doctor told the nurse to open the windows wide and check my temperature every hour. The windows were opened and I was left lying on the bare bed in my underpants. There was a strong, cold, autumn wind blowing and the curtains were flapping like the Union Jack at the top of Mount Everest. I curled up into the foetal position with my hands tucked into my skiddies clutching my genitalia for warmth. I'm telling you now, that a squirrel with a magnifying glass could not have found my nuts that night.

The nurse came in every hour and stuck a thermometer in my ear and after a couple of hours my temperature began to come down one degree at a time. The icy wind continued to blow across my naked back and I kept drifting in and out of these hallucinations where I was watching a nature programme on an imaginary television in the corner of the room. When I was lucid, it was like being in a prisoner of war torture camp so I quite looked forward to the hallucinations. By morning my temperature was almost normal and the doctor told me to inform the nurse at once if I got the shakes again because I had been in a dangerous position. It did happen two or three more times but not as bad. Next they noticed that my heart was starting to get faster and nothing they did was slowing it down. Eventually they got worried and sent for a heart specialist to come and see me. By the time she came my heart was beating at 160 beats per minute and I was feeling decidedly unwell.

I wasn't in pain I just felt dreadful and to make it worse I was remembering that my brother Bob had just died after coming out of hospital when his heart was beating at 160 per minute. He only lasted a couple of weeks after he came home. I was put on all sorts of medication, both orally and intravenously. It took days to see any improvement and it stayed at around 120 well into the second week of my stay in hospital. They wanted to send me home and carry on taking the tablets to reduce my heart rate further. My little darling wife Margaret told them that I wasn't going home until it was below 100 because it was safer for me in hospital. I have to say that I was relieved when they conceded to her request, my heart still felt like an outboard motor in my chest. In the third week they managed to get my heart rate down and it was fluctuating between 80 and 90 beats per minute. The trouble was that I had developed Atrial fibrillation, meaning that half of my heart was beating faster than the other. This is apparently quite a common occurrence after someone has had pneumonia. I would have to go onto Warfarin to thin my blood because the fibrillation made it frothy and could cause clots. When my blood viscosity was at the desired level, I was given the two paddles on the chest treatment where they zap you with electricity to get your heart beating properly. After a couple of failures, the third one did the trick and I started ticking with a normal beat. I'm glad they put me to sleep for the zapping because I had two burns on my chest from the paddles and I don't think that it would have been a pleasant experience had I been awake. I found out later that my brother Bob had refused to go onto Warfarin for some season, so we will never know if it could have given him the same chance. Perhaps if I had gone through this episode before him I could have given him some advice and hope of recovery.

Unfortunately, the steady heartbeat only lasted a few months and reverted to fibrillation. I was put back onto Warfarin and fitted with a defibrillator pace maker implanted into my chest. The good news is that I can still drive a car and if I was able to, fly a plane apparently. So my demise would not seem to be imminent I'm pleased to say.

This interlude from my early life story only accounts for a couple of months of my time, the rest of the time was wasted on feeling sorry for myself I'm ashamed to admit. I wallowed in self- pity like a pig in shit. You could say that it was traumatic to be so near to cashing in my chips and understandable. That wasn't it because I have had the grim reaper breathing down my neck before without going belly up. I felt like an invalid and I was as weak as a kitten. The doctor told me that it was common to be depressed and short tempered when you have heart trouble. Well I'm usually an upbeat, glass half-full sort of bloke and I did not deal with it very well. It culminated when I made my darling wife Margaret cry because of the way that I had spoken to her. This was the woman that had been through Hell for me and had remained loving and strong. I sorted my pathetic self out immediately and even now if my tongue gets a bit sharp I address it. I had lost my sense of humour and it took a while to regain it. If anyone reading this has been considering contracting pneumonia or heart failure I would advise you against it, its complete crap, take it from me.

✦✦✦✦✦✦

CHAPTER 7

Back to senior school

Where was I? Oh yes, I had just spied on the girls and discovered that I was considered to be the best kisser in the gang. Well this may have been true but to be honest I was still as green as grass when it came to the fair sex. Catchy kiss was one thing but when it came to a one on one situation with a girl I simply didn't have a clue as to what I was supposed to do. Twelve and thirteen year olds of today would be able to advise a Gynaecologist, I was still playing marbles.

I recall when I was that age I took Marion Morgan to Doctor Aitchesons old place to show her the skeleton of a dog I had discovered in the bushes, (you won't get a romantic tryst like that in a 'Catherine Cookson' novel). After Marion had made her inspection of the decaying canine we lay in the grass (upwind of the putrid pooch) and began to kiss. I freely admit that this had been my dastardly plan from the start and the demise of poor Fido had simply given me an enticement with which to lure the lovely Marion. I kissed her upturned face, eyes and mouth as the dappled Sunlight shone on her golden hair through the leaves of the orchard canopy, (romantic or what?). Then I stopped, at a complete loss as to what came next. I don't know if Marion had any idea of courtship rituals but I was clueless on the subject. Whatever was supposed to happen, didn't. I don't know whether I had a stirring in my twelve year olds loins, or if it was the long grass up my short pants. The upshot was, we lost the moment, got up, picked the bits of grass off each other and went home, never to try and pair up ever again. Marion was a bonny lass and when I think of her now I liken her to a young 'Shirley Eaton' the girl who was painted gold in the James Bond film 'Gold Finger' starring Sean Connery.

I mentioned short pants earlier. Well, when a boy was about thirteen years old it was almost a tradition in those days for him to get his first long trousers. I remember how I was bursting with pride when I went to meet my pals in Carville Gardens with my new grey flannel long trousers on. The girls were ooing! And aahing! And the lads looked suitably impressed. It was always grey flannels in those day's, 'Jeans' didn't hit the scene for another few years.

When I was about thirteen years of age a girl called Norma Grounsel took a shine to me and began to follow me about. She never spoke to me at first, she just followed me from school every afternoon about ten paces behind me. Then when I came out of the house she would just tag along wherever I was going. She never tried to hide from me at all and just stayed a short distance behind me. She always wore a green Anorak and had fair hair. I would speak to her and ask her what she wanted and she would just shrug and say, "I just want to be beside you". I suppose they would say that I was being stalked today but it was just an innocent crush she had and it did wonders for my ego and 'street cred' with my mates. Norma was quite a pretty girl and when I got over the strange circumstances I decided to show her more attention, (how magnanimous of me). One winters night when I came out of the house Norma was there in the back lane as usual so I walked over to her and struck up a conversation. She was obviously pleased to be acknowledged by me and we walked around the streets in the soft, warm glow of the street gas-lamps. She was happy and smiling and I found her to be good company. We wound up in the alcove of the Salvation Army hall back door. I started to kiss her and she eagerly responded to me. This was the first time that I had kissed a girl in earnest so to speak, like a grown up. We were both dressed for winter, woollen jumpers, woollen hats and woollen gloves. I was wearing my topcoat and Norma was in her faithful Anorak. I resembled 'Scott of the Antarctic' and Norma resembled an overstuffed green duvet, (not that I knew what a duvet was back then).

Like the unspeakable bounder that I obviously was I decided that I should proceed to the next stage in the ritual that I had been told about. I began to move my gloved hand around to the front of her stuffed and quilted Anorak. When Norma realised what I was attempting to do she jumped back and smacked me right in the gob, telling me that she wasn't that sort of girl. I was full of apologies and felt genuinely ashamed of myself. Norma would have none of it and stormed off. She never followed me again and I never got the chance to tell her how sorry I was. I don't know if this incident taught me a moral lesson making me a better person, or stunted my growth as a potential ladies man. All I can say in conclusion is, "good for you Norma, I hope you don't still despise me". As far as an erotic experience goes, I suppose it would have to be compared to reading brail while wearing a boxing glove. Strangely, I still find green Anoraks slightly arousing, (kinky or what?).

I got myself a job delivering papers at around this time working for Mr Wynn who had a shop opposite the Thermal Syndicate on Neptune road. The Wynn family lived next door to us in number one Union street. I referred to it as a paper round but it was in fact several paper rounds. I did one round in the mornings delivering about two hundred papers all over the bottom half of Wallsend between the High street and the river. I had to be at the shop for seven- o-clock in the morning to finish in time to get to school. Then after school I had the same round plus an extra fifty in Daisy Hill just over the boundary into Newcastle delivering the Evening Chronicle. This was six days a week and then on Sunday mornings I delivered the Sunday papers over the same rounds plus another hundred or so in Walkerville and West street estates. Mr Wynn would let me use his old pushbike on Sundays because I couldn't carry the newspaper bag it was so heavy. You were taking your life in your hands using his bike because it only had half of a handle bar. Yes it was the dropped handle bar racing style bike but somehow the right hand half had been snapped off. This meant that you could only steer and brake with your left hand while the paper bag hung on the stump of the right hand bar. I kept asking him if he would buy new handle bars but he just said that he rode it to the shop every day and didn't have any trouble, (about three hundred yards, un-laden).

I worked for him for about two years until I left school and I received the princely sum of ten Shillings (fifty new pence) per week. This was rubbish money even in those days for delivering papers seven days a week, twice a day. I had mates who only delivered 150 Evening Chronicles at teatime and were getting ten shillings more than me (one Pound) for six evenings only. Mam wouldn't let me tell him where he could stick his job and his bike because he was our neighbour. My Saturday afternoon job delivering meat (on a proper bike) and sweeping the floor earned me five Shillings for three hours work. I kept the five Shillings from the butcher and I gave the ten Shillings from the penny pinching Mr Wynn to my mam.

My brother Bob was seeing Mr Winn's daughter Eileen at the time and I remember that she had enormous breasts on her otherwise slim body, which probably accounts for the fact that I don't recall her face at all. I do have another reason to remember her though. The first two records that I ever bought were 'Teddy Bear' backed with 'Heartbreak Hotel' by Elvis Presley and 'When I fall in love' by Nat King Cole, (vinyl 78 rpm). This was an enigma due to the fact that I did not have a record player and indeed would not acquire one for about another eight years. Never the less I liked the songs and bought them. Bob loaned them to Eileen and I never saw them again. And so, Eileen was immortalised in my adolescent mind by the enormity of her statuesque upper protrusions and the fact that she purloined my records.

There was one plus to having the paper round, it saved me

from getting beaten up on one occasion. I was playing with a couple of my pals in the local recreation ground on the border between Wallsend and Daisy hill (Newcastle). A gang of Daisy Pushers (sworn enemies) chased us and only managed to catch me. They explained the error of my trespass and were debating the atrocities they considered suitable for the occasion. Urban myth was that they favoured putting hot tar on the legs of their captives. Although I had never heard of this story ever being substantiated, I still felt that my afternoon was about to be ruined in some way. Then like a miracle, a voice rang out from the baying throng, "He's OK, he delivers our Evening Chronicle". They released me and I legged it like a Greyhound chasing a Hare. When I caught up with my pals, I no doubt regaled them with stories of a heroic escape.

On another occasion I made my escape from the Daisy pushers due to my brother Bob. This was a couple of years earlier and I was climbing a tree in the recreation ground with a lad called Brian Metcalf. A gang of Pushers surrounded the tree and requested that we should descend at our first opportunity (well, words to that effect). So, we climbed down expecting to get a good kicking but then one of the Neanderthals said, "Are you Bob Blevins's brother". I told him that I was and he told us that we were free to go. As he explained to his mates that Bob was a real hard lad from Wallsend, I thanked my lucky stars for my family likeness. I have told this story many times before to people but I always said that I had been obliged to leave Brian there to get a good smacking. This seemed like a more amusing anecdote to me but the fact is, we both made our escape together and for the sake of the integrity of this opus I now tell it as it really happened.

My next story involving the recreation ground is vulgar and crude but in my eyes quite funny. The sports field had a railway line running along its northern side flanked with dense trees and shrubs. It was inevitable that if you played there all day you would need the toilet from time to time. The public toilets were a long walk and were horrible dark smelly places. Having a pee was easy there were shrubs everywhere that were seemingly designed for the purpose. When we needed a cacky (shit) we had developed a more manly solution to the problem. Each of us had our own Cacky tree with a forked branch to sit in and no shortage of leaves to use as toilet paper. It was wise to choose a forked branch directly above a large shrub to accommodate the excremental bombardment. We found that the unwise choosing of forked branches led to faecal landmines on the dirt pathways between the trees. I still get the urge to go back and see if I can find my Cacky tree if it is still there. It was so well fertilized it should look like a Californian Redwood by now.

Next to the sports field there was a huge wooden pavilion, I've never seen one as big to this day. It was square with a footprint as big as Doctor Aitchesons house with two stories and verandas top and bottom going all of the way around. The ground floor I assume was for all of the sporting activity equipment storage, changing rooms, meeting rooms etc! The upper floor was function rooms and kitchens. My sister Joan had her wedding reception in one of these rooms and I remember running around and around the veranda. The ground floor stood on a platform about three feet high and the veranda had two large steps so that people could sit and watch the sporting activity under its shelter. We found a loose plank that allowed us to access the underside of the pavilion, (or it may be more honest to say, we loosened a plank). We could crawl all of the way underneath the structure and the perimeter underneath the highest step of the veranda. We could not be seen in the dim light but we could see and hear the people above us between the gaps in the planks. It was like being a spy eves dropping on conversations and we learned quite a lot of grown up stuff in this way. It was also quite lucrative because people would often drop small change by accident and some would make its way between the planks. This wonderful structure has also been torn down, so much for posterity.

✯✯✯✯✯✯

I'm going off on a small tangent now because of a recent event that I want to record before I forget.

On the Christmas of 1947, I was given a book called 'Tiny Tots' annual 1948. This was the first book that my mam and dad ever bought me and I loved it. I was six and would be seven in January and I was a good reader for my age. The book had everything, short stories, comic strips, puzzles and lovely drawings but the things that I liked the most were the little poems. I would lie in bed between my brothers Alan and Bob, cosy under the blankets and dads army greatcoat. The frost would form on the inside of the window and I could see my breath as I exhaled but I never seemed to feel the cold. I was lost in the world of Tiny Tots annual, by the light of my little black and chrome torch as my brothers slept beside me.

Luckily, I read it over and over again and so I never forgot the magic that reading can give you. I say luckily because with two older brothers the book did not survive very long. The reason I am telling you this story is because I have been looking for the book for the last sixty-two years without any luck. Every time I have been to an old bookshop, flea market or car boot sale, I have always rummaged through the children's books in the hope of finding it. We were having a few day's holiday last week, stopping with friends Angie & Willie McLennan at their home in Aultbea on the west coast of Scotland. Angie was showing off the prowess of her computer skills, downloading music onto C Ds, showing us Google Earth and asking it random questions. I was suitably impressed due to my being a technophobe, not I hasten to add because I'm thick but because I'm too lazy to learn. I enjoy being one of those smug types who go around saying things like, "what happened to the art of writing a letter". I do lament the old and in my eyes nicer ways of communicating but I also recognise progress and my own reluctance to embrace it. As I have said, I am bone-idle. I asked Angie if she could find old books on her computer and told her the story of my Tiny Tots annual 1948. I described the front cover as having three horses wearing coloured pom-pom's on their heads and standing on their hind legs. There was a young girl wearing a pointed hat and a Tu-Tu and carrying a whip. She was obviously their trainer and it was in a circus ring. To my amazement Angie found one almost immediately for sale on E-bay. I couldn't believe it, there it was exactly as I remembered it I could hardly breathe and tears filled my eyes. Angie said that she would keep an eye on the bidding until the deadline and try to get it for me.

The book came to me by post yesterday and it took me on an emotional journey through time. The pictures, the stories and the poems are exactly as I had stored them in my brain. I admit that I have shed a few nostalgic tears as I once more became the little Billy Blevins, huddled under my dads army greatcoat between my two big brothers sixty two years ago.

There is one poem that I liked the most called 'The Sticklebacks escape' and I have been reciting it to Margaret since we first met.

"Oh, how unlucky. What a shame!
My jar has fallen in!"
Cries Johnny, as the little fish
Their way to freedom win.
Says grandma fish, "It serves you right.
A lesson that should be
Why were you not at school my dears?
Come home at once with me".

The poem has an illustration showing above and below the waterline of a stream.

Above the waterline Johnny is dipping his net into the stream and trying to retrieve his jar. A little girl is kneeling beside him watching the proceedings and there is a small white dog with them. Below the waterline the little fish are making their escape from the submerged jar, as grandma fish looks on sternly with her mouth open. If I had been asked, I could have made an accurate drawing of this scene except that I had forgotten about the dog.

I would like to thank Angie for her prowess on the computer and for getting me my book. (She wouldn't let me pay for it). I would also like to thank a little girl called 'Yvonne Haywood', who according to the inscription was given this book by her 'Mammie and Daddie' for Christmas 1947. Thank you Yvonne and God bless you for taking better care of it than I did mine and giving me this second chance.

CHAPTER 8

Brownrigg

OK, back to the plot. Back at the Western Secondary Modern senior school when I was about thirteen, we were told about two great adventures that we could put our names down for if we wished. The first was to live on board a training ship that was anchored in Portsmouth harbour I believe. Lads from all over were to be picked and I think that three places had been allocated to our school. Whoever was selected would be taken down by train and given a berth aboard the old square rigged sailing ship, learning seamanship for two weeks. This really appealed to a lot of us and we had visions of swashbuckling about the decks and swinging from the rigging. The other great adventure on offer was to go to 'Brownrigg' camp school at Bellingham Northumberland. This was for a full school term between the summer holidays and the Christmas holidays. You would do regular schoolwork plus outward-bound type stuff. Nobody really fancied going to Brownrigg but I got it into my head that if I put my name down for both, they would see how keen I was and were certain to let me have my pick. It turned out that I had been the only one in the school that had put my name forward for Brownrigg and so inevitably I was earmarked for this and not considered for the training ship. I was gutted, not only would I be living away from home for months but I would be going on my own. I put a brave face on for my mam who wasn't very happy with the idea of her little lad going off into the wilds of Northumberland. She came to see me off and I told her not to give me a kiss in case it made me seem soft in front of all of these strange kids. She adhered to my wishes and just waved me off as the bus full of kids moved away from outside of St Nicholas's cathedral Newcastle. When I looked out of the bus window I could see that she was crying and I felt the pang of guilt realising how much it was hurting my mam not to kiss me goodbye. I vowed that it would never happen again and it never did, even if I was only going to the corner shop I always kissed her.

The village of Bellingham is nestled among the Cheviot Hill's in the lovely county of Northumberland. There are many hill farms breeding sheep and beautiful moors surrounding it. Brownrigg looks like it could have been an old army camp or prisoner of war camp with its rows of wooden barracks on two-foot stilts. Or I suppose it could have been purpose built as a boarding school, as it was then. When we arrived we were segregated and the boys were billeted at the bottom end of the camp while the girls were taken to the top end. The classroom, administration, dining and assembly huts stood between the male and female dormitories. The barrack rooms were all named after northeast rivers and I was assigned to 'Wansbeck'. We each had a bed, a bedside locker and a footlocker. They showed us a room where we were to put our suitcases when we had unpacked and told us to make our beds up from the pile of bedding on the footlockers.

I have no idea what I was expecting but it had never occurred to me that I would have to make my own bed. By the looks on the faces of the lads around me I wasn't the only one to have the mat pulled from under him. This is the result of being spoiled rotten by my mam and three older sisters, I was bone-idle and didn't realise it. Two older lad's who must have been almost ready to leave school, introduced themselves and told us they were prefects. They had been at Brownrigg for a couple of years and their job was to show us the ropes and give us our daily tasks during our stay. "There they go again, daily tasks, making beds" I thought, "what happened to the fun stuff, I've been conned,

I'm not designed for domestic toil". Protesting would have been a sign of weakness, so I set about making my bed.

At first the prefects were very helpful and showed us the ropes and the little jobs that we were expected to perform daily. These tasks were given out on a rota system to make it fair. The tasks were sweeping the dormitory, dusting the lockers, washing the windows, cleaning the toilet block and keeping the outside perimeter and underneath of the huts clean. Then it was discovered that another lad and myself were non-catholic in an otherwise catholic hut. After this we were given every dirty smelly job that came up. If it was raining or freezing cold, we would be outside and under the hut picking up rubbish and fallen leaves. Yes religious bigotry was alive and well and I was experiencing it for myself, heart warming isn't it. We weren't bullied physically in any way and I know that I would have given them a hard time if they had attempted it. They spoke to us and were civil but we were never included into their activities or the little cliques that evolved. The other lad took it badly and he got a bit depressed. I took a more pragmatic point of view, due probably to having been a hot water bottle for my two brothers from time to time. If someone is higher up in the pecking order, they will favour themselves or their friends with the cushiest jobs. So, unless you're in pain, go with the flow until a practical solution reveals itself to you. Apart from the prejudice thing, I am aware that I would very likely favour friends and family in a balance of choice situation.

We were only allowed to have 2/6- (twelve and a half new pence) per week at the school, so all of our mail was opened and if anyone received more than 2/6- the excess was confiscated until the end of term. My fellow non-catholic whose name I can't recall had taken all of the victimisation that he could and saved his half crowns up until he had enough money for his bus-fare home. He sneaked away after morning classes and caught the bus from Bellingham to Newcastle. He was missed almost immediately when he didn't take his place for lunch and one of the teachers went after the bus in his car. The teacher waited at the Gallowgate bus station in Newcastle and when the lad got off the bus he just bundled him into the car and brought him straight back to Brownrigg. That night, after we had eaten our evening meal the headmaster brought the escapee out onto the raised area in the dining hall where the teachers ate. There was a nervous silence among the pupils as the lad stood with his head down looking very sheepish. The headmaster was looking, how shall I put it, 'stern and grave' or perhaps pompous would be more descriptive. He then spoke these immortal though stupid words to his captive audience, "This boy is not going to be punished for running away but he is for having more than half a crown when he knew that it was not allowed". I swear that this is true and I would have burst out laughing if he hadn't picked up a cane from the table and told the lad to bend over. He proceeded to give him six strokes of the cane across his buttocks in front of the entire school. To be fair, the other teachers looked as uncomfortable as I was feeling. The lad then had to leave the dining room with tears running down his face due to the pain and worse the humiliation.

It wasn't all bad at the school and I suppose that I tend to paint a blacker picture of it than it deserves. We did have Saturdays to ourselves to go into Bellingham and spend our 2/6- pocket money. Once a month they had a film show in the village hall that was very popular with the locals because it was a long way to travel into Newcastle for the nearest cinemas. In those days almost no one had a television and even if you did own one, I doubt if you could receive a signal for the one and only station 'BBC' out in Bellingham. Mostly, we spent our money on sweets or comics but I remember that there was one budding entrepreneur in my hut who bought a tin of 'Nestles' condensed milk. He then sold it to us at 3d for a teaspoon of this delicious nectar he must have made a fortune from it. I have to admit that I did succumb to temptation when I had three pence to spare. He is probably a retired drug baron now and my spare three-penny pieces helped him on his inglorious climb.

On Sundays we all had to assemble into our religious denominations and march down to our respective churches in the village. My brother-in-law Val Borthwick had given me one of his old suits to wear for best. Although he was very muscular due to him being a diving and swimming champion, he wasn't very tall. It was a smart double-breasted silver grey suit and although it hung on me drooping at the shoulders I thought I looked like a film star. Unfortunately my body had decided to have a growth spurt and each successive Sunday the trousers were an inch or so shorter. I had to keep letting my braces out a bit more and wear them lower and lower on my hips to make the legs reach my ankles. I was confident that this would go unnoticed because of the jacket being double breasted and hiding the waistline of the trousers.

After church we got changed into our sports kit and did the outward-bound stuff that I had been so keen to embrace. Our first walk was a tour of the village and it was surprisingly informative. There was a field as you entered Bellingham where the victims of the Bubonic (black death) plague were buried in a mass grave. I found that I was moved by this revelation because it brought the reality of it home to me. I knew from history lessons that up to 80% of the population of Britain and Europe had died from the plague but it had no real impact on me. Looking at this field and knowing that hundreds of men, women and children had been buried here without ceremony in one big grave was very moving.

We also went for hikes over the moors and up the cheviots and rock climbing in the crags. I liked climbing up the rocks but I have to say that climbing down was scarier. I once got threatened with being given the cane because I refused to climb down one particular crag. It was down a steep sloping rock and then blindly over a cliff so that you couldn't actually see where it was leading. It was pouring with rain and the water was cascading down the rock slope and over the cliff. I was soaked to the skin in my shorts, vest, soggy sandshoes and socks. My feet were slipping on the rocks and he wanted me to be the first one to lower myself down. There was no climbing gear like you would have today, just a rope tied to something. He had shown us how to put the rope over our shoulders and feed it out through our hands as we descended. I asked him what was over the cliff and he said, "You will find out when you get there won't you". All character building stuff I'm sure but I sometimes wonder what turnover of pupils he had in his outward-bound class.

Normally I was keen to prove that I was the bravest / daftest one there but on this day I was feeling less than intrepid and flatly refused. He then tried to get a volunteer from one of the other lads. They all realised the obvious wisdom I had uncharacteristically displayed and declined his request. The teacher was furious, shouting that we had all walked miles for nothing. I thought to myself that I could probably live with the disappointment, given time. He was adamant that I would get the cane when we got back for disrupting his class. I didn't get the cane or even a telling off perhaps he'd had time to think about it on the trek back.

We had to write letters home once a week in the classroom and the teacher would then collect and read them. He would then edit them for anything that in his opinion may upset our parents, then we had to write censored versions for him to collect and post. I was feeling increasingly like a prisoner with all of this regimentation. The classes often went on until six-o-clock in the evening and we only had Saturdays to ourselves with very little to do. Then the final straw came in the dining hall at lunchtime. There was a girl called Hazel that sat at my table and was also in my class. Her name is the only one that I can remember from my entire stay at Brownrigg. This may be because I always called her 'Hazel Nut' with my usual razor sharp wit, (sad I know), It may also be because I fancied her a bit. Anyway, as I was saying, the final straw came when one of the female teachers came to our table and told Hazel to follow her. She then went to another table and collected another girl. She took them both up to the raised area in the hall and stood them together in the middle. Everyone was silent not knowing what this was all about. The teacher then told us in a loud smug voice that she had noticed that these two disgusting girls had borrowed each of the others jumpers to come for their lunch. The wearing of other people's clothes was unhygienic and would not be tolerated at Brownrigg School. She then made them take off the offending garments and change them back in front of the whole school. I can still see these two thirteen year old girls crying and swapping back their jumpers, while being paraded like pariahs for this simple girly act. I was disgusted and vowed that I was going to get away from this place. Hazel came back to the table and sat quietly sobbing, not touching her food. I would like to tell you that I said something comforting to her but I can't remember if I did, or just thought it. We were probably all too embarrassed to mention it to her ever again.

The following Saturday was half term and I knew that my mam would be coming up for parents day. I told myself that this was my chance, I would just go home with my mam and this purgatory would be over.

We all had to dress in our Sunday best and wait at the school gates for the busses to arrive. Two busses came and went with no sign of my mam and I was getting a bit frantic. I was sitting on the fence feeling sorry for myself and crying. I didn't care if anyone could see me because all of the kids were crying when they greeted their parents. Everybody melted away and I was still sitting there crying all alone, it was like a Catherine Cookson melodrama. I looked down the road towards the village and there in the distance was the wonderful sight of my mam and my sister Alma walking towards me. They had missed seeing the school gates and went on into the village with the bus. I was ecstatic with joy as I ran down the road to hug my mam. I blurted out that I wanted to go home with them and preferably on the next bus.

They couldn't understand because my letters were always so cheerful and full of the interesting things that I had been doing. I explained that they were censored and that the teachers dictated most of what was written. They seemed a bit sceptical and mam said that she had just bought a single return ticket and didn't have enough money to get me a ticket home. She said that she would come back for me on the following Saturday because she couldn't afford to take time off work through the week. I knew that this was true of course but I was devastated at the prospect of spending another week in what I had now elevated in my mind to be a 'Hell Hole'.

I began to walk away with my tail between my legs so to speak, calling over my shoulder plaintively, "Nobody cares about me, just go and leave without me". (Tear jerking stuff). My sister Alma told me in later years that it was the funniest thing she had ever seen. Me, walking down the road, my jacket hanging over my shoulders by about four inches each side, the back of it in folds like a theatre curtain, my trousers at half mast with the crotch almost down to my knees. To top it off, I have always walked splay footed so apparently I looked like a lanky version of Charley Chaplin. The pathos must have worked because she shouted that she had some money and would buy my bus ticket. I was on cloud nine as we walked back into the school and into my hut 'Wansbeck'. As luck would have it, my housemaster was in the hut and Alma told him that they were taking me home. The teacher would have none of it and said that they would have to go through the education authority to secure my return to a normal secondary modern education school. This was like a red flag to a bull to my sister Alma and she said, "Is this establishment some sort of correctional facility for young offenders then". The teacher looked aghast and said, "No of course not". Alma then replied, "Then as I have already informed you, my mother and I will be taking my brother home with us now", she put the stress on the 'Now'.

The teacher, still trying to be authoritative said pettily, "You can take him home with you but you will have to come back for his suitcase because I don't have the key to the storage room". Alma looked him in the eye and said, "listen here you smug little pen pusher, my mother can't afford to come back up here for his suitcase so you had better toddle off and get the key as quickly as you can". (I didn't mention that Alma was a 'Chief Petty Officer' in the Royal Naval Reserve did I). At this the teacher realised that he was out-gunned and went to fetch the key. I was blissfully happy once we were on the bus heading back to Newcastle and home. I was also eternally grateful to my drama queen sister Alma for her confrontational eloquence in my hour of need.

CHAPTER 9

Return to normal education

And so I returned to the Western Secondary Modern school in Wallsend with a happy heart and a spring in my step. I brought back only one happy memory from Brownrigg, it was the small outdoor swimming pool. The teacher would get two lads to stand on either side of the pool holding a rope between them. We would then take turns holding the middle of the rope while the two lads ran up the length of the pool towing us through the water, it was quite exhilarating. I am also grateful to them for getting me to clean my teeth regularly, which I hardly ever did before going. I am turned seventy now and still have all of my own teeth.

Back at school I was to find that I had a new teacher 'Mr Wilson Taylor'. He had come to the school for the start of the term, at the same time that I had gone off to Brownrigg. We didn't hit it off at first, he made some comment about me not being able to stick it at boarding school, which hit a raw nerve because I knew it was true. He did treat me fairly but was a bit cool towards me, in my eyes anyway. Things came to a head one day when we were doing physical training in the school hall. I was told to bend over from the waist and hold my knees while he demonstrated how to vault over me to the rest of the class. I heard him running up the hall behind me and decided as a joke to crouch down at the last second, causing him to sail over me and crash to the mat 'Anus over Breast' in front of me. The rest of the class were falling about laughing at my jolly jape but I was already having doubts about the wisdom of my attempt at slapstick humour. On this occasion Mr Taylor's sense of humour was noticeable by its absence and he was furious. He took off his Sandshoe and told me to bend over to get a whacking with it. I refused to bend over and told him he could give me the belt on my hands but that I wouldn't bend over and be hit on my backside. At first he was dumbstruck and then he told me to wait in the classroom for him.

I thought that I was in deep manure, what with my stupid joke and then refusing my punishment. After the PT lesson the other lads went out into the schoolyard for playtime and Mr Taylor came into the classroom to see me. He had calmed down and asked me why I had crouched down at the last moment, was it an accident or had I been a bit nervous of a grown man vaulting over me. I looked sheepish and told him that it was just a stupid joke that I had thought was a good idea at the time and I apologised to him. He actually smiled at this and then asked me why I had refused to be punished when I knew that it was a stupid thing to do. I reminded him that I hadn't refused to be punished, just that I wouldn't be hit on my backside in front of all of my mates. I explained that I had witnessed a lad having to bend over and be caned in front of the entire school at Brownrigg and the two girls having to change their jumpers in front of everyone and how humiliating it had been. I was amazed when he smiled at me again and said that we both understood each other much better now and sent me out for playtime without giving me the belt.

Wilson Taylor and I got along like a house on fire after that and he became my favourite teacher from my schooldays. (Not counting Miss Pinkerton that is). I remember that he decided to give us a general knowledge quiz in class one day and I won it by miles. I've always had a good memory as far as trivia goes, although very little else seems to stick for long. The prize was a small framed oil painting of a Tugboat coming into the River Tyne between the piers at Tynemouth and he had painted it himself. He said that I would probably prefer a football or something but I assured him that I wouldn't and I think that he could tell from my face how delighted I was. It was a lovely little painting and I could hardly wait to take it home to my mam. She was over the moon when she saw it and you would think I had won the finals of 'Mastermind' she was so proud of my obvious genius. It hung on our living room wall until my mam died and I moved out of 3 Union Street. Sadly it went missing during the move as often happens unfortunately but I would like to think it is still hanging on someone's wall. It would be a tribute to Wilson Taylor's skill as an artist and a memorable teacher. Oh, just as an after thought, the lads that went to the sailing ship rather than Brownrigg had a great time. They never tired of regaling me with stories of climbing the rigging, diving off the deck into the sea and learning how to handle a sailing dinghy. I was really pleased for them, honest, (if you believe that you are daft).

It was about this time I suppose that I decided to give smoking a try. A couple of my pals had started but I had always refused to have a drag of their fags not wanting to slavishly follow the trend. I was curious though and decided to experiment on my own. I went to the corner shop near to my school and bought five 'Wills Woodbines' and a box of 'Puck' matches. The Woodbine cigarettes were sold in open-ended paper pouches and were the cheapest and most popular. I think they must have been made from the sweepings from the floor of an animal cage in a zoo. I took them up to the top of the 'Powder Monkey' hill for privacy and smoked them one after the other. I remember feeling dizzy and standing up trying to walk but my head was spinning so much that I fell and rolled from the top to the bottom of the hill. On reaching the bottom I was violently sick, bringing up things that I had never heard of never mind eaten. The vomit and red dust was all over me and I had a hell of a job getting cleaned up before I could go home. I think that I went to my sister Joan's for a wash down. It is true that you can always find diced carrots in your puke whether you have eaten them or not, it is a widely documented phenomenon. In truth, I could not be happier with this turn of events because I have never had the urge to try smoking again since that day.

✦✦✦✦✦✦

When I was about fourteen years of age, my pal Robert Gray and I went to Wallsend swimming baths. We were having a rough and tumble in the low end of the pool. A lad who lived a couple of streets away from me at the bottom end of Benton Way told us that he wanted to wrestle with me. His name was Colin and he was about a year older than me. He had a reputation as a bully and had been in trouble with the police a couple of times. He started wrestling with me and I took the fight below the water knowing that I would have more of a chance if we were submerged. After we had grappled for a while I accidentally kneed him in the nose. I apologised to him as soon as we surfaced but Colin was holding his bleeding nose and shouting that he was going to get me when we left the swimming pool. My pal Robert said that we should get dressed as quickly as we could and do a runner before Colin could stem the flow of his blood. I told him that I was sure to bump into Colin because he lived so near to me and I may as well get it over with. We met Colin and his pal in Vine Street that ran between the 'Territorial Army' drill hall and the swimming pool. I removed my black Onyx ring that my mam had bought me for my fourteenth birthday and gave it to Robert for safe keeping, I treasured it and still do. Colin was telling me what dastardly things he was going to do to me when he suddenly jumped on me and tried to wrestle me to the ground. I managed to get the better of him and succeeded in getting him into a headlock with my left arm. I can still see his ginger head poking out from under my left armpit as I punched his right lughole and his already sore nose repeatedly. Then ironically, an old lady came over and started bashing me with her handbag telling me to stop hitting the poor lad. Yes, because I had the upper hand it appeared to her that I was the 'Baddie'. The fight broke up and we all started to make our way home. Colin shouted that it wasn't finished and that he would get me later. This made me feel a bit uneasy because as I have said, he had a reputation as a bully.

When I got home, my brother-in-law Val Borthwick was there, I told him the whole story and about the threat that Colin had made. Val asked me if I knew where Colin lived and I told him that I did. He said that it was no good waiting for him to take me by surprise and that I should go to Colin's house and sort it out on my own terms. I was a bit apprehensive as I walked down Benton Way but I could see that Val was right. I didn't fancy going around waiting for Colin to jump me and take his revenge. I knocked at the front door and waited, holding my breath. Colin's sister answered the door and told me to go around to the back door because he was in the back yard. I went around to the back and opened the gate into his back yard. He turned to see who it was and his jaw dropped when he recognised me. I then came out with a line worthy of the script in a cowboy film. "I'm here to finish what we started", I said. Colin looked flustered then said, "Oh! lets just forget about that, come in and see my rabbits". I have to admit that I was relieved at this turn of events and he did have some nice rabbits as it happens.

A funny incident that involved Colin took place a couple of years earlier. A few of my pals and I were playing on our bogies, whizzing down the 'Boatie Bank'. This was the steep hill at the end of Benton Way that ran down between Swan Hunters shipbuilding yard and Wallsend Dry Docks. It ended at the riverside and the Tyne ferry landing. Its termination point was a wooden jetty from which the gangplank down to the ferry landing was attached. Colin didn't have a bogie, so he took a tricycle from a little girl and offered to race us to the bottom. We all set off down the hill gathering speed rapidly with the little lass screaming for her tricycle behind us. Then I noticed that the screams were now coming from in front of us. Colin was ahead of the pack and still accelerating. It looked quite comical, this ginger youth on a child's three-wheeler with his legs sticking out and screaming in fear. There were no brakes on the tricycle and he was out of control. We on the other hand, all had a rudimentary braking system on our bogies. Usually a piece of wood on a pivot that you could push, causing the bottom section to come into contact with the tyre on the back wheel, this was my preference. Or you could pull it, causing the bottom of the wood to come into contact with the road.

Colin's purloined transport was sadly bereft of such technological advancements and he now found himself straddling a projectile whose destination was to be the River Tyne. There were no railings between the jetty and the river in those days, only a wooden beam running along the edge of the jetty that was about twelve inches high. Colin and his trike hit this barrier and somersaulted in an arc into the river twenty feet below. His trajectory almost took him to the ferry landing, which allowed the workmen waiting for the ferry to drag him out of the murky water. I can still see him being helped up the gangplank looking like a drowned rat but unhurt. This was probably one of the times that he had a brush with the police, stealing and destroying the tricycle of the little girl.

After our run in at the baths and subsequent bonding with the rabbits, Colin and I were on nodding terms but not pals. He did save me from getting a good kicking a couple of years later though. I had been in Armstrong's shop on Denham Terrace, otherwise known as the penny drink shop. This was because Mrs Armstrong sold soft drinks that she made from fruit flavoured soluble tablets. They were mixed with water in a globular dispensing machine on the shop counter. If you put your penny in the slot it would fill your little paper cup. If the machine needed filling when you were there, she would fill the glass ball with water and put two tablets in it. The tablets were not agitated in the ball, just allowed to dissolve turning the water into the colour of whatever fruit flavour was on sale. If the machine needed filling when there was nobody in the shop, I suspect that she only put one tablet in the ball because some days it tasted like gnats piddle.

On the day that Colin saved me, I was leaving the shop and accidentally bumped heavily into a lad called Danny. I only knew Danny by his evil reputation and had never spoken to him. I say evil because he was one of those predatory types who spent his time making other peoples lives a misery. He was about eighteen years old and looked like a particularly ugly Neanderthal with the disposition of a rabid Baboon with haemorrhoids. I was only too keen to apologise for my clumsiness, in the hope that he wasn't in his usual homicidal frame of mind and that my early demise wasn't imminent. Danny had regressed into the slavering beast that he undoubtedly was and advanced on me uttering incoherent noises that I assumed were threats of violence. I began to walk backwards not wanting to turn my back on this drooling troglodyte when I heard a voice say, "It's OK Danny that's Bill Blevins a pal of mine and he is a bit of a hard case as well". It was Colin, who turned out to be Danny's pal and he had come to my rescue. Danny said, "If you're a pal of Colin, you're Ok with me". Then he turned and walked back into the shop. I had never been described as a bit of a hard case before and I left the scene with an exaggerated swagger. This was all an act of course because I was wondering if I would have had to change my pants had I not been rescued.

I heard that Danny had died when he was just in his forties. At least he was true to himself and had remained an objectionable drunken thug right up to the end. I don't think Wallsend grieved too much at his passing. I found out later that my brother Bob had been obliged to physically chastise him on a couple of occasions over the years. This may have been a factor in Danny's back down at the 'penny drink shop'. Either he thought I might actually be as hard as Bob or he was afraid of Bob's undoubted retaliation.

✻ ✻ ✻ ✻ ✻ ✻

I miss the halcyon days before puberty when everything was an adventure and life was for playing with your mates and not competing with them for the attention of the fair sex. (OK, so I don't miss it that much). I do though recall fondly when Micky Mulligan or Jimmy Sutherland and myself would help on 'Longies' pig cart. Mr Long had a pig farm on the village green in Wallsend. It's no longer there but I think that it was situated where the old peoples cottages are now, at the southeast corner of the green. Mr Long would ride his horse and cart around the back lanes of the terraced houses and collect buckets of Swill (left over unwanted food) out of the backyards. Everybody had a swill bucket for his collection and it served two purposes. Dumping leftover food in the dustbin meant that the ashes from the coal fires would turn to slime. This would make it harder for the lads on the dust bin wagons and leave you with a messy dustbin. The second purpose of course was that it meant Mr Long got the food to feed his pigs for free. Everyone was happy and in effect it was an early form of recycling. His cart looked like a large Roman chariot, open at the back and low to the ground so that you could step on and off easily. It had two car wheels with pneumatic tyres and two large oil drums standing in line fore and aft held in a cradle. He only came to our house once a week so he must have divided the town up into seven collection areas to assure a daily supply of food for his pigs. He always allowed two of us to help him and because I had been the one who had volunteered in the first place, I was always one of the chosen. He would stand on the right hand side and drive the cart while Micky or Jimmy and I stood on the left. We would jump off, run into the back yards, collect the swill and then hand it up to him to pour into the oil drums. We would then ride our chariot to the next street and repeat the task until the area had been harvested of pigswill.

It must have been on a Saturday or a Sunday because we seemed to be with him for hours. Then when he had finished his round we would go back to his farm on The Green. This was our favourite bit because he would let the big dapple-grey horse trot all the way back. The wheels were almost silent with the pneumatic tyres but the noise of the horse's hooves on the road was like poetry. The smell of the swill sloshing about in the open topped oil drums was enough to make you gag but it was worth it when he allowed me to take the reins. All I can remember about the pig farm is a large cobbled courtyard surrounded by pigsties and a shed containing a large vat in which the swill was boiled before being fed to the animals. I feel sorry for the occupants of the affluent looking houses that surrounded The Green, because the stench was dreadful. Still, we ourselves had to live with the bone yard that boiled horses down to make glue out of their bones a mile or two up the river at Walker. If the wind was blowing from the west it was nauseatingly putrid.

✦✦✦✦✦✦✦

A lot of people used horse and cart transport for their businesses in those days. The rag and bone man was a regular every week, blowing his bugle tunelessly to attract attention. We would take him some old clothes or the bones from the Sunday roast and he would give us a balloon or a gold fish if we took our own jam jar. Talking of jam jars, there were a couple of cinemas in 'Byker' that would accept jam jars or bottles as your entrance fee and they would give you a comic too. I think they were the Brinkburn and the Rabie. You could say another early example of recycling after the war. We also had trades people with handcarts that came around the streets plying their trade. There was Dostunies and Gracco's ice cream, although strictly speaking they weren't hand carts because they were three wheeled pedal carts. There was a bloke who had a grindstone mounted on his cart that he made spin by means of a foot treadle. He would sharpen your knives scissors or axes while he pumped the treadle. A very enterprising way to earn a living in those austere times I would say. I can remember 'Tommy Wilson' our coalman changing from a horse and cart to a petrol lorry, I think it was a 'Bedford'. He was really proud of his new acquisition with its maroon livery and 'Wilson and Son' on the side in I think, gold lettering.

They would deliver how ever many bags of coal, coke or anthracite that you ordered and tip them through a two feet square hole in the backyard wall, straight into your coalhouse. After a delivery we used to close the little wooden door and bolt it from the inside. I could never see the point of this because we never locked any other doors, so if someone wanted to pinch our coal they just had to come in through the back gate. We were only robbed once, when my mam was upstairs changing the bed linen. Her purse was stolen from the kitchen table and she was really upset by it. She only had a couple of shillings in it at the time but it was just the idea of someone doing such a thing. When our neighbours heard about it there was almost a lynch party formed.

As it happens, a lady came and returned the purse and money. She had her young daughter with her and she explained that the child was a bit simple minded and that she had just came through the open door and took the purse as a present for her mam. She got the girl to say how sorry she was for all the trouble she had caused and my mam gave them a cup of tea for putting her mind at ease.

People didn't start locking their doors until the 'fifties', when they started to have desirable acquisitions such as record players or even televisions if you were really doing well. We never owned a TV while I lived in Union Street, but the parents of a girl that lived near to my sister Joan did. Evie Conway was a year or so older than me and was always at Joan's house. She took me to see their new television because owning one was a bit of a status symbol. Her dad was a manager at the 'Rising Sun' colliery so they were relatively well off compared to the rest of us. The TV was the size of a refrigerator and had a nine-inch screen. They had a stand in front of it holding a huge magnifying glass to make the tiny screen look bigger. I think that the picture was only transmitted in 405 lines at this time, so the images were blurred and grainy to begin with. Through the magnifying glass it seemed as though you were watching ghosts through frosted glass and a Venetian blind. None of this mattered because this was 'state of the art' technology to us at the time and I was suitably gob smacked.

Evie was a bonny lass and I had a bit of a crush on her at the time although the year or so seniority she had on me robbed her of her chance to reach the stars. This may have been bolstered by her penchant for eating tealeaves. Yes, she loved to sit with the empty teapot and eat the warm tealeaves with a spoon as though it was ambrosia. I don't know about you but I only have to get one tealeaf in my throat to make me gag. I still see Evie now and then and she still appears to have teeth, which surprises me. I would have thought with her strange penchant for teapot dregs that they would have turned brown and fell out.

✶✶✶✶✶✶

When I was fourteen I had yet another saucy experience with a female of our species, or perhaps it would be more accurate to replace the word 'saucy' with 'farcical'. I had been hanging about outside Armstrong's penny drink shop with my friends one night and everyone began to drift off home as it was getting late and dark. In the end I was left talking to a girl that I knew only casually called Margaret, (not my future wife). She was an attractive girl and we began to kiss and cuddle. Then she took me by the hand and led me into the backyard of a house on the corner of Denham Terrace and Benton Way. She led me into the washhouse in the yard and climbed up onto the wooden bench. The washhouse served the families of both of the two flats that were accessed off the yard. It contained a zinc washtub over a coal fired heating stove and a wooden bench on which to scrub your clothes. Margaret was now reclined on this bench and looking up at me longingly. Her lips were moist with expectation as the Moon shone on her dark hair and pretty face. The mood was set her eyes said it all as she awaited my manly embrace and the intoxicating touch of my lips on hers. (Sounds promising would you think?).

I stooped over her, kissing her eager mouth, her neck, her eyes. Yes, I knew all the relevant moves I just needed the work

4

experience. Being a callow youth, the effect on me was the obvious one. I struggled but held myself in check, remembering the smack in the ear that Norma had administered a year earlier in the Salvation Army doorway. (It's risky getting frisky). I kept up this animated kissing for some time, with Margaret clutching the back of my head and attempting to eat my face. There was more steam on the windows than there was on a washday. At this point I realised that she was becoming agitated and moving her lithe young body spasmodically. Her breathing became laboured and rapid as she arched her back. I pulled away from her full pouting mouth looking into her wild eyes and she said huskily, "Billy, Oh Billy". (Erotic literature is obviously my 'Genre').

This was the moment in my life when I came to what was probably the daftest conclusion that I have ever made. "She must be having an Asthma attack", I told myself, Yes, 'ASTHMA'. (I told you it was farcical). I had no concept of female arousal or even if there was such a thing and I decided that it would be in her best interests if I took her home. She looked bewildered when I helped her off the bench and I suspect that she didn't in fact think that her best interests were being catered for.

I walked her home up Benton Way with a supportive arm around her waist and holding her left forearm. She didn't offer me a kiss goodnight and I don't recall her ever speaking to me again. I went to bed thinking that I was a knight in shining armour for saving a damsel in distress. Margaret probably lay in her bed with her motor still running and thinking that I was a 'Eunuch' or something.

I like to recall this little anecdote because it summons up a time in my life of innocence and naivety that I don't see in today's young people and I feel that it is their loss. (Did I really just say that? I must be older than I thought).

✷✷✷✷✷✷

Another exciting landmark happened when I was fourteen years old, I learned how to drive albeit four years before I was old enough to do so legally. My brother Alan was demobbed from the Army having served for three years, two of them in Kenya during the Mau-Mau uprisings. He got himself a job driving a truck for Ferguson's builder's merchants in Newcastle. He delivered sand, bricks, cement, bathtubs, fireplaces, in fact anything for the building trade all around the north east of England.

Sometimes I would play 'the wiggy' (Truant) from school and help him for the day. He would write me a note in his truly excellent hand writing to explain whatever debilitating malady we had chosen for that day. It was heavy work and there was no pre-packed stuff in those days. Alan knew the number of shovels of sand it would take to fill a one hundredweight sack, so if someone ordered a ton of sand we would have to fill twenty sacks and load them onto the truck by hand. If someone wanted a thousand bricks, I would stand on the back of the truck and Alan would throw them up to me to stack in neat piles. When we delivered them, the bags of sand had to be unloaded and carried to wherever the customer wanted them placed luckily he was allowed to use the hydraulic tipper to unload the bricks. He had to plan his drops so that he didn't have to unload other things, for example bathtubs etc, before he could tip the bricks. This wasn't always possible and they would have to be taken off the truck till the bricks were tipped and then reloaded. He did all of this on his own when I wasn't helping him but although he was slim like my dad, he had also inherited my dad's strength. I remember being amazed one day when he got a bath off the truck onto his back and carried it upstairs for an old couple. Remember that the baths back then were all made out of cast iron, not fibreglass. He looked like a bandy legged Ninja Turtle but I was well impressed. He did all of this for a wage of seven pounds per week and he still had to wash the truck before he could go home at night.

You may be wondering why I would prefer to do this backbreaking work instead of going to school. Well, there were many things that made it appealing, the excitement of driving to all of these lovely places in Northumberland and Durham. Places that I had never heard of along tiny roads that led to quaint little villages. Then there was the sense of achievement doing hard grown up work. Also the camaraderie with my big brother who was seven years older than me but treating as an equal, this bonding has stayed with us.

The most exciting part though started with Alan allowing me to steer the truck while he was driving or changing the gears for him while he operated the clutch. Then one day he stopped at the wrong house and the truck needed to go further up a back lane. Alan just stood on the running board on the driver's side and told me to shuffle across and drive it. I pulled away without stalling the engine pleasing us both but I looked down at the gear stick as I changed up into second gear and almost crushed him against the backyard walls. He had to reach through the open window and steer clear shouting for me to stop and screaming less than flattering expletives at me. He made me climb back into the passenger seat with my tail between my legs. I thought that this would be the end of my driving tuition but I was wrong.

Alan you must realise is somewhat of a free spirit so to speak. I was four years too young to be legally driving on the roads and seven years too young to drive a four-ton truck at that time, except in the armed forces. These facts would never have crossed his mind for a second. Legality, morality or sense of fair play, are things that he deals with only should he have no other option. If sidestepping were a dance, Alan would give Fred Astair or Gene Kelly a run for their money. He has no real concept of guilt, or if he does it is extremely short lived. If you think that this description makes him sound like a bad person you would be wrong. Everyone that knows him likes him, even those who are aware of his moral lapses. He is intelligent, well read and highly imaginative his surreal sense of humour is truly unique. Like Peter Pan, he just never really grew up to accept his responsibilities, (Sounds good).

Anyway, before long he had me driving on little country

roads like a professional. The old Austin truck had cable brakes, no power steering and a crash gearbox. This meant that I had to learn how to double de-clutch to change gear. When it was fully laden, it was a bit of a handful for me but I was developing muscles that I didn't know that I had with all the hard work I was doing. Alan was given a brand new Austin truck after a while and it was a beauty. It had hydraulic brakes and the luxury of a heater in the cab. It still didn't have power steering but it felt much lighter to drive than the old one. It also still had a crash gearbox but you only needed to double de-clutch when you were changing down through the gears.

I have never lost my love of driving since those far off days and trucks, buses, cars, tractors and motorbikes still fascinate me. I have driven most forms of motorised transport from two wheelers to eight wheelers. I have also driven a few tracked vehicles such as bulldozers and even a Centurion tank while in the army. I have even piloted a single wheeled mode of transport if you include the times when I tucked myself into a bus tyre and rolled down hills.

Riding inside a bus tyre is an anecdote that I feel is worth sharing with you so I will regress a few years to when I was about eight or nine years old. My pals and I would sometimes go along to the 'Green Bus' depot next to the 'Thermal Syndicate' on Neptune Road'. We would go into the workshops (health and safety laws were very lax in those days) and ask one of the workmen if they had an old tyre we could have. Quite often they would oblige us and we would happily roll one away with us.

We would make our way along Neptune Road to Victoria Terrace to play our favourite game. The top of Victoria Terrace was a short, steep, downward slope that became a shallower gradient that ran between the old terraced houses. The railway line wall ran across the bottom of the street and was the termination point of our game. The bus tyre stood as high as most of us and we took turns to sit inside it. To do so we had to pull our knees up to our chins and curl into the foetal position, gripping the inner rim with our hands. The game was to be pushed down the steep slope at the top of the street by the other lads. We would reach a good speed in the first thirty feet or so and the momentum would carry us down the lesser slope to the wall at the bottom. The winner was the lad who got the furthest down the street without mounting the kerb and crashing into the walls of the houses. The maximum accolade went to the hero whose tyre stayed on the cobbled street until it crashed into the railway wall ejecting its bilious passenger.

Once the tyre and passenger had started its roll, the rest of us would run along side and shout encouragement to the spinning occupant. Needless to say, you could almost guarantee that at least one of us would be sick during one of our rides. I can't remember being sick myself but I did witness a few spectacular regurgitations. This event was naturally a great source of amusement to the rest of us as we pursued the tyre. It was like watching a gastric 'Catherine Wheel' with all of the colours but none of the sparks. By the end of the day they would all have been spun-dry so to speak. It would then just have been the matter of shaking the organic bits from their hair and clothing. I have to say that they did remain somewhat pungent.

On one occasion we decided to roll our tyre to the 'Burn Closes', which is a deep valley at the east of Wallsend. We were on a footpath running between Boyd Road and St., Peters Road at the southern side of the Burn Bridge. The idea was to see who was daring (daft) enough to roll in the tyre down the steep grassy slope into the valley and over the stream. As we walked along the path looking for a nice straight run down into the valley we heard strange noises coming from some deep grass down the slope. We crept down to investigate and came across a young couple, shall we say getting to know each other. He was lying on top of her and his trousers were around his ankles. We honestly had no idea of what they were doing and probably thought that she must be deflating and he was trying to pump her up again. The diligence with which he performed his re-inflation was commendable because he was unaware of our furtive scrutiny.

We crept back up the grassy slope and once we were at the top we hatched our new diabolical plan. We would roll the tyre down the hill to see if we could run them over. We gauged where we thought they were, aimed the tyre and sent the rubber projectile on its way. It ran as straight as an arrow, bouncing over bumps as it went. As it reached their position it bounced about two feet into the air and came down on what I assume was his oscillating backside. There was a male grunt followed by a female squeak and then as we stood transfixed, a red faced youth stood up pulling his pants up as he did. His utterances were explicit and crude, which I think we can forgive him for, considering the circumstances. We decided to make a hasty retreat and abandoned our tyre, which did in fact succeed in crossing the stream during its onward journey. I hope the sudden weight and downward thrust of our tyre didn't cause this young man to impregnate his girlfriend. I know that he would never again achieve the velocity or impact of this memorable pairing. I suppose to look on the bright side of things, they could have named a daughter 'Pirrelli' or a son 'Michilin', very original and trendy.

****

I told you that it was a good anecdote didn't I and all of it is true, I promise. OK, so now let us get back up to date, I am in my fifteenth year and building up to leaving school at the Easter holidays. I had been on a couple of school visits to factories in the area to see what was available to us. To be honest, it was like falling off a log getting a job in the mid nineteen fifties. With all of the young men still having to answer the compulsory conscription for their national service in the armed forces, the employers had less to choose from. You were exempt from the call up if you were serving an engineering apprenticeship or working down the coalmines. Both of my brothers went down the Rising Sun colliery in an attempt to avoid being called up for their national service. They both hated the coalmines so much that they went up to the recruiting office and joined the army voluntarily. Ironically they were obliged to sign on for three years and they would only have had to serve two years if they had accepted conscription in the first place. Still, they were happy to be out of the pit and they were paid slightly more than the conscripts. As it happens, they both enjoyed their time in the Army and both regaled me with fascinating stories. One of Bobs mates in the army was the singer 'Englebert Humperdink' (Jerry Dorsey) before he became world famous. They remained good pals until Bob's death and Bob and his wife Mary stayed at his beautiful home on many occasions.

The description of life down the coalmines by my brothers put me off ever considering it as a career prospect. I chose not to bother going on the school visit to the Rising Sun but now I regret missing the experience. I won't have the chance again owing to its wilful destruction by the malevolent bovine 'Margaret Thatcher. (HOICK, SPIT).

I had got it into my head somehow that I wanted to serve an apprenticeship as a marine fitter. This would enable me to go to sea as an engineer officer and see the world. My brother in law Jimmy Ducker (Alma's husband) got an application form from the personnel department of 'The Wallsend Slipway & Engineering Co, Ltd'. He worked there himself as a 'Brassfinisher', a branch of engineering that specialises in instrumentation and small pipe work. Thus I was offered an apprenticeship as a Brassfinisher, to start after the Easter weekend. My wages would be £1-10-00, (150 new pence) for a forty-eight hour week over five days. I was lucky because the Unions had just won the battle to reduce the length of the working week from 52 hours to 48 hours. Before this time I would have had to work on Saturday mornings as well as weekdays. By the time I retired from work in 2006 after fifty years of heavy work, the working week had been reduced to 39 hours. It has taken half a century to gain nine hours of our life, well 'Whoop-De-Do'.

I remember being excited at the prospect of starting work and on the other hand feeling robbed. This was because I would have to start work after the three day Easter weekend and I would miss the usual two weeks school holiday that I was used to. My mam was excited too and she had been to the shops and bought me two pairs of bib & brace overalls. This was in spite of the fact that I would have to work for a year as an office boy somewhere in the company. This was the practice because you didn't start your apprenticeship until you were sixteen and you finished your training when you were twenty-one years old. The school leaving age was fifteen, so that meant you had to be an office junior until your sixteenth birthday.

I was surprised to be told that I would have to present myself to the head Timekeeper at the 'Swan Hunters' shipbuilding yard on my first day, instead of the Wallsend Slipway & Engineering Co., Ltd., as I had expected. I was informed that the engines were built at the Wallsend Slipway. Then transported the three miles or so up river on the massive floating crane 'Titan 11' to either Swan Hunters or the Neptune shipbuilding yards to be installed into the newly built ships. This meant that there was always a contingent of Slipway workers in the Swan Hunter yard. So, the end of another era was almost upon me and I was about to leave my boyhood behind and begin my working life. My last school report placed me at the top of my class for the first time ever in my ten years in education. If I had put as much effort into my studies in previous years I could have ruled the world, (or at least our street).

On our last day at school before Easter 1956, we were given the "Good luck for the future" speech from the Headmaster and then we just talked among ourselves. Mostly it was about the jobs that we were going to, I don't remember anyone in my class who hadn't got themselves a job. My three best pals at the time were John Moulden who was to be an apprenticed Welder, John Bartlay an apprenticed Butcher and Brian Ewing who started an apprenticeship as an engineering Fitter in a small factory at

Point Pleasant, near to the Wallsend Slipway but left to join the Royal Air Force and trained to be an Airframe Mechanic. The rest of the class had opted to go down the Rising Sun coal mine or be Van Lads on retail delivery trucks or the Co-Op Laundry. One lad I remember went to work for the Post Office as a Telegram Boy and I used to see him riding around town on his red GPO pushbike. When he was older they gave him a red BSA Bantam 125cc motorcycle and he could cover a larger area.

When the last day began to become a bit of an anti-climax I decided that I should acquire myself a souvenir to mark the end of my incarceration. I know now like most people, that these had been ten wonderful years to be treasured in hindsight. The souvenir that I decided on was the piece of wood between the two lids on my old- fashioned school desk. It had two brass screws holding it in place and it took me all afternoon to remove them using a halfpenny coin as a screwdriver. I was elated when it finally came loose and I admired my well-earned trophy.

It was about twelve inches in length, two inches wide and three quarters of an inch thick, with the male half of a Mortise and Tenon joint at one end. It was covered with initials etched into the wood by penknife, including my own of course and to me it seemed like a Totem.

As I walked across the schoolyard towards the iron gates for the last time, someone jumped onto my back clutching me roughly around the neck. He was shouting, "This time we'll settle it". I realised that it was my old enemy Alan from my first day in the Western school you may remember. 'He' of the red white and blue willy. So, with my new work honed muscles I just reached over my shoulders, grabbed the back of his head and heaved him over the top of me to land flat on his back. There was no need to chastise him any further because it was obvious that he had no fight left in him. He wheezed up at me, "I was only messing about Bill, honest". "Aye, of course you were Alan", I chuckled down at him as I swaggered away. He must have been secretly building up the courage to try for a rematch.

I should have stamped on his 'Patriotic Willie' while he lay there do you think? No, I couldn't have, because in my own mind I see myself as one of the good (ish) guys.

There is a 'Geordie' actor with the same surname called Alan that I have seen on TV a couple of times, although he now speaks with a middle of the road vaguely northern dialect. He always reminds me of the Alan that I knew back then. He looks like an older version of him and he has a pock marked face just like him. Alan was extrovert enough to have become an actor and should 'Pocky Alan' in fact be the 'TV Alan', then I have to admit that he is a very good actor and I am genuinely pleased for him, I love success stories. Perhaps we will meet someday and we can have another comeback tussle if he still fancies his chances. 'EAT MY SHORTS ALAN'.

✸✸✸✸✸✸

CHAPTER 10

Starting in the timeoffice

It was in trepidation that I made my way down to Swan Hunters Shipyard but I managed to find my way to the Slipway time office on the riverside. I was to report to a man named Mr Southern who claimed to be the 'Head Timekeeper' for the Slipway workforce at Swan Hunters. The fact that he was the only Timekeeper for the Slipway workforce seemed to have slipped his notice. I suppose that if you are the pedantic type, he was indeed the Head Time keeper under the circumstances. (The ego is a fragile thing). He had a surly demeanour and tended to be abrupt with people. He was full of his own importance and was regularly referred to as "That little Hitler" by the workmen. He showed me what was expected of me, such as sorting out about 150 time clock cards and putting them into a rack in numerical order. The men would come to a little window in the exterior wall of the office and call their clock number to me. I then had to look up and down the rows of time cards and give them their own numbered card. They would then put their card into a slot in the time- clock next to the small window and stamp the time onto the card by the use of a brass handle. This procedure was known as clocking on or clocking off, depending on whether they were starting or finishing a shift. They were obliged to clock (in) 7-30am, (out) 12noon, (in) 1-0pm, (out) 5-30pm. If they worked a half-shift they would then be required to put their cards through a letterbox in the little window.

The men were always in a mad rush to clock in at the start

of the shift because if they were three minutes late they lost fifteen minutes pay. Some sort of punitive incentive scheme introduced no doubt by some other snotty timekeeper who did not have to 'clock-on' due to his 'staff' status. It was also chaotic when the men were waiting to clock out because they were not allowed to get their cards until the knocking off buzzer blew at 5-30pm. This meant that they had to stand in a line of 150 men waiting to get their timecards and they weren't being paid for the privilege. Also of course, a lot of the men had buses and trains to catch very few people had their own transport in those days. My initiation was utter pandemonium, and there were timecards all over the floor. The men were screaming through the little window obscenities that I had never heard before and threats of violence so graphic they would have made the Gestapo cringe. I was almost catatonic waiting for the next shift change but I need not have worried. Because most of the men stayed in the yard for their lunch and they only came in dribs and drabs usually clocking out and immediately back in. I had time to get some practice in and although it was still fraught and eventful I eventually got the hang of it. I even started to recognise the men before they could call their number and had their cards ready for them. I also got to know the men who were habitually late and I would have their card standing next to the window to save them a few seconds.

The room that I occupied was only about 8ft by 6ft, with a small table and a wooden form. The little window was in the end wall facing the river with the rack for holding the timecards fastened to the wall on its right. There were two other pre-sixteen office boys waiting to start their apprenticeships but I was last in the pecking order due to being the last one to start. The oldest lad was called Billy Porter and he only had a couple of weeks to go before he would be sixteen and start his trade training. The other lad had started in the office after the Christmas holidays so he only had a few months seniority over me. The strange thing is that I remember Billy's name even though I never saw him again after those first two weeks and yet I can't for the life of me think of the other lad's name. This is strange because he also became an apprentice engineering fitter and I knew him all through my training. It may have been because Billy had the same name as me or it may be because he gave me more help in the two weeks that he was there.

Our little office was only a cubical attached to several other offices that housed the Managers and Foremen of every trade represented at Swans by the Slipway. Our boss Mr Southern had his office next to our cubbyhole. Our job was to be gophers for the Managers and Foremen as well as distributing the timecards. During my second week on the job I was given the task of going up to the Wallsend High Street at lunchtime to get the pies and pasties for a few of the Foremen. The Gateman would let an office boy out of the yard half an hour early for this purpose. I had the paper bags containing the pies Etc. in a shallow cardboard box and was on my way back when it started to rain. I didn't have my jacket on and I was soaked as I handed out the food to the men. They were all very sympathetic and told me to keep the few coppers change I had for them. Then I went back to my little office with pies for Billy and the other lad. Billy thanked me and began to have his lunch but the other lad just looked at the wet paper bag and said, "Look at the state of this, you stupid bastard". I hit him so hard that he went right over the table and landed full length on the bench seat. I was on my way around the table to continue rearranging his features when Billy stopped me saying, "you'll get the sack if you're caught fighting". I told him that nobody could call me a bastard because that was insulting my mother. I was so unworldly that I really did consider it to be an insult to my mam. By now the other lad was sitting up rubbing his jaw and saying how sorry he was and that he hadn't meant it the way that I thought.

Working in the shipyards would mean that I would have to hear a lot worse things than that said to me, you have to grow the skin of a Rhinoceros. I had never heard my dad swear other than the odd 'Damn and Blast' if something wasn't going too well. Nobody in fact swore in general in those times apart from the odd drunk who would be admonished by others if he did so within earshot of women or children. The working environment was different and the use of swearing was the norm. Some blokes would often split the syllables in a word with an expletive, making communication colourful but sometimes unintelligible.

The lad that I chinned and whose name I still can't recall got his revenge a couple of years later you may be happy to hear. A group of us apprentices were standing on the jetty at the Slipway yard and throwing old nuts and bolts at a condom floating in the river. Suddenly I saw stars and flashing lights in front of my eyes and then I found myself lying on the jetty with my mates standing over me. I had been hit on my cheekbone by a rusty nut. The lad I had chinned years earlier in the time office was saying how sorry he was and that the nut had slipped out of his hand when he was throwing it. He looked fearful and suitably remorseful, so I had to accept that it had been an unfortunate accident, (Or, was it revenge?). If it was in fact revenge, I feel compelled to give him 10/10 for his patience and you could say that I deserved it, even if it was a bit sneaky.

One of my tasks as an office boy was to answer the telephone and take messages for the various Managers and Foremen. The group of offices only had one phone shared between them and it was situated on the wall in the corridor. You know the ones that you have to lift the earpiece off a hook and hold it to your ear and then talk into a trumpet shaped mouthpiece projecting from the instrument. I hated having to answer a call for a foreman because they were rarely in their office and I would have to take a message. Invariably these messages were of a technical nature and I could barely tie my own shoelaces without a workshop manual. I couldn't write them down because the phone was halfway up the wall, I was holding an earpiece on a short wire and there was no table to rest the paper on to write. So I would try to remember what I was being told, hang up, run to my office and write down anything that I could recall. My short-term memory is pathetic today and sadly it was pathetic then too. Needless to say, the notes that I left on any given foreman's desk were like one of those Chinese whispers and could not have made any sense.

One day I was asked by someone on the phone if I would go onboard the ship tied up at the wharf. I was to seek out a particular Manager because it was urgent that they spoke to him as soon as possible. He was to be located in the engine room and he would be wearing a white boiler suit. I had never been on anything bigger than the cross Tyne ferry and this was the ocean going liner 'Bergensfjord'. She had been recently launched by Swan Hunters and was now being fitted out with her engines and luxurious interior. I climbed the gangplank not knowing what I would be going into, a bit wary and nervous to say the least. As I entered through the side of the hull I was met by a cacophony of noise, Riveters, Caulkers, Grinders as well as manual hammering and sawing. Then there was the flashing from the Welders and the sparks from the Burners and Grinders. It was like entering the mouth of Hell and I was in a state of shock from that point. When the sparks and flashes paused now and then the corridors became dark obstacle courses, lit only by a string of dim temporary electric bulbs. The decks were strewn with welding cables, riveters and grinder's air pipes plus fat flexi-hoses for the extraction fans. I think that I was expecting to find a nice passageway with a signpost saying Engine room this way. I made my way through this infernal labyrinth up and down temporary wooden ladders between decks. My fifteen-year old heart was beating like a steam hammer but I didn't have the sense to ask somebody the way to the engine room. The men that I passed all looked demonic in the stroboscopic lighting as they shouted and swore at each other over the noise. The smell of burning and electricity in the air made me think of 'Dante's Inferno' and that I was trapped inside his painting. I was totally lost on the huge ship and I had no idea how long I had been wandering aimlessly in its noisy, dim, smelly warren of an interior. I heard the muffled sound of the noon buzzer and like a miracle the noise and the flashes stopped within seconds. I realised that everyone was moving in the same direction and I joined the mass exodus heading for daylight and fresh air once more. I had not found the engine room or the elusive Manager that I had been sent to find. It had seemed like hours to me and could well have been in reality, so I just didn't mention it to anybody. There were no comebacks from anyone concerned, so I just stored it away in my memory and put it down to experience.

I explored the liner after that during my lunch breaks when it was quiet and eventually found my way about, at least to the engine room and boiler room. I learned from the experience that if you don't know something it is wise to ask for help from someone who does. It is amazing how many people would rather guess than ask for directions. It was wonderful to watch the ship becoming more and more beautiful day by day as she was fitted out. I never got used to taking messages on the phone and I still have a phobia about talking business of any kind. I'm OK with friendly banter but for anything else I prefer to conduct my conversations face to face.

✦✦✦✦✦✦✦

I didn't have to stay in the office for the full year because the personnel department told me that I could transfer into the Brassfitting department at the Slipway. They told me that if I did, I would not have to go into the apprentice-training department. I would start pre-apprenticeship training a few months earlier than the other lads if I decided to go. I jumped at the chance because I was bored out of my skull with time cards. I had become aware that my mam had bought me the wrong sort of overalls. Dealing with all of the different tradesmen coming to the time office I realised that only the Joiners and Painters seemed to wear Bib & Brace overalls and the engineering tradesmen all had blue Boiler suits. I was worried that I would be the odd one out among the other blokes, shallow and insecure, I know. I knew that my mam could not afford to buy me any more and she had kept them too long to exchange. I didn't say anything to her and just decided to bite my lip and live with it, "How magnanimous of him" I can hear you sneering. I was indeed the only person in the Brass-fitting department wearing a Bib & Brace but nobody ever mentioned it, even the other apprentices. I admit that I could still hardly wait for them to wear out so that I could get a boiler suit.

I reported to the Foreman 'Brassie' on the following Monday morning at the Wallsend Slipway. He was a big pleasant looking man called 'Billy Duncan' and he was wearing a three-piece suit and a battered old Trilby hat. All of the yard foremen wore dark suits and either Trilby or Bowler hats. They only put on their white boiler suits if they were required to go onto one of the ships. Billy took me up to the far end of the workshop and introduced me to my first Mentor he was a tall slim man of about forty years of age. His name was Fred Armstrong and I could not have wished for a better tradesman to get my basic training in the use of the tools of my trade. Fred was a meticulous craftsman and taught me how to use all engineering hand tools correctly. He would not tolerate rough, sloppy or careless workmanship and instilled in me, that if a job is worth doing it is worth doing properly. He had a work mate at the same bench as him called John Naylor who was about the same age as him. John was a nice bloke too but I didn't learn anything from him. Except that he lived on Fisher Hill in Walker, the same street that my dad had grown up on half a century earlier and that he was a bachelor who liked his beer.

Fred had one eye missing and a glass one in its place, so I had to remember to always look at his real one. This was difficult for a curious fifteen years old lad who had never seen a glass eye before. Fred was in an amateur operatic society and used to sing arias in a very good tenor voice all day. I think that the other blokes got a bit sick of it. I on the other hand thoroughly enjoyed listening to him, due probably to me having my sister Alma do the same thing since I had been a child. He really took me under his wing and wouldn't let anyone use foul language in my presence. This fatherly protection almost caused a fight one day. One of the blokes gave me a little pamphlet telling me that it was a Port Said book. He told me to go away and read it somewhere in private. I had no idea what a Port Said book was but with my innate curiosity I felt compelled to investigate it. I went to the toilets and sat myself in a cubical with the door bolted to ensure privacy during my perusal. It is fair to say that I had guessed that it was something shall we say saucy. In those days, censorship was very strict and there were no such things as glamour magazines or sex instruction books. The only thing on sale at the time was a thin booklet promoting nudist camps called Health and Efficiency. I had seen one of these pseudo-educational booklets showing naked women playing Tennis or Volley- ball. The women all had their nipples and pubes blurred out of the photos and this is how I thought that a naked woman looked for years, very confusing. Port Said books were purchased in the middle-eastern ports by seamen and brought into the country on their return. They were absolute filth with dreadful spelling and grammar with some of the text printed upside down. I can remember the engaging if morally bereft little tale as though it was yesterday. Without being as sordidly graphic as the anonymous Egyptian that penned it, it went like this. A wicked old witch kidnapped a beautiful princess and tied her spread eagled on a bed in a dungeon. After this she was subjected to being repeatedly raped by an ugly wart-covered dwarf as the witch cackled gleefully. She was eventually rescued by a handsome prince who killed the dwarf and impaled the witch on his sword, in what I can only describe as a phallic manner. This sadomasochistic dross was written in disgusting detail and I was shocked to my core, it was hardly Pantomime material after all. When I returned to my workbench Fred could see that I looked a bit shaken. He asked me if something had upset me and I told him that I had been given a book to read and handed it to him. He went berserk and went straight to the bloke who had given it to me even though I hadn't told him who it was. He had him by the throat and was shaking him like a rag doll. Apparently he was well known as a bit of a sleaze and had a draw full of these books. I thought Fred was going to kill him but the other lads stopped it from getting out of hand. The pervert kept well away from me after Fred told him what he would do to him if he so much as spoke to me again. The other blokes shunned the pervert after that for trying to corrupt a lad as young as me. It saddens me to think how much morality has gone downhill since those days. Fred became one of my hero's and because he lived in Dene Crescent in Wallsend I would often see him around town for many years. We always stopped and had a catch up chat when we met.

Fred and John specialised in building oil fuel burners for the front of ships boilers. These burners replaced the heating method of the old shovel fed coal furnaces. They were a Slipway patent and world famous for there efficiency and were fully automated. Fred involved me in all aspects in the assembly of these burners and I was getting a sense of achievement in my work. When parts didn't live up to Fred's high standards he would put them into a scrap bin. I would secretly take a scrapped part home every night until in time I had all of the parts required to build a complete oil fuel burner. Apart that is, from its heavy brass outer casing with which it was mounted onto the furnace door. I then summoned my mam into the kitchen and proceeded to assemble it on the kitchen table which took me about twenty minutes. I was explaining to my mam as I worked that all of the parts had to be made to fit and that I was just assembling it at this time. She started to cry because she was so proud of her little lad's obvious technical genius. I know that it wasn't brain surgery but her reaction to my little display filled me with pride and did wonders for my self-esteem.

I returned all of the burner parts inside my ex-army haversack and put them back into Fred's scrap box. (Every workman in the shipyards carried an ex-army haversack).

One day Fred was asked to build a special one-off oil fuel burner. This one would have cut-away sections in the brass housing so that the patented world famous working parts of the burner could be viewed in operation. It was to go on display at the Industrial Museum in Newcastle. Fred was even more meticulous than normal. This was to be the Rolls Royce of the oil fuel burner world. He carefully cut viewing holes into the wall of the brass housing body. He had positioned them in places that would allow the viewer to see the most interesting working sections of the unique patented oil fuel burner. All of the inner steel working parts had to be chromium plated for show. They were not of course normally chromed and when Fred made and fitted them he had to allow for the thickness of the chrome in his tolerances. The brass cutaway body was polished to a mirror finish also and it was indeed a thing of beauty. Fred allowed me to stamp the part numbers onto each component and fasten the brass 'Wallsend Slipway Patent' badge to the outer body. This was so that I could claim to have had a part in the creation of this masterpiece. It went on display in a glass case at the Science Museum in the Exhibition Park in Newcastle. I took my mam up to see it and she was so proud that she told everyone in the museum that her son had helped to make it, 'Magic'. The museum had it on display for many years until they moved from the Exhibition Park into the lovely old Co-op building on Blandford Street in Newcastle. They changed their name to The Discovery Museum and it is a wonderful place to spend a day. They probably still have the oil burner in its glass case gathering dust in the cellar or somewhere because these places don't throw stuff away. It will be over sixty years old now, so it is rapidly becoming an antiquity in its own right, just like me.

The middle section of the brass-shop had a row of ancient belt driven centre lathes. The machines were all driven off one big electric motor at the bottom of the workshop next to the

Gaffa's office. A shaft ran along the ceiling of the shop with a multi diameter drive wheel above each lathe. A leather belt ran from the motor up to a wheel that turned the shaft at a constant speed. Each lathe had a leather belt connecting it to the driving wheel on the shaft via a multi diameter wheel on the lathe. To change the speed of the lathe spindle, the operator had to force the belt to change its position on the different diameter wheels, giving it a different ratio. It was an antiquated system even back then and the lathes themselves were museum pieces. It's a tribute to the Turners operating these old mangles that they produced such accurate parts. I used to watch one man in particular because Fred had told me that he was the best Turner in the shop. His name was Albert but I can't remember his surname. I was fascinated watching him produce these intricate components out of lumps of steel, brass, or iron castings. He was indeed highly skilled and I picked up on some of his methods and learned a few tips that I used myself in later years. He did try to teach me how to calculate the chain of cogs needed in the gearbox of the lathe to cut the different screw threads. It all had to be done by hand on these old lathes but it involved a lot of maths and as I have said earlier my grasp of maths is tenuous at best. I would watch and listen to him and I would smile and nod in what I thought would be the right places but sadly it was mostly over my head. Luckily for me, all of the lathes that I have ever operated have had gear change levers. They also had instruction plates telling you what threads you could choose and what spindle speeds you would need. Albert also had to make all of his own cutting tools for the lathe out of carbon tool steel. He would get a blank roughly forged tool and shape it on the grindstone to suit his exacting requirements for each job. It turned out that with a bit of coaching from him, I was a natural at making these tools. My mentor Fred told me that I was privileged because Albert had never let anyone else make a tool for him. I was doubly pleased because Fred seemed proud of me.

On the other side of the brass-shop were a row of semi-automatic 'Turret' or 'Capstan' lathes. These were designed to produce high volume parts, nuts, bolts, spindles etc. These machines were classed as semi-skilled turning because every cutting tool was pre-formed even the threads were cut by a preset die box. All tools required to manufacture the component were fastened into a revolving capstan. After each operation the capstan would turn automatically and present the next tool required for the job. The skill in operating these machines was in the setting up at the start and adjusting the various limit stops and speed settings. There is no question that the centre lathe turner is more skilled than a capstan lathe turner. Even in these days of 'Computer Controlled Machine Centres' the skills of a high calibre centre lathe Turner are like gold dust to any engineering firm.

During my time working at the bench with Fred I invented a few tools and jigs of my own to make my job easier. Fred and John were so impressed that they adopted my ideas and used them to their own advantage. I have found during my working life that I have a flare for innovation. I have always made tools and gadgets that would make repetitive work quicker and easier for me. This is probably because I am bone idle at heart, why run if you can walk, why walk if you can ride, that has always been my motto.

After a few months working with Fred, Billy the gaffa decided to put me to work on one of the capstan lathes to see how I would manage. One of the last year apprentices was given the task of showing me the ropes so to speak I think his name was Alfie. The machine was set up to make burner cap nuts, which meant that I did not have to be shown the setting procedure. Alfie was a good teacher and I was operating the small 'Ward' lathe in no time. The capstan operators were on a piecework bonus scheme, which meant that they were given a price for each component that they made. He showed me a work sheet and told me that I had to fill one out every day and then hand them all in on Friday. He then filled a sheet in to show me how it was done and left it as an example for me.

Left to my own devices I plodded on making my cap nuts and dutifully filled in my worksheets every day. It was boring work but I was becoming more and more proficient at operating the lathe. The following week my pay packet had £3 in it. This was double my usual £1.10. 0. To say I that was overjoyed would be an understatement because my pay had doubled due to my own sterling efforts. My joy was to be short lived alas because the foreman summoned me to his office. He greeted me cheerfully and said, "Well Billy my lad, you seem to have had a productive first week on the lathe". I smiled broadly and replied, "Aye, I've doubled my wages, I can't believe it". "No son, neither can I", was Billy's cryptic retort. "Show me where all of these cap nut's are", he requested. I took him up to my lathe and proudly pointed to the sack and a half of completed burner cap nuts. Shaking his head he said, "The trouble is son, there should be about seven sacks full according to your worksheets". I just stood there dumbstruck and couldn't understand what had gone wrong.

He took me back to his office and told me to sit down. "Have you noticed that all five of your worksheets are exactly the same for each day, the exact same number of nuts for five separate days?" he said. I went onto the defensive and replied, "They are bound to be, that's what Alfie wrote on my example sheet". Billy was silent for a bit while he considered my statement and then he burst out laughing and rocking in his chair. I just sat there looking at him and wondering what was so funny. When he had composed himself he explained to me that I wasn't supposed to just copy everything off the example sheet, I was supposed to record the number of nuts that I had made myself, not the fictitious number that Alfie had given as an example. He told me that I had been grossly overpaid due to my false claim. It wasn't until this point that I realised what piecework actually was, I was mortified at my own stupidity and it was all crystal clear to me now. I was convinced that I was going to get the sack (fired), not just for cheating the company but for being a half-wit as well.

I thought of a brilliant solution to the problem and put it to Billy, "I'll work Saturday mornings for nothing until I have paid it all back". Billy looked at me incredulously and started to smile slowly, he then began to laugh again like before. He turned to me with tears in his eyes and said resignedly "Bugger off back to your machine before I piss myself". I asked him what was going to happen about me being overpaid and he replied, "Nothing son, it was worth it for the entertainment but don't let it happen again". I made my way sheepishly back to my lathe feeling every bit the idiot that I was. No one ever mentioned it so Billy must not have told anyone about the sorry incident I would have had the Micky taken out of me mercilessly if he had.

A hilarious if excruciating event took place one day involving Alfie when he got a hot cutting from his lathe down the open neck of his shirt. He was working on the next lathe to mine and I heard him shout with pain and jump backwards into the walkway. He was bending over and shaking his shirtfront to keep the hot metal shaving from burning him. His hope was that it would work its way down and out of his trouser leg. Unfortunately the sizzling sliver was destined to come to rest somewhere other than the shop floor. Alfie gave out the most bloodcurdling scream and clutched at the front of his trousers. We had to restrain him and force him to let go of his crotch so that we could unzip his fly and check his wedding tackle. Sure enough there was a small crescent moon shaped piece of brass on the bell end of his 'Willie' where it had burned its way in like a branding iron. There was no blood because it had cauterised its self. One of the blokes pulled it off and told him to go to see the nurse in the ambulance room. He didn't want to go but he didn't have much choice. It may have been an attractive little scar and certainly an icebreaker on certain occasions but you wouldn't want it to go septic would you. We were all still laughing when he returned to the shop but he got into the spirit of things by displaying his bandaged appendage without coercion.

After a month or so of making nothing but burner cap nuts I

was getting bored and restless. I had been speaking to Alfie and he told me that he had been stuck on the lathe for the last three years and had learned nothing else. He told me that he had been accepted for the Police Force and would be leaving soon. I wasn't very happy with the idea of stagnating on the lathe for the rest of my apprenticeship. I still had my dream of becoming a marine engineer and sailing the seven seas. I didn't want to join my first ship knowing nothing about engines. So I decided to go to the personnel department and have a talk to the welfare supervisor Mr Brown. All of the apprentices liked to go to the personnel office because it gave us the chance to chat to Mr Brown's secretary. Her name was Sheena and she was known among the lads as 'Sheena the Jungle Queen', after a popular comic book heroine of the time.

I think that she was attractive but I can't actually remember what she looked like. Her popularity may have had more to do with the fact that she was the only female that we had access to. She loved the attention though and I remember her as being a bit vacuous and egotistical. This description may be a bit unkind to her and perhaps my dubious charm just didn't push her buttons. (No, I just can't grasp that concept).

The upshot was, I spoke to Mr Brown and told him of my nautical aspirations and my worries about my future training. To my surprise he was very sympathetic and suggested that on my sixteenth birthday he could change my training direction. I would begin my apprenticeship as a 'Marine engine fitter' instead of a 'Brassfinisher'. This was a good result and I returned to the Brass-shop with a happy heart.

Before I left the brass-shop, Fred Armstrong decided to show me how to make a shovel as a present for my mam. He got a sheet of mild steel $1/8^{th}$ of an inch thick and showed me how to mark off the pattern onto it. Then he talked me through the procedure of panel beating the shape of the shovel using a hammer and a vice. After this I had to flatten the end of a short piece of steel pipe for the handle. Then after drilling holes in the handle and the shovel, I riveted them together. The end result was a really good looking and strong shovel. Not like the little tin things with wooden handles that we bought for getting coal for the fire. In my usual sardonic way, I stamped (FRONT) along the edge of the blade when it was finished. Over the years I must have made dozens of these shovels for other people. Taking it home was a bit of an ordeal for me though. It was what we called a 'Govie' job this was an abbreviation for 'working for the government'. This term was a euphemism for a job that you did for yourself, in works time and using works materials. In other words, you weren't supposed to be doing it. I had to push the shovel down the front of my trousers with the handle up my jumper and my Bib & Brace over the top. I then had to push my bicycle out of the works gate past the security police like a zombie who had shit himself. Once outside I carefully mounted my bike and gingerly pedalled away, painfully aware of the guillotine action of the shovel across my genitals as I rode. When I reached Wallsend High Street I tucked myself in behind a green bus to slipstream him.

As we were passing the 'Boro' cinema at Park Road I was eyeballing some girls instead of watching the road. The bus stopped suddenly for some reason and I ran into the back of it. The pain was eye watering I can tell you that. Luckily the shovel didn't part me from my family jewels but it did come down hard on my thighs. Stoically I picked myself up and pretended that I was more concerned about my bike, checking the front wheel, that sort of thing. I remounted and rode away with a fixed expression of normality on my face, while inside I was in agony like a cartoon character looking for somewhere private to scream. All of the time that this little tableau was taking place the girls that I had been ogling were in fits of laughter and pointing at me. I wanted the ground to swallow me up until I got around the corner and out of their line of sight. I had acquired two nasty bruises on my thighs.

Anyway, my mam loved her new shovel and used it until she

died. I made one for my brother Alan and it was passed on to his son Craig who believe it or not still has it. It is almost sixty years old now and is still in remarkable condition. It is not as shapely as the one I made for my mam but sure enough, along the blade of the shovel I have stamped 'FRONT'.

✻✻✻✻✻✻

CHAPTER 11

Apprenticeship

True to his word, Mr Brown the welfare supervisor had my apprenticeship training changed from Brassfinisher to Marine Engine Fitter on my sixteenth birthday.

I said my goodbyes to Fred and John and the rest of the blokes in the brass-shop and then ironically I swapped one Ward capstan lathe for another Ward capstan lathe. I had been transferred to a department called the 'Yankies'. It was so called because most of the machines were American Ward lathes of different sizes. There were two small Herbert lathes, one multi-spindle automatic lathe and a profile turning lathe that were British but the other thirty or so machines were 'Yankies'. It was a long narrow machine shop with a line of lathes running along each side of a walkway leading to the Foreman's office. The shop Foreman was a man called 'Herbie Anderson', he was in his fifties I would surmise and he looked like an ex-pugilist. He was stocky of build, had a broken nose and a cauliflower ear. He put me more in mind of a nightclub bouncer than a machine shop Foreman. Herbie was afflicted with a stomach ulcer and if he had suffered a bad night with it, everyone knew about it. He would prowl the shop looking like thunder and giving the men and boys a hard time. If on the other hand his ulcer wasn't bothering him, he was a different bloke all together. During my time on the Yankies I grew to like and respect Herbie a lot. He would come and demonstrate how to make something on the lathe for me and he would only use inside and outside callipers (basic measuring tools). The inspector would arrive to check the accuracy of the component using micrometer and vernier gauges (precise engineering instruments) and it was always spot on to the parameters required. I was well impressed, as I always am when I see a true artisan at work.

The difference being on a lathe in the Yankies department was that I was more involved in the engineering side of things. If I got a batch of fitting bolts or dowels for use in the engine erecting bays for instance, I would have to go to the Fitter on the job with the first of my batch. He would then try it in the engine component to see how good a fit it was. If it proved too tight or too slack he would take a new set of readings and give them to me. I would then go back and re-calibrate my lathe settings to compensate. When the Fitter was satisfied with the fit, I could rattle off as many parts as he required, checking every tenth part that I made with him. This procedure made me feel more creative and part of things.

There were three more apprentices of the same age as me in the department so we had a few laughs as you can imagine. It was at this time that I started swearing I am ashamed to say. I am not usually prone to peer pressure but I seemed to be the only one in my work environment that didn't swear constantly. I realised that I was the odd one out and made the conscious decision to slip the odd expletive into my vocabulary so that I would blend in, how pathetic is that? It was actually hard work at first to get the syntax correct in my conversations. I must have sounded like I was trying to overcome a stammer. As I have said before in this journal, although men used bad language at work, they seldom swore in front of women or children. Now of course a lot of females are more foul mouthed than the men, equality of the sexes you may say, 'how endearing'.

The reason that I am mentioning the swearing is because it was the pivotal part in one of our running jokes. We would wait until Herbie the Gaffa was walking past us and one of us would pretend to sneeze loudly. Instead of the usual 'Ah-Tishoo' sound, we would substitute 'Ya-Bastard' making it sound as much like a sneeze as we could. Sometimes we would change it to 'Ya-Shitbag'. We thought it was hilarious and so did the other blokes. We were too daft to stop while we were ahead and began to incorporate more obscene words into our sneezes. We still thought that it was side- splitting humour but the more mature blokes told us that it was wearing a bit thin. Eventually we caught Herbie on one of his bad ulcer days and he took the four of us to one side for a little talk. His face was purple and the veins were pulsing in his neck and temples. He said, "You must think that I'm as daft as you lot, I've put up with your infantile humour long enough". He was walking up to each of us in turn and talking menacingly an inch away from our faces. He continued, "You must all think that you are hard cases. Well, why don't I take you around the back of the shed and prove that you're not by kicking the crap out of you, all at the same time".

None of us had any doubts that he could do it, he looked like a Silverback Gorilla and I half expected him to start beating his chest. We were all cringing and saying how sorry we were and that it was just a bad joke. One of the lads, 'Geordie' was a quiet and timid sort and he had tears in his eyes. Herbie calmed down a bit and told us to get back to our machines, which we did with our tails between our legs. When he had left we all started laughing nervously but without humour, it was just a face saving exercise for our own benefit. I for one didn't feel like laughing, as I have said earlier I really liked Herbie and I was afraid that he wouldn't want anything to do with us after this. My worries were unfounded because the next day he came in full of the joys of spring as though it had never happened. His ulcers must have allowed him to have a good night and I realise that he must have had to deal with countless numbers of obnoxious apprentices over the years.

Apart from Geordie, (I'm not sure of his last name), my other two pals were Nicky Smith and Lenny Button. We were all sixteen and full of ourselves, well apart from Geordie that is. He was a gangly serious lad with very little sense of humour, or to be more accurate he did not appear to understand my sense of humour. Most of my so-called jokes went straight over his head including one that I had adapted from our run in with Herbie. I remembered my abject fear at his anger, then the utter relief when he let us return to our machines followed by the absolute joy when he was nice to us the next day. I utilised these three emotions to create what I considered to be a hilarious practical joke.

I would leave my lathe and walk down to where Geordie was working and say in a menacing voice, "If you ever say that about me again, I'll punch your lights out". Then I would return to my machine and continue working. Geordie would come up to me with a terrified look and say, "I didn't say anything about you Bill, honest". I would then turn to him pretending to be furious and say, "You had better get out of my sight Geordie before you lose your teeth". At this he would scuttle back down to his machine and not make eye contact with me. After a couple of hours I would go down to him and give him a toffee or something and have a friendly chat. The relief on Geordies face was tangible and he never once mentioned my little make believe tantrum or asked who had accused him, he was just happy to be off the hook. I performed this sick scenario two or three times over a period of a few weeks and Geordie never realised that it was supposed to be a joke.

I'm not proud of this story because it was obviously mental bullying and I profess to be anti-bullying in any form. I honestly did not think that it was bullying at the time, just a well constructed practical joke. I am even more ashamed to reveal to you that it still made me smile writing about it. What does that say about me now? I still see Geordie now and then in Wallsend and he still looks gangly and humourless.

Nicky Smith was a bit of a character, his real name was 'John Smith' but he thought 'Nicky' was less ordinary. This got him into trouble with the police on one occasion though. He had been to a dance at the Memorial Hall in Wallsend when a fight broke out. He wasn't involved but the police had been called and along with a lot of other lads he was questioned. He told them that his name was John Smith, this sounded a bit suspicious to the boys in blue due to it being such a common name. He insisted that it was his real name and they eventually accepted it. Sadly, one of his pals from work was passing and called out, "I'll see you on Monday Nicky". To which he automatically replied, "Aye OK mate". The Coppers were furious thinking that he had been lying about his name. They threw him into the 'Black Maria' and took him to the cells for the night. His parents had to go and confirm his name before they would let him go. On another occasion Nicky came to work with a pirate style hoop earring in his left ear. He was the first lad that we had seen with an earring and we were all fascinated by it. A man having his 'left' ear pierced and wearing a stud or hoop earring was acceptable but still rare and usually confined to merchant seamen. If on the other hand a man had his 'right' ear pierced for a stud or hoop earring it was assumed that he was homosexual. If a man had 'both' ears pierced for earrings it was a foregone conclusion as to his sexual leanings. I don't know if this was a worldwide folk-law in those days or a local concept, I only know that it was rigidly adhered to as a definitive tradition in my day. These days of enlightened acceptance mean that it is of no interest or concern how balanced a person's auricular perforations are distributed. I am not homophobic but I still find it strange if I see a man with his 'right' ear pierced, unless of course he is in fact homosexual.

Nicky told us that his parents had refused to give him permission to have it done, so he had done it anyway and just kept taking the ring out every time he was at home. One day after a week or so he came to work with his left ear bandaged up and told us that he had forgotten to take it out when he entered his house. His mother had spotted it and in her anger she just grabbed it and pulled it out, ripping his earlobe in the process. This was slapstick humour at its best and everyone in the machine shop was laughing for days afterwards.

The last of the three lads was Lenny Button and he was a complete gobshite with delusions of grandeur and worst of all he was a supporter of the Conservative party. In spite of this we became best friends and have remained friends throughout our lives. When we were in our thirties Len went to work in the Middle East and as often happens we drifted apart. We still bump into each other now and then and it's like old times for a while. He embraces Buddhism now and has become a socialist. (Good man). When we first met there was a lot of friction between us due to the fact that I was the new boy and Lenny had been the Alpha male so to speak among the apprentices. He was shorter than me with a half-inch crew cut hairstyle on his bullet head. He was always on about how hard he was and how he had grown up in a tough neighbourhood in North Shields. He never actually threatened me out right but he was always making veiled threats to me in front of the other lads, obviously trying to establish a pecking order. In the end I had swallowed enough of his verbal diarrhoea and said, "OK Lenny lets quit this dancing about and go behind the sheds to see how hard you really are". Len was taken aback but replied. "Aye OK lets just do that". The other lads were excited at the promise of a Gladiatorial event as we walked through the shop to the back door. I was planning my strategy for the showdown as we neared the exit when Len put his arm around my shoulder and said, "This is daft Bill we're mates aren't we". I was secretly relieved at this turn around and said, "You're the one that has been pushing for this Lenny". He started to laugh and said, "Na Bill, I was just messing about man". And so we made our way back to the Yankies with our pals disappointed at their bloodlust being unquenched. The pecking order had been stalemated but stabilised without anyone's feathers getting ruffled. After this we spent our time playing stupid jokes on each other. Geordie did not partake in this inane behaviour, perhaps because he was aware that there could be adverse consequences. This is admirable if true but it is more likely that he just did not have the imagination.

We would wait until one of us had gone to the 'Netty' (Lavatory) and then we would take out one of the cutting tools from the capstan on their lathe. We would then either leave it out, or put it back in upside down or backwards, depending on how much time we had. It only took seconds to remove the tools but it took ages to set them up again using measuring instruments and gauges. Or for a change we would alter the stops on the machine so that components being turned would be too thick, thin, short or long. As before it only took us seconds to alter the stops but ages to reset them. As you can see it was all childish and tedious stuff but it amused our adolescent minds time after time.

All of these so-called 'pranks' were of course dangerous but this fact obviously went straight over our heads. That is until Lenny played a new one on me that went horribly wrong. I was making dowels for the engine erecting shop out of 3/4 inch, round steel bar. The bar came in twenty feet lengths so I had to cut it into four to make it more manageable. To do this I had to remove the tail stock from my machine and feed the bar through the capstan and the chuck of the lathe until it stuck out of the back of the machine. This meant that I had fifteen feet of bar sticking out of the chuck. The shop labourer had to hold the excess of bar while I cut it into the five foot lengths on the lowest speed. This was perfectly safe because the chuck was only turning at about 50 revolutions per minute. While the labourer and I were feeding the bar through the machine, Lenny decided that for a laugh he would alter the speed setting for the chuck. Without looking, he just walked past and flicked the rotating handle on the speed dial. The Ward lathes were capable of speeds in excess of 1000 revolutions per minute and he had changed it up into the high end of the scale. The labourer held onto the bar and nodded, letting me know that he was ready for me to start. I started the lathe and instead of the chuck turning slowly it just became a blur of speed. I slammed the control lever back into the braking position and the chuck stopped almost instantly. I was aware of people shouting and pointing frantically. When I looked towards my assistant the steel bar was bent at a grotesque right angle and there was no sign of him. He had been flung across the shop and was lying behind the machine opposite. He was conscious but obviously in a lot of pain so they sent for the first aid man. He sent for an ambulance immediately and had him taken to Hospital. I was really shaken and Herbie the Gaffa had his arm around me, I told him that the lathe seemed to go too fast before I could stop it. We went over to my lathe and the speed setting was on the perfectly safe 50 revolutions per minute. Herbie said, "It wasn't your fault son, it must have been a flaw in the steel bar that allowed it to bend with the centrifugal force". He told me that I had done well to stop the machine so quickly and that accidents happen. I was still shaken but it was a relief that it had not been my fault. When Herbie had left me and I was on my own, Lenny came up to me white faced and shaking. "I didn't expect that to happen Bill, honest", he said. I did not know what he meant until he told me that he had altered my speed setting as a joke. I was speechless the poor labourer was in Hospital with God knows what injuries because of a stupid joke. At least Len had saved my bacon by turning the speed control back down to 50 rpm during the aftermath. I have to give him ten out of ten for telling me what he had done because I am not sure that I would have owned up to it if it had been one of my jokes. I would like to think that I would have because we learned a valuable lesson about practical jokes that day. Like my dad had told me years before, it always pays you to think of possible consequences before you speak or act. We had a fearful couple of days, waiting to hear how bad things were for the poor victim. It turned out that he had broken his hip but was otherwise OK and he was off work for quite a long time needless to say.

On a lighter note, I acquired my first (Yes I said first) fan club at about this time. Our pay packets were delivered to the shop on Friday afternoons and we were obliged to check them for mistakes before we went home. One Friday there was a note in with my pay telling me that I was lovely (How very wise) and would I look at the window of the pay office opposite the gatehouse when I left the yard that night. I was delighted at this female attention and the kudos it gave me with the blokes on the other lathes. So, as I left the yard that night with my hair neatly brushed, (OK, so I carried a brush) I flashed my heart-stopping smile at the office window. There were three girls waiting at the open window leaning out. When they saw me the two outer ones began jumping up and down with their hands to their faces. The girl in the middle, who is the only one that I can still picture in my mind smiled and waved coyly to me. I waved back immensely pleased with myself and had I have known what a celebrity was back then I would have definitely felt like one. This went on for two or three weeks with me getting little notes from the girls and me smiling and waving every night. Then one night the girl in the middle who had blonde curly hair and was quite pretty called me over. I thought, "At last, they have drawn straws and one of them has won the chance to ravish my adolescent body, with any luck". I went to the window flashing my teeth at her as I approached. She smiled down at me and asked, "We were just wondering how old you are"? I replied, "I'm sixteen". She looked shocked and the other two girls started to back away from the window. Blondie said, "OK then, thanks", she then returned to her desk not looking back. I couldn't understand what had gone wrong until one of the older blokes told me that the girls were all in their early twenties. He told me that they would probably have thought people would consider them cradle snatchers. After that, the notes stopped and they never came to the office window again. Silly girls, I was up for it.

Although they may have had to give me a few clues as to 'what' I was up for.

✱✱✱✱✱✱✱

CHAPTER 12

One life long love and one eternal passion

Let me talk about motorbikes for a while, indulge me. At around this time my brother Bob bought an old 500cc side valve 'Norton'. It had rigid front and rear forks only the springs in the saddle to lessen the bumps in the road. He hand painted it bright blue because it was his favourite colour, which made it gaudy but unique I have to say. He could never get the timing on the engine right so every couple of minutes it would backfire like a gun going off. You could always tell that he was coming long before he arrived by the racket it made. One day he decided it was about time that I knew how to ride a motorbike and got me to sit astride it. I was over the moon and jumped at the chance to acquire yet another skill. I sat there in the back lane and listened as he explained the controls to me. The clutch lever was on the left handlebar, the front brake on the right handlebar and the back brake pedal just in front of the left footrest. The gear change lever was just in front of the right footrest. All British bikes had this configuration for the position of the rear brake and the gear change lever. Foreign machines were the exact opposite with the gears on the left and brakes on the right. Our motorcycle industry eventually conformed to this European and American arrangement and quite rightly so. Bob explained that I had to pull the clutch lever then put my toe under the gear lever and lift it up for first gear. Then after that I had to put my foot above the gear lever and press down for second, third and forth gears.

Changing down was simply a matter of putting your toe under the lever and lifting it up three times and then easing it down between first and second to engage neutral. I knew the principle of changing gears from driving my older brother Alan's truck but this seemed unreasonably complicated to me. "Well, off you go" he said, "I'll see you when you get back". I was dying to ask him to go through it all again for me but my ego wouldn't let me. (Egos are dangerous things). So off I went, it was a relief to me that I didn't stall the engine as I let the clutch out because I knew that Bob and his mates would have laughed. I rode up the back lane and made sure that I changed up into second gear before I turned left onto Roman Wall to show Bob how competent I was. When I got to the end of Roman Wall I turned right and made my way up The Avenue. By the time I had reached The High Street I was feeling confident or even cocky to be honest. I remember the exhilaration and joy of the wind blowing through my hair (No helmet) and the people turning to stare every time the old Norton backfired. I made a circuit of the town riding along The High Street and down Park Road then along Buddle Street back home to Union Street. I even managed to find the elusive neutral position with the gear lever, 'eventually'. The problem then was getting off the bike without it falling over. I couldn't see a stand anywhere on the bike when I looked down and after a few tenuous attempts to dismount I chickened out. I had to resort to tooting the horn until I attracted Bob's attention in the house. He came out and held the bike until I got off and then he just heaved it backwards onto its rear stand. I was grinning from ear to ear in my elation and Bob just smiled and said, "There you are, you can ride a motorbike now". He was right because I can't remember ever having any doubts about riding any make, size or type of motorcycle since that day. I don't think I slept that night just thinking about the thrill of it all and I have had an undying love for them since that day.

I was riding my pushbike up West Street to visit my sister Joan when I heard the distinctive engine noise and intermittent backfire of Bob's exhaust. Sure enough he pulled alongside me and asked, "Are you going up to see Joan"? To which I replied, "Aye". He grinned and said, "You'll get there quicker with a push". Before I realised what he was doing, he got hold of the back of my saddle with his left hand and accelerated. At first I was enjoying being pushed up the road without having to pedal. Then he started going faster and faster and giving me a running commentary of the speedometer reading on his bike. When he said," 30mph", I was quite excited and still stupidly enjoying it. Then he continued accelerating and saying, "40mph, 45mph, 50mph". By this time I was rigid with fear and my knuckles were white with the way I was gripping the handlebars and I was shouting abuse at my mad brother. He reached 55mph before he let go of my saddle to allow me to slow down and stop at my sister's door. I have to admit that I enjoyed the thrill of the adrenalin rush but it doesn't take a genius to know that bicycle tyres are not designed for those speeds.

****

And so it came to pass, early in that year of '1957' I would meet a girl that would convey me into an eternal passion. I still feel that we have transcended all other boy girl relationships, after sixty years I am still in love with her. (OK so I'm a romantic). I saw her from my sister Joan's front window talking to Joan and her own elder sister Connie who were sitting on a garden bench. I had never seen such a lovely elfin creature, with long wavy dark hair that reached down to her incredibly tiny waist. She had a delicate face with a very kissable little mouth, which in fact she still does. She was wearing a sleeveless dress with a white collar and a patchwork coloured print pattern. It was close fitting around the bodice with a wide, flared, calf length skirt. (I sound like a dressmakers advertising brochure). I approached her and went into what I thought was charm mode but I think I was in overdrive. I most likely came across as Joan's daft younger brother.

I established that her name was Margaret Magee and that she was visiting her sister Connie who lived across the back lane from Joan. It turned out that it was the same Connie Magee that Joan had taken me as a baby to see. As you may recall from the start of this journal I was laid down beside Connie's baby sister, yes, the very same Margaret Magee. This was when Joan and Connie were delighted to relate the tasteful account of my copious intestinal expulsion into Margaret's little hat. Not perhaps the best opening stratagem for a love affair I hear you say, well I have to admit that I was thinking the same thing. Never the less, I was smitten by this four foot eleven inch beauty and I was determined to pursue her until I could claim my God given prize. I kept up my charm offensive and was able to make her laugh, which as every would be 'Lothario' knows is half the battle.

It was slow progress because I was too busy playing the clown to make my true feelings known to her. If she had an inkling of how I felt about her she was in denial because she kept trying to fix me up with one of her pals, Hazel Park. Hazel was a lovely lass but I only had eyes for Margaret and Hazel eventually met and married a mutual friend of ours, Fred Weldon. Meanwhile Margaret kept coming to my sisters and I kept on making her laugh and walking her home to 61 Gerald Street Wallsend which was actually only a couple of streets from mine.

When the summer holidays came, Margaret went with her mam for a week or so to stop with family friends in a small place called Millom in Cumbria. I was like a fish out of water without her and thankfully she must have missed me too. When she came home it seemed like a black cloud lifting and the sun coming out again for me. From then on we became closer and closer and it became obvious to everyone that we were indeed a couple and not just friends.

As I write this, Margaret is 70 years old and she still has an exquisite little face with a mouth that is still irresistibly kissable to me. Making her laugh is even easier for me now because all I have to do is take my clothes off. The telling of the next few years of our courtship could have become torrid, salacious, daring or even unequivocally filthy. Should this journal ever be published with this inclusion it would no doubt have become a best seller in the erotic literature genre. As it is, my darling wife has banned any lurid reference to our, shall I say 'awakening'. There was no workshop manuals on the art of love in those days in fact there weren't even any 'Girlie' magazines to glean any sort of knowledge from. Luckily I have always had a good imagination combined with an adventurous streak. For years I swear to you, I thought that I had invented everything in that department and that I must be some sort of deviant. I would like to say that in my eyes it was a blossoming of legendary proportions and a tragedy to the literary world not to allow me to record it for posterity. In reality of course, it was more likely to have been a lot of inept but enjoyable fumbling and experimentation.

AS WE WERE WHEN WE MET

THE BRASSFITTING
DEPARTMENT AT
'THE WALLSEND SLIPWAY.'

(ME) WITH MY HAND ON THE
SHOULDER OF MY FIRST
MENTOR, 'FRED ARMSTRONG'.
1956.

IT WAS OBVIOUS
TO ME THAT SHE
HAD JUST FALLEN
FROM THE TOP OF
A CHRISTMAS TREE

THE LOVELY 15 YEAR OLD
MARGARET ROSE MAGEE.
1956.

'ME' LOOKING
SMUG.

BILL BLEVINS AGED 18 YRS (1959)

THE REASON
THAT I AM
LOOKING SMUG

MARGARET ROSE MAGEE AGED 18 YRS (1959)

CHAPTER 13

Back to the Yankies

OK, thank you for indulging me. We will return to my apprenticeship and the Yankies machine shop. I was becoming very proficient on the lathe and because I had taken an interest in the larger machine opposite mine, the operator Bob Cook asked the Gaffa if I could go onto the vacant one next to his. Herbie was impressed that Bob thought that it was worthwhile because apprentice fitters usually just stopped off for a matter of months as part of their training. To my delight I was installed on the big Ward lathe under Bob's supervision. He too was an excellent mentor and I quickly became proficient on the bigger and more complex machine, the other lads were well impressed and even envious.

Lenny, Nicky, Geordie and I were all afflicted with the dreaded teenage malady 'Acne' at this time. Geordie was the worst afflicted and his face was just one mass of eruptions. It was hard to tell where his nose ended and the spots started. I was bad enough with my forehead and cheekbones covered by them. I always seemed to have a huge one in the bottom corner of my nose and my top lip. My worst area though was on the front of my thighs, especially my right thigh. I blamed this on the White Water coolant from the lathes splashing my legs. The coolant was a mixture of soluble oil and water that was fed by a movable pipe onto the metal as we machined it. My mam even made me a plastic apron to wear while I was working. One of our favourite jokes was to play the White Water onto the spinning chuck of our lathe as people were passing so that it splashed all over them. We would be very apologetic pretending that it was an accident and offering them a piece of rag to dry themselves. (Was there no end to this mirth)? These teenage spots of mine were to become a bonding ritual between Margaret and me. It was the same sort of thing that you find with Apes or Monkeys but instead of grooming, it was spot and blackhead squeezing. It turned out that the lovely Margaret had a natural talent for extracting organic matter from puss filled protuberances. We would lie on the beach at Tynemouth and she go from one end of my body to the other, tirelessly coaxing the 'Goo' from my numerous 'Zits'. You don't get that sort of fervent endeavour in modern romance novels do you? I think perhaps not. At the end of these excavations, I would look as though I had been through a mincing machine. It would take a couple of days for me to lose the multitude of little nip marks but Margaret would be happy with her prowess, (Ah! Young love).

****

When it got close to the Guy Fawkes celebrations, shops all started to display the usual fireworks. This is when I hatched one of my stupidest and most dangerous plans to date. I decided that with all of this gunpowder at my disposal I would make a working gun. I crafted the barrel on my lathe using one-inch diameter steel bar and I drilled out the bore for a projectile six inches deep with a calibre of $3/8^{th}$ of an inch. I had decided to keep it simple for my first attempt and make a Cannon. I cut off the length of the barrel at six and a half inches, giving it a breach chamber back wall of one half of an inch. I then drilled a $1/16^{th}$ of an inch hole through the barrel into the bore of the breach chamber to enable me to ignite the gunpowder. Lenny Button who was as daft as me was intrigued by my project and asked if he could be involved. I told him that he could make the ammunition for it if he wanted to and he was eager to make a start. He produced three shell shaped projectiles that were one inch long and had a diameter that was two thousands of an inch smaller than the 3/8th of an inch calibre of my barrel, 'perfect'. We fastened the barrel to a block of wood with steel clips and it did indeed look like a crude facsimile of a miniature cannon.

We took the finished gun up to Len's house because it was the nearest in Rothbury Terrace next to the 'Tynemouth' bus depot in North Shields. I had already bought a couple of 'Little Demon' bangers from the corner shop for our gunpowder supply. I stuffed a piece of knitting wool down the ignition hole in the breach then I poured what I considered a suitable amount of gunpowder into the barrel. I then crammed a small piece of rag in after it to compact and contain it. Then Len dropped one of his bullet-like projectiles down the barrel and I stuffed another small piece of rag after it to hold it in. We stood the gun on the dustbin and aimed it at the backyard door. The honour was left to me to ignite the woollen fuse using a long piece of burning newspaper. I touched the flame to the wool and then we stood back to witness this historic event. Nothing happened for a few seconds as the woollen fuse smouldered and then there was an almighty 'BANG'. The cannon had shot backwards and crashed into the house wall, knocking a small chip off one of the bricks. On inspecting the wooden backyard door into the back lane, we found a neat 3/8th of an inch hole right through it at about head height. As we were looking at the ragged hole on the outside of the door, Lenny's dad came running out of the house to see what was going on.

When he found the cannon and Len had told him what we had done he went crazy. It's hard to believe that up until that point when his dad was screaming it at us, it hadn't occurred to us that we could have killed somebody passing the back gate. Needless to say, the gun, two remaining shells and what was left of our gunpowder went into the bin. I was sent on my way after having it explained to me, not for the first or last time I have to confess, that I, along with his son was an idiot in the first degree. Lenny was dragged back into the house having the back of his head smacked profusely. It's a pity because I had some great plans for a breach loading mechanism.

It just isn't fare, that bloke called 'Nobel' got a peace prize named after him after he invented 'Dynamite'. (Where is the justice).

✦✦✦✦✦✦✦

I have just remembered another amusing little story involving Nicky Smith. He was invited to meet one of his pals from work at the 'Jackdaw' coffee bar on Station Road, Wallsend. Nicky lived in North Shields and rarely visited Wallsend even though the two towns are only about three miles apart. The Jackdaw was one of three coffee bars in Wallsend at the time. The other choices were the Luxor on the corner of Park Road and High Street East, or Marchi's, which was more of an ice cream parlour. In the 1950's, coffee bars were the meeting places for teenagers who were too young to frequent Pub's because the licensing laws were much more strict then. Nicky found the Jackdaw and ensconced himself in one of the little booths that lined the wall opposite the counter to wait for his pal. The place was full of 'Teddy boys' and their girlfriends as usual and one well intentioned Ted approached Nicky and said, "You don't want to sit in that booth mate, that's where the 'Twinnies' sit". Nicky decided that bravado was called for and replied, "The Twinnies can sit in another booth for a change, OK". The Ted just smiled and said, "Aye, suit ya'self mate" and walked away. Nicky should have done his research before opting for this course of action because the Twinnies, (Twins, as the name suggests) were two identical brothers aged about eighteen. They were both quite short, about 5ft-5ins., tall but they were also both as hard as nails. Their names were Jimmy and Cornelius Pike and they were the undisputed leaders of the Wallsend and Daisy Hill Ted's. They always wore the full Teddy-Boy gear (Based loosely on Edwardian garb, hence, Teddy-Boy). It consisted of a fingertip length drape jacket with a velvet collar styled like the frock coats of the Edwardians, a white shirt with a bootlace tie, drainpipe trousers, fluorescent socks and colourful quilted suede shoes with inch thick crepe rubber soles, (Known as brothel creepers). They were reputed to carry bicycle chains around their necks that they would pull out if they were in a fight with other Ted's. It was also rumoured that they had razorblades sewn behind their jacket lapels. This was a common practice among Ted's in case anyone grabbed them by the front of their coats to head-butt them. I know this is true because I saw a lad with both of his hands bleeding after attempting this in a fight at the yearly travelling fairground in the Burn Closes one Easter.

Anyway, back to the Jackdaw and Nicky. After a short while, the Twinnies arrived and walked over to the booth. One of them, probably 'Cor' (Cornelious) looked down incredulously at Nicky sitting there and said, "You must be a stranger here mate, shift your arse now". Nicky looked at this comparatively diminutive Teddy-Boy and in his ignorance said, "You shift it, if you think you're hard enough". At this, Cor grabbed Nicky and nutted (Head-butted) him about six times on his nose. He helped Nicky to another booth and then continued with his own social intercourse for the rest of the evening.

The first that we heard about it was when Nicky came into work, sporting two of the blackest of black eyes that I have ever seen. His nose was just a big tender blob and his top lip looked like an over-ripe Banana. The daft thing was that he was proud of it because his pal had turned up and told him about the Twinnies reputation. Although he told everyone the story with gusto, he swore that he would never go back to Wallsend again. Luckily I always got on well with Jimmy and Cor, due I suspect to the fact that they knew my brother Bob. He was about three years their senior and his reputation as a hard man would have impressed them in their formative years. I have worked beside Cor in the shipyards and he was well respected as a hard working natural leader. I appear to have always commanded respect over the years among my peers as someone who is not to be messed with. I can talk the talk and look the part if I have to but I don't have the temperament to actually be a hard lad. I can honestly say that I have never lost a physical fight in my life (up to now) but I have never enjoyed a fight either. I think that to be a genuine hard man you have to enjoy the conflict, whereas I have always felt sick after a physical confrontation. Each to his- own I suppose.

✶✶✶✶✶✶

As I neared my seventeenth birthday, Herbie the Gaffa told me that I was going to be transferred into the erecting bay to learn about Diesel engines. As the name suggests, this is where the main propulsion engines were built and tested before being taken to pieces in large units. They were then transported on large flatbed rail trucks down to the riverside, pulled by the yards own steam locomotive. This internal railway had tracks all over the yard with sidelines to every department. It culminated on the wharf next to the huge hammerhead crane that stood like a Colossus next to the River Tyne. The crane had a twin standing next door at the North Eastern Marine yard, although ours had an auxiliary smaller hoist to augment the main hoist. The only crane on the river that was bigger than ours was the one at the 'Naval Yard' in Newcastle. This gigantic hammerhead crane has a smaller crane that runs along the top of it and is truly impressive. This crane was given the honour of becoming a listed building ensuring its continued existence. The Slipway crane and the North Eastern crane were demolished along with all of the other cranes after the shipyard closures during the subhuman Margaret Thatcher's years as prime minister. (Hoick, Spit.).

When the engine units had been conveyed down to the riverside, the crane would lift them onto a floating platform or directly onto the 'Titan 11' floating crane. Titan was the largest floating crane in Europe at the time and had two immaculately maintained small triple expansion steam engines driving two propellers. They were only used to help manoeuvre the crane and Titan 11 was not in fact supposed to be a self-propelled vessel as was widely believed. The Tyne Tugs would pull and push the platforms up river the three miles or so to Swan Hunters and the 'Neptune' shipbuilding yards.

Herbie asked me if I would like to stay and let Bob Cook show me how to operate the multi-spindle and the profile lathes because I seemed to have the aptitude. Thanking him for the offer, I told him about my ambition to go to sea as an Engineer and sail the world. He wished me luck and said that there would always be a job on the Yankies for me if I changed my mind. His offer of further training and promise of future employment should I ever ask was good for my self-esteem I have to say.

✦✦✦✦✦✦

Writing about the yard locomotive has reminded me of another amusing story. It took place when I was fifteen and still in the Brass-Shop so I'm backtracking a bit. The rest of the men were out on strike but the apprentices were bound by their indentures to the company and not allowed to take industrial action. The strike lasted for a couple of weeks, so the yard Managers and Foremen were obliged to keep an eye on us. They gave us little jobs to do to keep us busy and a couple of the apprentices in their final year scored for the job that we all coveted. They were shown how to drive the saddle tank Locomotive and spent their days shunting stuff around the yard to different departments. To say that the rest of us were green with envy is a massive understatement. One day, they were coupling a flatbed truck to the 'Loco' when one of the lads got his left thumb crushed flat between the buffers. When he eventually returned to work he was inundated with lads wanting to see his thumbless left hand.

He was delighted to tell us that the company had promised him a job for life. Nowadays he would have sued the Slipway and got enough money to never have to work again.

This isn't the end of the story because I now have to travel about twenty-three years into the future from that time. I was working in the 'Wallsend Dry Dock' when I met him again. We were having a laugh talking about his crushed left thumb when he raised his right hand and showed me that he had lost his right thumb as well in another workplace accident. God knows how he got the beers in if there were more than eight people in his company. After we both had a laugh at the irony of it all, he told me that they had promoted him to Foreman because he could no longer use the tools. I told him that if he ever wanted to be a manager he might have to sacrifice a limb. True to their word though, he still had a job for life and now due to his odd and yet equal misfortune he had a more lucrative job.

✦✦✦✦✦✦

In the September of 1957 while I was still working in the Yankies department, I started going to night school as this was expected of an apprentice. They were held on three evenings per week at the Wallsend Grammar School on High Street East. I would be lying if I said that I enjoyed the experience because as I have said before I am not exactly academically inclined. To make matters worse I had just started courting the lovely Margaret Rose Magee, so my limited brain cells were well and truly pre-occupied. I managed to pass my exams that first year by the skin of my teeth and signed on for the following year. The second year was one full day and one evening, I ground to a halt in the first month. It wasn't my fault, (I keep telling myself), the Maths teacher who was called, shall we say 'Mr Smith' for charitable reasons, was as much use as an ashtray on a motorbike. Maths has always been my Achilles heel and it would have been an uphill struggle for me anyway. 'Mr Smith' was more interested in telling us about his son 'Alistair' (yes, I have even remembered the kids name) and how good he was at playing his Violin and at his drama class. He would also show us how to do the Waltz or the Quickstep because he and his wife were going to dancing classes. I can't remember him ever giving us any Maths tuition at all.

At the end of the class he would hand us all our homework assignments and tell us that they would count towards us passing our exams at the end of term. At first I would try to make as much sense of it as I could and make an attempt at doing what I was able to. By the forth week of his asinine drivel about the talented Alistair and his own prowess on the dance floor, the homework he dished out had surpassed my limited capabilities. When I handed in my homework he was astute enough to notice that I had given him a blank piece of paper. He asked me why I had made no attempt to do my assignment. I told him that when he gave me some questions about the Foxtrot or the Waltz or his son Alistair's achievements I would be able to comply. Otherwise he was wasting everybody's time by asking Maths questions. The other lads were falling about laughing at my one-man rebellion but 'Mr Smith' seemed less than amused. At his reluctance to respond to my sardonic humour I chose to vacate the classroom or should I say dance floor. Really, I should have gone to see the head of the college who was a nice approachable sort of bloke and put him in the picture. He could probably have put me in with another class or at least have a word with 'Mr Smith'. If I am honest though, I think that I was glad of an excuse to walk away. 'Mr Smith' probably went on for years making a good living while wasting student's time.

The trouble now was that I thought I might get into trouble for walking out of my studies. I should have realised that my ensuing course of action was doomed to failure due to its abject stupidity and yet I inanely thought that I could pull it off. My master plan was, to just stop off work on the day that I was supposed to go to college. They would then assume that I was at my day-release education and all would be well. I really find it hard to believe that I was so naïve that I even contemplated this imbecilic plan or for that matter how I have survived into adulthood.

After about three weeks of accepting payment for days not studying or working, the time office sent for me. I was taken into the head Timekeepers office and he asked me why I had not been attending day release classes. I told him the whole sorry story and how I thought I would get into trouble for walking out and then just coming back into work. So I had just thought it best to not come into work. He shook his head and said, "So you think that accepting three days wages from the company and not actually being here won't get you into trouble". I sat silent, thinking that this was the end of the line for me. The head timekeeper and the bloke that had brought me to his office huddled together and talked for a short time. The head turned to me and said, "Do you realise that if the Bosses hear about this you will be sacked on the spot". "Yes" I muttered with my eyes looking at the floor. "Well, no one outside of this room knows about it, so as long as you keep quiet we'll let it pass this time", he said. I couldn't believe it they were going to cover for my stupidity. "Before you go, I hope you're going to enrol again at the college next year, it's in your own best interests", he wisely suggested. Unfortunately I never did go back to college and yes he was correct, it would have been in my own best interests.

God bless both of these men wherever they are, their compassion for a young half-wit enabled him to learn his trade.

✦✦✦✦✦✦✦

Well, so much for further education. The next step was my move from the Yankies and into the Main Engine erecting bay.

Lenny Button was placed in the steam turbine erecting bay and I was in the Diesel engine erecting bay next to it. I have no idea what happened to Nicky Smith because I never saw him again after I left the Yankies. As for Geordie Byers, I never saw him again in a works environment, although I have seen him in Wallsend. When I started, they had one four cylinder 'Doxford' engine almost finished and the massive bedplate for another with its crankshaft installed. I was put to work with a fitter called 'Geordie Hayes' who was about thirty years old and a giant of a man. He was about six feet four inches tall (1-93 metres) and built like the proverbial brick shithouse. He was a smashing bloke and always full of fun. He told me that he had several brothers and that he was the runt of the litter, being the smallest among them. I remember that he came from 'Byker', which was known as a tough area. I am willing to bet that his family never had any trouble from the neighbour's. His favourite joke was to grab you by your shoulder with his massive hand and squeeze it with his vice like grip until your entire arm went dead. One day, he must have caught me in a bad mood or something and I decided that enough was enough. I grabbed him by his tie with my one still functioning hand and jumped up to try and nut him. My novice head- butting attempt fell well short, luckily for me. Geordie picked me up by the front of my overalls with one hand and held me out in front of him, "I'm sorry if I hurt you son, so if I put you back down you're not going to try that again are you", he said good humouredly. My anger fled as I dangled there, realising the futility of my ambitious gambit. I reached out with my good arm and patted him on his immense shoulder and said, "I'm OK now Geordie, I just lost my blob (temper) for a second". He put me down and as I walked away he shouted, "That was a gutsy attempt though son". This made me feel better as I waited for the circulation to return to my arm. I met him twenty years later when he was in his fifties and he still looked formidable but he was still just as affable too.

It wasn't long before the first Doxford engine was completed and ready to run. I was given the job of climbing up the eighty feet high tower outside, to sit all day next to the diesel oil fuel tank. It was situated on a platform at this height to give it gravity feed to the engine. It was much heavier oil than that used in diesel trucks or cars, and it had to be heated by coiled steam pipes inside the tank. It was my job to keep an eye on the temperature of the oil to assure that it was at the correct viscosity and fluidity for feeding to the engine. I could adjust the temperature up and down by the use of a valve in the steam pipe.

Every morning I would climb up the 80ft steel ladder inside the safety hoops to the platform, turn on the steam and wait until the oil had reached its optimum temperature. The Charge-hand who was called 'Jacky Frost' (no not a nick name) would keep coming out of the erecting shop every ten minutes or so and shout up, "Is it ready yet". Eventually, I would be able to answer in the affirmative and Jacky would shout back, "Cover your ears then bonny lad". This was good advice because they would then blast the engine with compressed air to make it turn. Then when the diesel was injected into the cylinders and the first piston fired it was like a bomb going off. The magnificent Doxford would roar into life like a gigantic primordial animal. When an engine was started for the first time after being built, all of the men would cheer for their achievement. The exhaust pipe stuck out of the outside wall right next to the platform that I was on and up into a huge silencer. The first 'BANG' always startled me even when I was expecting it and with the din of the exhaust from the engine right next to me all day I was almost deaf when I came down from the tower. It was inevitable that I would develop 'Tinnitus' in my hearing due to that and working next to Riveters and Calkers in confined spaces on ships. No one was issued with ear protectors in those days and so now I have a constant hissing in my ears. The same was true of working with Asbestos, we were not told of its dangers. We now know that they were aware of the risk even then and we weren't given masks. Hence I have Pleural plaques causing a thickening of the tissue in my right lung. "Hard work doesn't kill you", they say. Well I am willing to bet that it was a Public school Conservative that thought up that platitudinous drivel.

They would run the engines for a week or so while checks and adjustments were made before it was accepted. During this time I was up my tower from morning till night and got paid for my lunch breaks which I was obliged to take up there on the job. The platform was open on all sides apart from a safety rail but it had a corrugated iron roof that kept the rain off, unless it was windy. Someone thankfully had taken a stool up, so I was able to sit with my back to the warm tank on cold days and read my book. If I needed to go to the 'Netty' (Lavatory), I had to climb down from the tower and tell Jacky Frost where I was going and then climb back up on my return but should I only need to pee, I simply peed off the top.

Jacky Frost had a little hut at the base of the tower in which he would sit for his 'Bait' (Packed lunch). I used to enjoy splashing a few drops of my pee onto his tin roof when I knew that he was in there. He would come running out shouting up to me, "I know what you're doing you dirty little swine". I did this a few times and he never told me off for it when I came down, I suppose he could see the funny side of it, he had been a young lad himself at one time after all.

This piddling off high places has become part of my psyche since that time. If I am at the top of any high structure or natural formation I always have a compelling urge to pee off it. I feel cheated if this urge has to be suppressed for discretion, safety, or modesty reasons. (Look, it's my fetish and I'll bet you're not perfect, 'Puritan'). I have peed off castles, cliffs, office blocks, bridges, waterfalls and trees, in fact anything that has a bit of noteworthy altitude. It would be safe to say that I have been fervent in my pursuit of elevated We-Wee's. My personal favourite is when I climbed to the top of the magnificent Slipway hammerhead crane during one lunch break. I must have been about seventeen at the time and I walked to the end of the jib that was turned out over the river. Looking down from this vast height no doubt stimulated my unwholesome piddling urge and I was spurred on when I spotted two 'Foy-boat' men in their rowing boat.

Foy-boat men were self-employed and hired themselves out to anyone who wanted a ship moored to a wharf anywhere on the river. They would catch a light rope thrown down to them off a ship. This rope would be attached to a heavy mooring rope that would hold the ship alongside the jetty. They would scull the rowing boat to the wharf and pass the light rope up to a squad of strong men waiting for them there. The shore squad would then heave the heavy hawser up to the jetty and loop the huge fixed noose at the end over one of the iron bollards. The ships own deck winches would then pull the ship alongside securely. You may think that being a Foy-boat man was a strange way to make a living but you would be wrong. These men were second and third generations of the same families and they all made a good living. They provided a vital service in the speedy mooring of ships because at that time the river traffic was prolific. Not now of course, after the tragic term of office of Satan's advocate Margaret Thatcher, (Hoick, Spit). Now the Foy-boat men are an extinct species like the Do-Do because not enough ships use the river any more. The once world famous River Tyne is now mostly a Marina for rich boys toys.

I looked down on these men sculling their boat up the river to their next job and it occurred to me, due to my juvenile sense of humour that it would be amusing to pee on them. Yes, from my lofty perch I would become the great God' Urineious' anointing them with my essence, (Come on, cut me some slack, I was just a callow youth). I watched the golden torrent falling towards its targets. It separated into an amber cascade, then a pale lemon precipitation. Finally, just before it engulfed the two men it became a fine spray that actually formed a little rainbow, it was really quite lovely. It was also a bit of an anti-climax because the men did not seem to notice the event. They probably thought that it was just wind blown river water that they could feel. In my defence, I think I should point out to you that the river water was considerably less hygienic than my piddle in those days, so stop condemning me.

✳✳✳✳✳✳

<u>THE SPLENDID HAMMER HEAD CRANE.</u>
<u>WALLSEND SLIPWAY + ENGINEERING Co., LTD.,</u>

Slipway, Wallsend-On-Tyne.

<u>MY FAVOURITE ELEVATED</u>
<u>PIDDLING PERCH.</u>

A FEW BONUS
SHOTS OF THE
LOVELY MARGARET
AT THAT TIME.

184

I enjoyed my time in the erecting bay and learned quite a bit from various Fitters along the way. It wasn't all work though and I made quite a few friends among the other apprentices. The lads that I remember are Martin Bell, Lance Hopper, Frankie Hall, Bill Davidson, Hudson Morgan and 'Tossa' Thompson, (I don't know his real first name). Tossa was really small, about 5 feet 2 inches and a bit chubby but I am sure that in his own mind he was 6 feet tall and built like 'Tarzan'. He was the most obnoxious, irritating little squirt that you could ever meet. He looked like a cuddly Teddy bear but he had the attitude of 'Genghis Khan'. I quite liked the cocky little swine but he was a bit wearing at times. He gave lip to everyone men and apprentices alike. I don't know how he didn't get smacked about a bit because he pushed his luck with everybody. It can only have been his diminutive stature and cherubic face that saved him. I remember one day when he was really getting up all of our noses, we put a rope sling around his chest and under his armpits. We then hooked him onto a hand operated electric jib crane and sent him up about 20 feet into the air. Then we left him dangling there and went to take our lunch hour. He was suspended there for about twenty minutes before Jacky Frost was forced to leave his little hut to find out what all of the shouting was about. When we came back from our lunch break Jacky took us all to one side and gave us all a good talking to. He told us that Tossa had refused to tell him who had done it to him but he knew that it was us. He said that he was fully aware that Tossa was an annoying little shit but it had still been a dangerous thing to do and that he would be watching us. I knew Tossa for the rest of my apprenticeship and he was always just as belligerent.

When we were not working we got up to all sorts of stunts. One of the stunts involved jumping off the top of the engine and grabbing the rope that was tied to the end of the electric jib and then sliding down the 30 feet or so to the ground. I had volunteered to go first as usual like the hero that I thought I was and successfully grabbing the rope I hung there in triumph acknowledging the cheering from the other lads. I was less jubilant after I had slid down the rope and the friction had burnt the skin off both of my hands. It was absolute agony and the skin was sort of rolled up my palms towards my thumbs. I would have let go of the rope but I knew that there were too many hard and sharp things to land on, so I just had to suffer until I reached the bottom. I went to see the first aid man, telling him that I had accidentally fallen off the engine but had managed to grab the rope. He told me how lucky I had been and bandaged them both up, no enquiry into an accident yet again, lax or what? They were sore for ages but it didn't stop us from doing the jump, although we did all wear our protective gloves after that.

Lance Hopper was a smashing lad he was always smiling and very soft spoken. He was by far the most intelligent of us but still game for a laugh. One of the older fitters was due to retire and he had a half built model of a triple expansion steam engine. He asked if any of us would like to have it and finish building it. None of us could honestly say that we were up to the task, except Lance. His eyes were shining with excitement when the old fitter handed him the box with parts that he had already made and the skeleton of the little engine. Over the next few months Lance worked on his model engine in his spare time until it was complete. He then built a small boiler to supply the steam to power it. Eventually, one dinner hour he coupled the boiler to the engine and we all stood by in anticipation of its first trial. I think he heated the boiler with a blow-lamp as a temporary measure before designing something more appropriate. When he calculated that he had a big enough head of steam, he slowly opened up a small valve. There was a hiss of steam and the lovely little Brass and Steel engine began to turn slowly. As he continued to open the small valve, the engine began to pick up speed. In the end it was just a blur of moving parts and the flywheel was going so fast that it looked as though it was standing still. A great cheer filled the erecting bay from all of us and the other blokes who had gathered for the occasion.

I was awe inspired by it and I knew then that Lance would go far. He did in fact go on to become the 'Head Ships Engineering Manager' at Swan Hunters Shipbuilding yard. Funnily enough, I bumped into Lance about two weeks ago in North Shields after not having seen him for thirty odd years. We had a good long chat in the middle of a wallpaper shop and he is still a good-natured softly spoken lad. He invited Margaret and me up to his static Caravan on a site near Long Horsely in Northumberland. We have not taken him up on his kind invitation yet, perhaps this summer I'll surprise him.

Frankie Hall was a bit of a character too, a bit larger than life personality-wise. He was absolutely full of himself and exuberant to the point of eccentricity. All of this in a good way I must add. You couldn't help but like him even though he never got tired of telling you how good he was at everything. The daft thing is, I think that we all started to believe him. I suppose this is how religions are started, the more that someone attests to something, the more that people will start to believe them. I worked with Frankie many years later in 'Parsons Steam Turbine' works in Newcastle. I wasn't as easily fooled by then and I realized that Frankie was just an amiable bluffer. He was always in trouble with the 'Gaffa' for making daft mistakes and they didn't keep him on after his trial period. I don't suppose that Frankie would have been bothered, he would have just talked himself into another job. I still see him in Wallsend now and then and I always feel better after sharing his endless buoyancy.

Bill Davidson was a tall dark haired lad who tended to get a bit obsessive about things at times. He had read an article about 'Charles Atlas' the American body builder who had invented 'Dynamic Tension'. This was a way of building muscles without the use of weights or any other apparatus. The idea is to use one set of your own muscles to work against another set of your own muscles. For instance, if you pretend to lift a heavy weight in the arm curl position and fight your biceps with your triceps you will make the biceps bigger and stronger. So, whichever muscles you are using, you apply a resistance with the opposite muscles. Bill was living proof that this system of exercise worked. He followed the instructions every spare moment that he had, doing the curl and another one for the forearm. The trouble was, he only ever exercised his right arm the result being that after a few months his right arm was huge and his left arm was normal. Charles Atlas had an advertisement in magazines showing two photographs of the same man in swimming trunks. In the first one entitled, 'Before' the man was quite puny. In the second one entitled, 'After' the man had an impressive physique. Bill could have demonstrated the validity of the Charles Atlas exercises with one photograph and his arm differentials put me in mind of a fiddler crab. I got on well with Bill but he was inclined to be a bit huffy, he would stop talking to people for days if they upset him. After finishing his apprenticeship he joined the Fire Service and went on to become a Chief Fire Officer at North Shields, (Another success story).

Martin Bell was a tough looking lad with high cheekbones like a North American Indian and he was as strong as a bull. We all used to do a bit of weight lifting during our tea breaks using one of the big stud bolts that fastened the cylinder heads onto the engine blocks. We would heave it up to shoulder height and then see how many times we could push it straight up with one arm. Most of the lads could only do three or four and I could do six or seven but Martin could do nine or ten, like I said he was as strong as a bull. Bill Davidson was good with his right arm but rubbish with his left arm, thanks to Charles Atlas, hilarious.

Another of our games that went painfully wrong involved the use of something called Elephant board. This is a very hard, tightly compact cardboard that is used in engineering workshops to make temporary gaskets between joints. Sometimes we had to do a water pressure test on the Doxford engine cylinder liners. To do this we had to cut three-foot circles of Elephant board out of three-foot square sheets. The remnants of the gaskets we had made were the four corners of the board with a curved hypotenuse. To us they resembled futuristic boomerangs so they were obviously made for throwing at each other.

We would each collect an armful of these corner pieces and get behind whatever cover we could find for ourselves. The object was to hurl these makeshift missiles at each other if given the opportunity. Once you were hit you were out of the game and any missiles that you had left were there for the taking. This applied to thrown missiles too if they landed close enough to you. By this method you could augment your own depleting cache of weapons. When there were only two players left, the one who ran out of missiles first would have the opportunity to concede defeat. Alternatively he could choose to leave his cover and try to retrieve a missile or two before he was hit. Being hit was indeed a painful experience and I collected a few bruises during these Gladiatorial encounters. One day during one of our skirmishes, I unleashed my weapon in the direction of Lance Hopper. Sadly, as luck would have it Tossa Thomson chose that moment to stick his head up from behind his hiding place. My Boomerang hit him with considerable velocity right on the bridge of his nose and felled him like a tree. He had fallen straight back and lay still on the workshop floor. We all gathered around his still form waiting for him to get up and shout abuse at us, but he didn't stir. He lay there unconscious with the gash in his nose oozing blood all over his face. We got him to his feet and he began to regain his senses. Frankie Hall and I walked him down to the first aid room holding a less than hygienic (OK filthy) piece of rag to his nose. He was still in a confused state and we kept telling him to say that his spanner had slipped off a bolt while he was tightening it. As he was led into the treatment room we didn't know if we would all soon be in deep manure or not. Tossa came up trumps and had repeated the version of events that we had given to him. Everybody seemed to be happy with the plausibility of the 'accident'. We decided then that our days of Boomerang battles would have to stop.

✳✳✳✳✳✳

The Gaffa asked if any of us would like to go onto the nightshift because things were getting busy. They needed two shifts to keep up with the workload for a short while. There were a few of us that volunteered, mostly to earn ourselves a bit more money and in my case out of curiosity. I liked nightshift because it was quieter and had a more relaxed atmosphere with no Foremen, just charge-hands. The charge-hand would give each man a particular task or tasks for the night. As long as this work was completed by the morning, no one bothered us.

If one person finished his work first, he would go and help somebody else. This was the practice in every shipyard and factory that I have ever worked nightshift in. Everyone helped each other until all of the work on the list was completed. This would mean that everyone finished together and the rest of the night however long or short was your own. There is no need to get the whip out when you have a mutually accepted co-operative workforce like this and I thought then and now that it was a successful system. It sometimes gave us an hour or two free, to do what we liked. Some of the men would catch up on their sleep, while others would do a bit of work for themselves. For me it meant that I could explore the whole of the Slipway yard. I could take a look inside all of the different departments. There was the Foundry, Blacksmiths, Pattern Makers, Electricians, Carpenters, Boilermakers and Riggers. They even had a department in which they did their own Chrome plating. When I tried to look around these departments on dayshift, I was always chased away by the Foreman or the Manager. However, on nightshift they only ever had charge-hands who were more amenable and because I was showing an interest they would show me around. They would explain the different procedures quite happily because most people are proud of what they create.

One night during my nocturnal wandering I came across a 'Dumper' truck parked next to some building work that was being done during the day. I decided that because I was the only creature stirring so to speak, I would climb up into the driver's seat and have a snoop at the controls. I realized that they were basically the same as my brother Alan's truck. It had clutch, brake and accelerator pedals on the floor and a hand brake lever and a gear stick to the left of the seat. I felt quite at home sitting there. The Dumper truck was parked at the top of a hill that led down to the Slipway dry dock. The ignition key wasn't there but there was no such thing as a steering lock in those days. I decided that it would be fun to release the hand brake and let the truck coast down the hill. It began to pick up speed and I tried to brake but they didn't seem to be working. They may have been servo-assisted and needed the engine to be running but my guess is, they were just knackered. The only thing I was sure of was that they weren't working at that time. I pulled the handbrake back on but it didn't make much difference, it was probably just a cable brake for parking. The hill took a shallow turn to the right to run along the top rim of the dock. I calculated that I could make the turn OK and then I would just coast to a stop. When I began to steer to the right, I got the fright of my life because the back end of the truck had veered to the left. I didn't know at the time that Dumper trucks steer with their rear wheels and I thought that I was skidding. I turned the steering wheel sharply to the left thinking that I was steering into the skid to correct it like Alan had taught me. This resulted in the rear of the truck being thrown sharply to the right. To say that I panicked would be an understatement and I was turning the steering wheel left and right like a madman.

I was completely confused at my inability to get it under control and the back of the truck seemed to have a mind of its own. Eventually it was lifting two of its wheels with every violent swerve and crashing down again as it lurched the other way. I had visions of crashing through the railings around the rapidly approaching dock and plunging to my certain doom. I decided that it was time to bail out and I jumped off the right hand side as its back end lurched to the left. This proved to be the expedient thing to do because the Dumper turned completely onto its left hand side. It slid in a shower of sparks to a juddering halt and if I had not jumped when I did I would have been under it. This was not the first and certainly not the last time that I have stared down the barrel of my own mortality. Apart from a couple of scrapes on my hands and elbows and a few bruises I was otherwise unharmed. I would like to tell you that I learned a lasting lesson from my foolish behaviour but I can't. I never mentioned the incident to anyone and I never heard a word about the overturned Dumper truck. They must have just thought that the handbrake had slipped you may recall that I had pulled it on again just before I jumped.

While I was on nightshift there was a horrible accident in the machine shop that shared the same sheds as us. There were only two horizontal drilling machines working in the machine shop that night. One of the operators got the sleeve of his boiler suit caught in the slowly turning drill as he was clearing away the cuttings. He was unable to pull his arm free and the revolving drill pulled him over the top. We all heard the screaming and rushed to his machine. The other operator had managed to switch off the machine but not before the poor lad had made several revolutions. The men were able to untangle him and they lay him flat on the floor. In my mind it is like a very bad surreal dream, he was still conscious and somebody gave him a cigarette. As we waited for the first aid man to come he was saying that his arm was hurting. It was like a nightmare as his left hand still holding the cigarette slowly reached across his body and gripped his right forearm. He just gave a little tug and his entire right arm came away from his shoulder and lay beside him. I can remember him moaning as I turned around and made my way back to the erecting bay. I had seen more than my young eyes wanted to see.

The horror didn't end there the first aid man said that he would have to be taken to hospital as quickly as possible. The men carried him to the gatehouse to get the keys for the garage where the yard ambulance was kept. The nightshift gatehouse coppers were real 'Jobsworths' and said that they didn't have the authority to allow the use of the ambulance. The blokes told them what they could do with their authority and broke into the garage to get the ambulance. This ludicrous delay may well have been the reason that the poor soul died on the way to the hospital. I only know that I wouldn't want to have it on my conscience, like I imagine those two gatehouse coppers must have had.

✦✦✦✦✦✦✦

I have witnessed deaths or the aftermath of deaths many times in the shipyards, I suppose it is inevitable if you work in heavy industry. When men died in the coalmines it was usually more than one person at a time, this made it news worthy and everybody heard about it. I would think that there were as many if not more men killed in heavy industry but they usually died alone and didn't always get reported.

I will list just a few that come to mind that occurred in my proximity. The first one that I will sadly relate was none other than my charge-hand 'Jacky Frost'. He had just retired and was enjoying his hard earned freedom, when the Slipway management begged him to come back for a couple of weeks. They needed him to oversee the completion of an engine because it was running behind time. It was only supposed to be for a couple of weeks so he agreed to help them. They were lifting a piston connecting rod into place with the overhead shop crane when something went wrong. The connecting rod came down on Jacky's head, killing him instantly.

On another occasion a bloke was walking in deep snow alongside a mobile crane in the yard when he slipped. Unfortunately when he fell, his head went under the huge tractor type wheel and he was decapitated, or to be more accurate his head was crushed. Morbidly, all of the apprentices me included went down to look at the bloody mess that was left in the snow before they had cleared it away, 'gruesome'.

When I was working up at Swan Hunters yard the Foreman

of the tail end squad (the men who fit the ships rudders and propellers) was killed. They were fitting the massive bronze propeller to an oil tanker that was being built. One of the chain blocks broke and allowed the propeller to swing, crushing the man against the side of the ship. We all went up to the deck of the ship that we were on to look across at the tragic scene. What was left of the poor Foreman was being taken away and there was just a long bloody smear along the side of the tanker. It was like the mark that is left on wallpaper when you swat a fly, only magnified.

Then when I was on loan to the 'Neptune Shipyard' up river, I witnessed a Driller who was taking his machine and coiled air pipe onto a ship. The access into the ship was over a wooden plank and through a hole burned into the side. Half way over, the plank rocked a bit and he fell into the river. He didn't come up again so they sent for a diver to try and find him. The diver discovered the poor bloke a couple of hours later and said that he was stuck up to his waist in mud on the bottom of the river. It would seem that although he had dropped his drilling machine and air pipe, his pockets had been full of large heavy drill bits. He must have sunk like a stone and got stuck in the rancid silt of the riverbed unable to free him-self not a nice way to go.

All of these fatalities occurred while I was still an apprentice and I have witnessed many more since then. The most spectacular one that comes to mind was at 'Smiths Docks' North Shields. A bunch of us were walking down a steeply inclined roadway that led down to the dockside. We were all keeping to a narrow single line path as we walked down the hill to allow for the passage of vehicles. Half way down the hill there was a blind curve to the left. An articulated truck approached us from behind carrying a heavy load for one of the ships. As it turned the curve the driver in cab of the truck could not see the rear of his articulated trailer. At this point a hook on the side of the truck normally used for securing loads snared one of the men's haversack straps. It pulled him off his feet and dragged him for a short distance until he was able to shrug it off his shoulder. Unfortunately, with the truck turning into the bend he fell under the double back wheels of the trailer. The driver could not see or even feel the event and carried on down to the dockside to deliver his load. He was supervising the unloading of his truck when somebody informed him that he had just killed a man. We can only imagine what a shock that would be for someone.

One of the saddest deaths that I witnessed was not an accident but natural causes. It also happened at Smiths Docks as I climbed the long flight of concrete steps that led from the dockside up to the gatehouse. There were hundreds of us knackered workmen on their way home after a hard twelve-hour shift. A little old bloke wearing a greasy flat cap and holding a plastic lunchbox collapsed onto the steps right in front of me. A couple of us went to help him up but he was unconscious. Someone went for the first aid man and a few of us stayed with him on the steps. He was pronounced dead as soon as he had been examined. I know that this was a natural death but it really upset me. I kept thinking about him saying goodbye to his wife that very morning and that she would never see him again. I also kept thinking, 'what a crap place to die'. Smiths Dock wasn't even a nice place to be alive in, as far as I was concerned.

✦✦✦✦✦✦✦

Let us go back to the more frivolous nightshift recollections shall we, before we become suicidal with despair. During my spell on nightshift, a group of fitters and us their apprentices were transferred down to the boiler shop next to the river. We were to put the finishing touches to a Babcock and Wilcox marine boiler for a ship at Swan Hunters. For one of the jobs, Tossa had to climb inside a pressure vessel at the top of the boiler through its small oval access door. He was inside checking the water tubes for an hour or so and he got very hot. It is always warm when you are working in such a confined space, I can attest to that. When he tried to climb back out of the access door he found that he couldn't. His chubby little body had swelled with the heat and he was unable to squeeze himself through the gap. We all responded to his cries for help and then we all stood around laughing at his predicament. Tossa was not finding it the least bit amusing and I can still see his panic stricken cherubic little face. It didn't matter how much the blokes told him to keep calm and allow himself to cool down. He kept screaming that he wanted to be out and struggling to free himself of his coffin like confines. All of the other apprentices were gathered around and were telling him that it looked like he would have to sail with the ship.

Eventually, an old Boilermaker told us that he had seen it happen dozens of times over the years. He instructed Tossa to take off his boiler suit and his shirt and then he produced a small tin of grease and told him to smear it all over his upper torso. Tossa complied, handing his clothing out through the door and giving his shoulders chest and back a good greasing. He stuck his arms out through the hole and a couple of the lads pulled him. He popped out screaming and greasy like he had from his mother's womb eighteen years earlier. There was a big cheer and Tossa was relieved and grateful for his successful extraction. I was glad to have been a witness to his rebirth, or shall we call it his Immaculate Misconception.

Another memorable event took place as we were all sitting around the hexagonal Welders table having our one-hour meal break. One of the apprentices mentioned that he had been to the 'Miners Hall' dance on the previous Friday night. A Boilermaker enquired, "Did you kop off then like bonnie lad"? Geordie translation, ("Did you make the acquaintance of a young lady then young man"?) The lad replied, "Oh aye, ah cud tell she was a ganna stright off ". ("Oh yes I knew that she found me attractive immediately".) The Boilermaker asked, "Well, did ya give her one like or what"? ("Did intercourse ensue",) The lad said, "Ya not kiddin man, ah hadda bent reet owa the Privit , gannin like a fiddlers elbow". ("I most certainly did and I was grateful for the support of her garden hedge assisting me in the velocity of my reciprocation".)

This callow youth went on enthusiastically due to having an audience describing the girl in detail, even revealing the street in High Farm that she lived in. By now it was getting ominously quiet around the table but he didn't seem to notice. The Boilermaker then asked in a casual matter of fact manner if he had managed to acquire the girl's name. The lad riding high on his perceived burgeoning repute, revealed the name of the young lady. There was a deathly silence and then the Boilermaker leapt onto the Welders table, knocking cups and flasks everywhere. He grabbed the lad and proceeded to knock hell out of him. It took the other blokes all of their strength to drag him off the well and truly battered youth. Yes, as you have guessed the man was incensed by the violation of his daughter. Either that or he was oversensitive about the blatant abuse of his garden hedge.

The Boilermaker was sacked and the lad was off work for a couple of weeks getting over his injuries. The daft thing is, the lad was probably lying as many teenagers do to gain a bit of kudos with their mates. The lesson we all learned that night was that if we were going to be naughty we should be discreet about it.

During one of our one-hour 'lunch' breaks I went out on one of my nightly reconnaissance expeditions. I was behind the Pattern Makers shop looking at some of the beautifully crafted wooden patterns. There were mock-ups of valves pumps and strange pipe manifolds that had been made as temporary patterns for the real ships equipment. I believe that Pattern Makers are the Crème de la Crème as far as wood working artisans are concerned. All of their work is a one off and must be absolutely accurate whether it is something hand held or the size of a house.

Anyway, as I turned to continue on my nocturnal wanderings I discovered a lean-to shed. It was really only an open sided angle-bar frame with a corrugated iron roof fastened to the back wall of the Gatehouse office. I couldn't believe my eyes when I saw what it contained. There was one of the little electric trucks that could be seen on dayshift dashing all over the yard carrying small components between departments. They were all red in colour and were locked in their own shed and plugged into an electricity supply to charge up their batteries at the end of each day. This one was orange in colour and I had never seen it before, it must have belonged to the Pattern Makers department. It was plugged into its own electric supply and it was easily accessible, the temptation was beyond my control. You would have thought my misadventure with the Dumper truck would have made me stop and think wouldn't you.

I had always wanted to have a scoot about on one of these little trucks but they had seemed to be out of my reach. This one was whispering, "Drive me, drive me" the little minx. I unplugged the charger and surveyed the controls they could not have been simpler to operate. The driver sat on the single seat behind a bull nosed console that was open to the elements. On top of the console was a pram handle type tiller for steering the single front wheel to which it was directly attached. A small handle with a knob on one end and a pointer on the other was positioned to the left of the tiller. It had three positions and the pointer was straight up in 'Neutral'. If it was pointed to the right it was in 'Forward' and if it was pointed to the left it was in 'Reverse, simplicity. There were only two foot-pedals, brake and accelerator and a hand brake. They were designed like a little pickup truck with a flatbed body and drop down sides.

This was an opportunity that I just could not miss, so I selected reverse released the handbrake and backed slowly out of the lean-to shed. (Would I ever learn? Well not in this lifetime I am obliged to tell you). A path ran along between the workshops and the 'Willington Gut' that is a small tributary that runs into the River Tyne. I drove along the path towards the river, getting the feel of the trucks handling. There was about an inch of snow on the ground so I could hardly wait to reach more open spaces to try skidding it about. It was quite a fast little thing and I had a good half-hour squirting about the yard and doing sideways drifts around the corners. I didn't see another living soul during the entire duration. This is probably because it was two-o-clock in the morning and anyone with any sense was indoors keeping warm. I made my way back behind the Pattern Makers shop to the little lean-to feeling elated. The whole thing had been performed in virtual silence, just the soft hum of the trucks electric motor and the swish of the wheels through the snow.

I parked it where I thought I had found it and plugged it into the charger unit. Stepping back for a final look I decided that it needed to be a couple of feet further back. I wanted it to be exact so that nobody would know that it had been moved. This way I could take it for a spin every night while I was on nightshift. I unplugged it again and got back into the drivers seat. I was looking over my right shoulder to judge how far I should back it up. At the same time I was reaching down to move the selector lever into reverse. I think that I had left my multi-tasking head at home because I must have selected 'Forward' instead of 'Reverse'. My error became evident when the little truck shot forwards and not the way that I was looking. My instinct was to stamp on the brake pedal but the rear wall of the Gatehouse saved me the trouble. The crash resonated in the corrugated iron shelter and I could hear the smashing of the cyclopean headlight in the centre of the bull-nose. I knew that the yard coppers must have heard the bang on their office wall, so I legged it back down to the Boiler-shop. When I got there the men were all still sitting there around the Welders table playing Dominoes. I climbed up to the Riggers loft and lay on some coiled ropes to watch them play and to get warmed up off the steam heated blowers.

After about ten or fifteen minutes, one of the yard coppers came in carrying the chrome ring of the smashed headlight. He walked up to the table and grabbed Tossa by the scruff of his neck (Yes, Tossa yet again). He had been sitting with his legs crossed and the copper pointed to the sole of his boot and informed him that he had followed his footprints in the snow from where he had smashed the truck. Tossa spluttered his denial saying that he had been playing Dominoes and all of the blokes attested to this. The copper was adamant because of the distinctive pattern of the treads on the sole. About four other apprentices showed him that their boots had the same pattern as Tossa's. The copper began waving the headlamp ring about and ranting that he knew that it was one of them and that somebody should own up. The older blokes started to laugh and told him to bugger off and harass somebody else.

Luckily, all of the apprentices had been given the opportunity to purchase 'Tuff ' toe-tector work boots from the personnel office for half-a-crown (12.5 new pence) per month. Before this we just had to wear whatever old shoes we had for working in. When I was in the Yankies machine shop, I used to wear an old pair of crepe soled brothel creepers. After a while the oil soaked into the crepe soles and they spread out like swimming flippers. I used to squelch about like a Scuba diver masquerading as a machinist.

If I had been down beside the Welders table when this scenario took place, I would have been captured. I would have been the only one with wet boiler-suit legs and damp boots. Once again, I had been saved by dumb luck and the discretion of anyone who may have seen me coming in and climbing up to the Riggers loft. Would I have saved Tossa by confessing if I had been put to the test? The honest answer is that I don't know, I would like to think that I would have. I don't think that my basic personality has changed that much since those days and I certainly couldn't live with myself if it happened now.

The last thing that comes to mind about nightshift in the Boiler-shop is a lesson that I learned one night. As I have said, everyone used to play Dominoes during the break times and one night they talked me into playing too. In no time at all, I had lost my bus fare home, seven pence (3 new pence) and this was all the money that I possessed. The outcome of this was that I had to walk three miles home through ten inches of snow in a Blizzard. By the time I got home I was soaked to the skin and blue with the cold. I swore that I would never gamble for money ever again and I never have. I know that any of my work mates would have given me the bus fare if I had asked them but I considered it my own stupid fault and didn't tell them of my dire plight. It was a lesson well learned because I have never again been drawn into games of chance where money was involved.

At last the boiler that we were working on was finished and I watched fascinated as the entire roof of the huge building was rolled back. This was to allow the big hammerhead crane to reach in and lift the boiler out through the roof and down onto the jetty. It would then be transferred onto a floating platform and be delivered up to Swan Hunters to a waiting ship.

CHAPTER 14

The white city

On the return to dayshift and the erecting bay the Gaffa had another proposition for us. He asked if anyone would like to be transferred into 'The White City' for a couple of months to help them with a backlog of work. (The White City is not as exotic as it sounds). I never found out where it got its name from but it was a machine shop that contained Horizontal boring, Milling, Shaping and Broaching machines. It was situated between the Yankies and the engine erecting bays in the same gigantic shed. The gaffa assured us that it was only for a couple of months to help them to catch up and that we would be trained to operate all of the machines. After that, we would be sent up to Swan Hunters shipyard to join the fitting out team.

I was the only one to volunteer because I was intrigued when I watched the machinists creating things on the various machines. Also, it had occurred to me that it would be more strings to add to my bow. I reported to the shop Foreman who was a nice bloke called 'Jimmy Gibson'. He took me to a Horizontal boring machine that was situated under the steel stairs that led up to his second floor office. One of his machinists stayed with me for a couple of days to show me how to set the machine up. They are different to a lathe in as much as the cutting tool is fastened into the revolving chuck. The component to be machined is fastened to a bedplate and is static in whichever position it is required to be at. This is to facilitate the machining of castings with awkward flanges or interior bores such as valves or manifolds. The setting up of these machines was completely different to a lathe but I had a good lad instructing me and I soon mastered it. Jimmy the Gaffa was delighted at how quickly I was able to start production work. There was one other apprentice in the White City and his name was 'Jimmy Gibson'. Yes, as you have guessed from his name he was the Gaffas son. He was a year or two older than me and you could not have met a nicer good-natured lad, just like his dad. We remained friends for many years and worked together in a couple of places. Jimmy senior didn't show Jimmy junior any favouritism and if you hadn't been told, you would not have known that they were related. I did not get the chance to work on the milling machines while I was there although I did in later years. I did operate the Shapers and Broachers from time to time. Shaping machines are too uninteresting to explain and the only thing to say about Broaching machines is that they turn round holes into square holes.

My position under the steel stairs to the Gaffas office turned out to be a teenage lad's fantasy. The treads of the steps were open mesh, which meant that when an office girl went up the stairs I could inspect their laundry so to speak. This was in the 1950s and all of the girls wore flared skirts, stockings and suspenders. Those passion killer tights had not been invented yet, thank God. Needless to say, I suffered from a lot of neck aches back then. I will not insult your intelligence by apologising for my licentious adolescent behaviour, I could have sold tickets but I didn't, decent or what? The best part was, my mate Lenny Button had started courting the Gaffas office girl 'Audrey'. Every day I would tell him the colour of the knickers that she was wearing (I find that this really is shameful, though still funny). Len always pretended to be amused by my revelations but he must have said something to Audrey. It wasn't too long before a couple of Joiners came and boarded the underside of the stairs. I can't blame Lenny I would have done the same under the circumstances. It was obvious that I was an utter cad and a bounder in the first degree. Really, I should have kept my mouth shut for the sake of future cads and bounders who may have operated the machine.

After about three months, true to their word, I was transferred but not to Swan Hunters. I was to go to another department housed in the same huge shed where they built the water coolers for the Steam Turbine erecting shop. I was disappointed not to be going to Swans but it turned out to be interesting and lucrative due to their excellent bonus system.

✦✦✦✦✦✦✦

At about this time my brother Bob bought himself another motorbike, a shaft driven Sunbeam S8 500cc. It was a thing of great beauty and one of the aristocrats of British motorbikes at the time. These beautiful machines were built in two guises, the S7 and the S8. The S7 was green and had balloon tyres like the American bike the 'Harley Davidson' and the S8 was black with conventional sized tyres. The S8 was considered to be the 'sports' version of the two. Compared to the bikes of today both of the models were sedate as far as speed goes, 90mph was their limit. They had a unique inline twin cylinder engine that looked and sounded like a motor car engine. It was smooth and quiet and transferred its power to the rear wheel via a shaft drive rather than the more conventional chain drive.

Bob magnanimously told me to get a provisional driving licence and I could learn to ride it legally and put in for my test. I was delighted and did so as soon as I could before he could change his mind. He would let me use it to go to work on when he didn't need it or when he was on nightshift. You can imagine how smug I was on these days, riding into the Slipway car park and standing it next to the other motorbikes. There was only one bike in the car park that was better than the Sunbeam and it belonged to one of the older blokes. It was a 'Vincent Black Knight' which was (and still is) the best motorbike ever made. HRD were the company that built them and Vincent 'Black Knight' along with 'Black Shadow' and 'Rapide' were model types,

The Sunbeam had one fault that Bob could never get to the bottom of. If it was left standing for a few hours, it was an absolute pig to get started. You could stand there for five minutes jumping on the kick-start lever before it came to life. Once it had been started it ran smoothly and never missed a beat. After that, you could switch it off and leave it for an hour and it would start at the first kick of the starter. Thinking about it now, I'm inclined to think that it was petrol starvation and the carburettor must have been draining itself slowly. At the time it was a real puzzler and I didn't want the embarrassment of being left standing in the car park every night and so, I devised a cunning plan.

The drawing office was situated outside of the works gates next to the canteen and car park. Every night I would get hold of one of the engineering blue prints that were lying around the department. Then I would leave the yard thirty minutes early waving the drawing at the gatehouse copper. It was usually the head Gateman who was a nice bloke known as 'Maurice the polis' to everyone. He would assume that I was going to the drawing office and give me the nod to leave the yard. Once outside, I would make my way over the car park to the Sunbeam, there was no such thing as closed circuit surveillance TV cameras in those days. I would then spend five minutes frantically kick starting the bike until it fired up. God knows what Maurice thought I had been doing because I was always red faced and sweating like a pig on my return journey. The cunning plan always worked and the bike never failed to start first kick for me when I left for home.

One day I was riding home after a shower of rain and taking a shallow right hand curve on High Street East Wallsend just beside 'The New Winning' pub. I must have been going too fast because the rear wheel skidded to the left and the bike went down. As is always the case it all seemed to happen in slow motion as I watched sparks flying and the rear view mirror smashing. All that went through my mind was that I was 'knacking' Bob's lovely bike and that he would justifiably kill me. A couple of blokes picked me up and made sure that I was OK. Then they picked the bike up and put it on its stand at the side of the road for me.

Only racing circuit and TT riders wore leathers in those days, a couple of the bikers at work had waterproof 'Barber' jackets. I was wearing a pale blue Tweed jacket over my boiler suit. Although I didn't have so much as a scrape on me, the right sleeve elbow of my jacket was shredded. Crash helmets were not a legal requirement at that time, so Bob and I never bothered to acquire one.

I sat at the side of the road for ages feeling sorry for myself and a bit scared to get back on the bike, so in the end I decided to push it home rather than ride it. Its about two miles from where I came off to Union Street and the Sunbeam was a heavy bike. I pushed it all the way to Benton Way, which was only a couple of streets away from home. As I stood there wheezing like an old steam engine, it occurred to me that Bob would be even more annoyed with me for not having the bottle to ride it home. So, I remounted the bike and she started with the first kick. I was pleased that the bike sounded and handled exactly the same as I rode the rest of the way home. I could have saved myself a lot of hard work and backache if I had came to this decision at the crash scene.

I went into the house and told Bob what had happened, to which he exclaimed, 'SHIT'! This was his (and also my) first expletive in times of duress. I left him to get his shoes and coat on and went to stand by the bike, hoping that my imminent demise would be swift and painless. By the time he came out, his mood had softened (time is a great healer) and he asked me if I was OK. When I confirmed that I was, he went to inspect the damage to his beloved Sunbeam. Remarkably, apart from the broken mirror and the end of his front brake lever being curled forward, there wasn't another mark on the bike. He went for a ride around the block and when he returned he declared that he preferred the brake lever curled forward on the end. He then went into the house and returned with a big pair of Pliers. I had visions of him extracting my teeth or crushing my nuts in retribution. Thankfully he used them to curl the end of his clutch lever on the opposite side to match the brake. I promised him that I would save up and buy him a new mirror. He just said, "Aye, right oh, as long as you have learned something from all of this". That was it I had not been put to death, beaten senseless, or even shouted at. Best of all he didn't even stop me from riding his bike. I have to say that I agreed with him, the brake and clutch levers were much better with the little curl on the ends.

✱✱✱✱✱✱

I now have to confess to something that I am deeply ashamed of even to this day. Like most people I know, I'm not averse to the odd bit of purloining from places that I have worked. (Recycling sounds less felonious). Even if it is only a paper clip or a pencil it is still wrong but we have all done it. What I have always found disgusting is someone who will steal from another individual. I was desperate to replace the mirror on Bob's bike but I was only keeping ten shillings (50 new pence) of my wages and giving the rest to my mam. This is not an excuse for what I did and as I have said, I still feel guilty about it to this day. There was a cycle shed between the Brass-shop and the Electricians shop and people were allowed to bring their pushbikes into the yard for safekeeping. Among the bicycles were a few Mo-Ped's and although they had small engines (50cc) they also had pedals so they were classed as bicycles. The men were not allowed to use the engine in the yard and had to push them to and from the gate. Usually they were 'Raleigh's' with the little motor mounted over the front or back wheel. These machines looked more or less like an ordinary bicycle and the power was transmitted directly onto the tyre via a little rubber wheel. Needless to say, the tyre being driven got worn out very quickly and was always having to be replaced.

One of them though was really only posing as a Mo-Ped

because I never 'ever' saw one of them being pedalled. It did have pedals and I believe that if you turned them backwards they operated the rear brake. And I suppose that they could propel the bike if it was required. It was the splendid German made 'NSU Quickly' and it was the forerunner of the small step-through motorcycles. Its 50cc engine was a little marvel and incredibly reliable, it would take the little bike up to 30mph. The Raleigh on the other hand was lucky to reach 10mph and it had to be pedal assisted up the slightest gradient. The NSU Quickly was a beautifully designed machine that still looks cute today and it even had a twist grip gear change on the left handle bar.

Anyway, enough of this digression, we will return to my shameful act. I was walking between the cycle rack and the back wall of the Brass-shop. I happened to notice that the mirror on the NSU was almost exactly the same as the one I had broken on the Sunbeam. I had a shifting spanner in my pocket and after a lot of inner conflict I removed the mirror in seconds and stuffed it into my boiler suit. After I had done it I was guilt ridden and felt really bad. Obviously it would seem, not as bad as I felt about crashing Bob's Sunbeam. I am sure that you as a reader feel as disgusted with me as I have always felt about this sorry incident. Bob was delighted to have his replacement mirror but I never told him where it came from.

All of this talk about guilt does not mean that I am the 'Prince of Virtue', far from it. As I have said, I never had any qualms as an employee about taking or making something for myself. This is no doubt immoral but universally traditional whether you choose to accept it or not. It is common practice, from the lowest paid workers to the Moguls of industry. A toilet cleaner will take home the odd roll of lavatory paper, and the manager will be over-imaginative with his expense account. The only difference is that the toilet cleaner could lose his job and the manager will only have to be more imaginative. I have known managers in the shipyards who have had entire kitchens built in the Carpenters shop on nightshift, transported to their homes in works vehicles and fitted by the yard joiners during works time. Then you have all of the top Bankers and Industrialists with creative accountants who manage to pay less tax than the average nurse. Even Prince William used to make huge detours in RAF helicopters to visit his girlfriend Kate, paid for by the taxes of the working classes. Politicians claiming expenses for houses they don't have, members of the House of Lords signing in and then going straight home but still being paid for the day. 'YES' from the top to the bottom we are all as 'bent' as a nine Dollar note. The only difference between us is the vast variation in consequences to the individual if we are found out. I'll bet the Bishop of Westminster has the odd swig of communion wine.

We at the bottom are aware of it but it seems that the higher up the social ladder you clime you begin to think that dishonesty is the prerogative of the lower classes.

I still find it abhorrent for someone to steal from another person. So there you have it, two sets of values and I am comfortable to live with both of them. I beat myself up over the mirror incident fifty years ago and yet I have never lost a wink of sleep over my other numerous, shall we call them corporate misdemeanours. Perhaps I am just a born paradox, so we will leave it at that.

✦✦✦✦✦✦

Talking about the NSU Quickly reminds me of a regret that I still have and it concerns my mother. She was still working at George Angus & company on the Coast Road in Wallsend. She told my brother Bob and me that she was thinking about buying one of these lovely little bikes to go to work on. She had worked it out that it would be cheaper buying the bike and running it than it was to travel by public transport. Plus, she wouldn't have to get up so early to walk up to the High Street for the bus and then have to walk back again after her shift. This was in fact true because they did about 200 miles per gallon and were quite cheap to buy. Bob and I wouldn't hear of it, pointing out how dangerous motorbikes could be. There were too many nutters on the roads Etc, Etc, in the end we eventually talked her out of the idea.

I truly regret that we did now because she had always been a keen cyclist and had even cycled all of the way to Bradford in Yorkshire. She and my dad had done the 200 hundred mile round trip to visit my dad's brother Joe and his wife Meggie. Dad had my brother Alan on a little seat fastened to his crossbar and mam was pregnant with my brother Bob at the time. This was on two bikes that my dad had built out of old parts that he had acquired. It's a bit of a chore to drive in a car to Bradford on modern motorways let alone those old meandering back roads of the time. So the thought of riding there and back on a pushbike just doesn't bear thinking about.

Mam always loved to get on the back of Bobs or my motorbikes and although she was a heavy woman she was a very good pillion passenger. I used to take her up to my sister Joan's house or to the 'Bingo' and I could hardly feel her on the back of the bike. I know that she would have made an excellent rider and it would have been a wonderful adventure for her. I wish now that I had supported her in what would have been her last mad 'Tilt at a Windmill' so to speak.

Three years later she suffered a heart attack and died at only 59 years old, ironically she was running for a bus when it happened. Here I am turned 70 years old and still riding my own 750cc Kawasaki motorbike and still loving it.

✦✦✦✦✦✦

During my apprenticeship I worked with a few premium apprentices. These were lads from overseas whose parents were wealthy enough to afford to pay the Slipway a premium to train their sons. The first lad that we were introduced to was from Toronto in Ontario, Canada, his name was Jimmy Salt and he was 24 years old. This was old to be starting an Engineering apprenticeship but as long as his parents were paying, the

Slipway happily obliged. He told us that he had been sent over by his dad to try and straighten him out. At his own admission he told us that he had always been a bit of a waster and liked to party too much. We were all fascinated by his stories about growing up and his life in Toronto. His parents had over indulged him all of his life. They had even bought him an old 'Cadilac' car when he was fifteen to do his paper round in. (This beats an old pushbike with half a handlebar). He told us that he had never held a job for more than a few days and that he was always drunk. I think that his dad may have been from Tyneside originally and had been a marine engineer who had settled in Canada. He hoped that Jimmy would get a sense of purpose in life and become more self disciplined by being taught a trade on the Tyne.

He had hoped in vane I'm afraid because Jimmy soon discovered 'Nukie Brown' the famous Newcastle Brown Ale. This is a Tyneside Beer that it is known locally as 'Lunatic Broth'. It is a very nice beer but some people have a propensity to become overly attached to it. Jimmy would increasingly come to work either drunk or suffering from a hangover whenever we spoke to him. He would greet us with bloodshot eyes in the mornings and then just disappear for the rest of the day. I never saw Jimmy do any work and when I left the department I never set eyes on him again.

The next premium apprentice was an Indian lad called Achuta Kuma Chatterjee. The other lads didn't have much to do with him at first but not through any racial prejudice that I could perceive. It was just that we never met people from different ethnic backgrounds in those days and nobody knew the protocol. Jackie Frost the charge hand noticed that I was the only one talking to Achuta. This I must point out was not because I was a paragon of interracial harmony. The fact is, I can't remember having any thoughts at all on that subject. I was though always curious about things and with Achuta being different to me he was therefore interesting. The outcome of my curiosity was that Jackie Frost asked me to take Achuta under my wing until he got the hang of things. I was only too happy to oblige and we got along very well, swapping stories of our lifestyles. He told me that his surname Chatterjee was as common as Smith was to us in Britain and there were thousands of them in the Bombay telephone book. Unfortunately he had no interest in the job and certainly not in any kind of manual labour. He would often go missing and I would find him curled up in some out of the way corner out of sight. Or he would be inside a Doxford cylinder liner hidden behind a piece of cardboard sound asleep. I would have to shake him until he woke up to tell him that it was time to go home.

The men soon realised that there was no point in them telling him anything because he just wasn't interested, so as you would expect they just stopped bothering. It wasn't a language barrier thing because he spoke and understood English perfectly even the 'Geordie' dialect didn't bother him. He was always friendly with everyone and we had some interesting talks during our lunch breaks. One Friday he told me about a nurse from Preston Hospital in North Shields. She lived in the same boarding house as him and she had asked him to go to the pictures with her that night. He didn't know what he should do or if it was acceptable behaviour. I told him that she was just being friendly and that he should go with her if he wanted to. He had said that he was lonely not having friends or family to go home to at nights. At least now he would have a friend to talk to when he was not at work. So on the following Monday, I asked him if he had went out with the nurse yet. He had a shocked look on his face as he told me the events of the evening. They had indeed gone to the pictures and on their return to the boarding house she had asked him if he would like to kiss her. He was taken aback by her forwardness but decided that it must be an English custom. He leaned forward and obligingly kissed her on her upturned mouth. At this, the nurse had reached over and grabbed his manhood. (And I am not talking about the cowl on his coat). I was all-ears by now, nothing like this had ever happened to anyone else that I knew of. "What happened then", I asked him agog with eager anticipation. "I slapped her face and went to my room" he told me indignantly. Talk about an anti-climax. (Nurses, what can I say, what happened to foreplay?)

One day as we sat and talked, Achuta said to me, "You know Bill, back in India I would not talk to you". I asked him what he meant by this, not knowing if I had heard him correctly. "Well you see Bill, my father is a doctor and you are a common worker, so it would be wrong for me to socialise with you". He said this in a matter of fact way without any trace of malice. I was taken aback to say the least by this statement and my reaction was of hurt and anger. I jumped to my feet and yelled at him to get out of my sight before I put his lights out. I could not believe that I had befriended him when he was alone and now he was telling me that I was beneath him socially.

I was unaware at that time of the 'caste' system in his culture and I know now that he wasn't being offensive in his eyes, just factual. I am sorry to say that every time he tried to approach me to talk after that I would threaten him until he left. Had I known about the 'caste' thing I might have been able to enlighten him about how awful a concept it was. When the other lads heard the story, none of them spoke to poor Achuta again. Worse than that, I remember that on one childish and potentially dangerous occasion I purchased a Jumping Jack firework and threw it into the cylinder that he was sleeping in. I was only seventeen at the time but that is my only defence and it doesn't hold much water does it? I find it disturbing and scary how quickly we can turn malignant given the circumstances. It would be a better world if rational thoughts were our first thoughts every time.

Then there was a premium apprentice who came to us from 'Sarawak' in Borneo. I can't remember his name but he was skinny and sallow skinned with Jet-black hair. He too was completely bone-idle and believe it or not he used to fall sound asleep while standing up holding onto a broom. One of the Fitters had a spare room and he offered to let him lodge with him and his wife at a reasonable charge. While the Fitter was on nightshift, his wife decided to supply the sallow youth with extra comforts or should we say 'extra-maritals'. (At least this explains why he was always so tired). Inevitably, the fitter became suspicious and went home early one morning catching them in bed together. I never heard the full details but the Sarawak lad never came back to work.

The only premium apprentice who proved his worth was a Chinese lad from 'Hong Kong' called Albert Leong. He like Jimmy Salt was in his twenties. He was a smashing lad and clever with it, always getting excellent results at night school and day release. The blokes all liked him because he was a good worker and always showed interest. I worked along side him right through until the end of our apprenticeships and we became journeymen. He was destined to return to Hong Kong to be a Manager in his fathers ship repair dock. He'd had his wife over here living with him and they had a flat down at 'Whitley Bay'. I seem to remember that they had a baby while they were living here. Albert told a few of us that if we ever wanted to, he would give us a Supervising job in his yard. This may have been just talk but Albert was such a genuine sort of lad that I like to think that he meant every word.

****

While I was in the department that built the coolers for the Turbines, a funny or even farcical and yet illuminating incident happened. It helped to shape the future me, so it was a worthwhile learning curve in my books.

One of my pals came to work wearing a 'Wyatt Earp' tie you know the type of thing, the ones that were worn in the American wild-west by the gamblers. Just a simple, thin, black tape under your shirt collar and fastened in a bow at the front. The one that my pal was wearing was quick and easy, with the bow already made. An elastic tape went under your collar and fastened with a stud. I thought it looked great and asked him if I could try it on because I fancied getting one. He said "OK" and we went into the washroom so that I could look in the mirror. I was admiring my self as I looked at my reflection, with the thin straight bow and the two tails hanging down from the knot. "I'll have to get one of these" I enthused. My pal replied, "Aye, it looks great Bill, it really suits your build". (This is where it gets farcical), after he had uttered these inoffensive words, I smacked him in the mouth. He looked stunned and said, "What was that for". To which I replied indignantly, "For taking the micky out of my nose". He looked even more stunned and said, "I only said that it suited your build". I was mortified I had thought he had said that it suited my 'bill' (as in 'beak'). Up until that moment, I had always been a bit self-conscious about my nose, thinking that it was too big. I couldn't believe how daft I had been, (I can hear you saying that I must have had enough clues by now). I apologised immediately and when I explained to him what I thought he had said we both had a good laugh about it. He must never have mentioned the ludicrous incident to anyone, otherwise I would have been known as 'Billy the Beak' for the rest of my apprenticeship. Nicknames are a common thing among workingmen and once you have acquired one you are usually stuck with it for life. At the beginning of this anecdote I said that it was to shape the future 'me'. The reason I said this is because it made me aware of that old saying, 'Sticks and stones may break my bones but names can never hurt me'. This is a genuine 'truism' and it makes all of this political correctness that everyone is obsessed with just pretentious rhetoric, 'crap' in other words. Now, if I feel offended by what someone has said about me, I ask myself if there is some truth in what they are saying. If there is, then I can't honestly be offended and I know that I should take a look at myself. If there is no truth in it, then I know that they are talking rubbish and I can decide whether to get angry or consider them beneath my contempt and laugh at them. If you still rise to the so-called 'offensive' remark then you should take a step back to inspect the fragility of your own ego. (After this fiasco I grew to love my big nose).

✶✶✶✶✶✶

On the subject of nicknames, I only ever got stuck with a nickname once and luckily for me it only lasted for a couple of years. When I finished my apprenticeship I left shipbuilding for many years and by the time I went back, it had been forgotten. I used the word 'luckily' because unfortunately my nickname was 'Hairy-Arse'. At the time, this was an erroneous description of my peach like 'Gluteus Maximus'. There were more hairs on a billiard ball than my teenage, Walnut cracking buttocks. The nickname came about when 'Jean Jackets' first came onto the market. I had seen Glen Ford the Canadian actor in a modern day Cowboy picture wearing a pair of Jeans and a Jean Jacket. I thought it looked great and decided to get one myself. They were not considered suitable for casual wear as they are today, they had been designed as work wear. I decided that instead of a boiler suit I would go to work in Jeans and Jean Jacket. I think I must have been the first in Swan Hunters if not every yard on the river to dress like this, how cool was that? It meant of course that I was a bit of a spectacle at first and one of the labourers remarked, "You look like a hairy arsed Norwegian". I am not aware of Nordic people having particularly hirsute posteriors, or more to the point, why he would know this. The result of his observation was that I was known as Hairy-Arse for the next two years.

I will now recall just a few of the nicknames given to some of my fellow workmen over the years so that you can see how they originated. The first one that comes to mind was the old yard labourer at Swan Hunters. He was widely known in the yard as 'Pot Pie'. I never found out why he got this nickname or what his real name was but he had answered to it for as long as anyone could remember. That is the trouble with nicknames your real identity becomes more and more obscure. He had been there for donkey's years and even the older men knew him only as Pot Pie. I remember him as being skinny, wearing a cloth cap and always in an old Trench raincoat tied at the waist with a piece of rope. All of the apprentices used to bait him by shouting

"Pot Pie" at him. He would then throw his brush at us and give chase to us. Then one of the other lads would pop up behind him and shout "Pot Pie" at him again, causing him to turn and chase in the other direction. This pointless and seemingly cruel game took place on a daily basis and had apparently been acted out by many generations of apprentices over the years. One day, one of the lads thought it would be a good idea to set fire to Pot Pie's barrow while he was in the toilet. By the time he came out, the rubbish was well ablaze and the wooden barrow was completely destroyed. I don't know whose idea it had been but I believe it was one of the older apprentices. Needless to say, we all did a runner when we saw how quickly the conflagration had consumed the barrow.

The next day, the Manager came into the fitter's workshop and gathered us all together. He told us that he could not prove anything but he knew that it was one of us who had lit the fire in the barrow. He said that the baiting of Pot Pie had to stop because he was an old man and a bit simple minded. He told us that we should all be ashamed of our behaviour and in fact we all were. There is a strangely heart warming conclusion to this otherwise sorry tale. After a couple of weeks of us leaving Pot Pie in peace, he came to see us while we were having our morning tea break. He stood in front of us with his cap in his hands and said, "What's the matter lads, do you not like me anymore, you never shout Pot Pie at me now". He looked really sad as he said this. We all assured him that we still liked him but that the Manager had told us to stop pestering him. He grinned from ear to ear and said, "Tek nee notice of him, ah like ti chase yi aboot". We told him that it would be back to normal tomorrow and he went away happy. As promised, we resumed our pointless and cruel baiting of Pot Pie and did so until I left the yard at the end of my apprenticeship.

Another nickname was Ten-Bob-Wilf. His name was Wilfie Thompson and I was his apprentice for a short time at Swans. He got his name because he liked to wager people Ten Bob (10

Shillings / 50 new pence). To back up the validity of his bet, he would take an old, tattered, folded, brown Ten Shilling note out of his waistcoat pocket and wave it at them. If he lost the bet he always paid up but not with his Ten Bob note. It had been in and out of his pocket hundreds of times over many years and would probably have fallen to pieces if it had been unfolded.

I have known two fitters who were given the title 'The Hollywood Fitter'. This was because they were always combing their hair and I mean virtually none stop. One of them was a Foreman in Swans and the other one was a friend of mine called Ronnie Waterworth when I was at George Angus & Co. Their combs would have had to be surgically removed from their hands.

'Fango' was a lad that I knew in Swans and he was so called because his Eye-Teeth were long and pointed like 'Dracula', they looked great and all the lads envied him of them.

I was seconded up to the 'Neptune' shipbuilding yard a mile or so further upstream for a short while and I worked with a big fitter who I only ever knew as 'The Strangler'. Yes, he lived up to his nickname and did make a habit of strangling people that annoyed him. He was a huge bloke and he settled every argument by grabbing his opponent by the throat and lifting them off the ground. He would hold them out in front of him with his massive hands but not quite choking them. The victims had to hold onto his wrists to relieve the pressure on their necks. I don't think he would have actually killed them, he was always happy when they conceded defeat. I only ever saw him do his party piece on one occasion but it left me with an indelible memory of the incident. A charge-hand came to the 'deck winch' that The Strangler and I had stripped down and asked us to stop what we doing and follow him. The Strangler said, "Aye, when we finish here". The charge-hand said, "This other job is more important". The Strangler stood up towering over the charge-hand and took him by the throat, then lifted him over the side of the ship. "Every job that I do is important you cheeky little bastard", he explained. The poor bloke's knuckles were white as he hung onto The Stranglers treelike forearms while he dangled over the murky river. His eyes were popping as he croaked, "Aye OK Strangler, finish the job ya on first". I don't have to tell you that I was always very polite to The Strangler and we got along very well. I must say that for a psychopath he was a very good fitter. Today of course, he would have been sacked, jailed or sectioned to the funny farm.

I can't remember where it was but I worked with a charge-hand who actually answered to the name, 'Billy the Bastard'. I have no idea which side of the blankets he had been conceived or the marital legality of his parents but he lived up to his nickname with other aspects of his demeanour.

When I worked at Smiths Dock in North Shields there was a labourer who worked with the tail end squad (propellers and rudders). He was a big powerful lad and he was the best man for using a sledgehammer to tighten the huge bolts. He was known throughout the dock as 'Captain Slog'. This was a clever and humorous play on words from the Sci-Fi TV show 'Star-Trek'. Captain Kirk would update the space ships computer data by starting his entry, "Captains log, Star-date Etc, Etc. I've always thought that this was the best-derived nickname I've come across.

When I worked for George Angus & Co, I was responsible for giving one of the lasses her nickname. Her real name was 'Pat Carr' and she asked me to make her a long steel hook to pull her tins of work about her department. All of the girls used to ask me to make them because I used to stamp their names on the shaft and put rubber handgrips on for them. The other fitters would just bend the end of a piece of 3/8" steel rod and give it to them. Pat was a self-confessed man-eater, so when it came to stamping her name on it I stamped, 'PAT, THE BEAST THAT ROAMED THE FLASH'. ('The flash' was the name of her department). Far from being offended by this, she was delighted by its exclusivity and went around showing it to everyone. From that day on, she was known as 'Pat the Beast' and proud of it.

My brother Bob worked at George Angus too and he used to answer to the name 'Walter'. This is because he was always regaling the other lads with stories from his colourful past. Most of the stories seemed unlikely to the average person and so Bob was likened to the fictional character 'Walter Mitty'. The American comedy actor 'Danny Kay' played the part in the film, 'The secret life of Walter Mitty'. In the film, Walter used to go through life fantasizing that he was the hero in different scenarios, saving damsels in distress. The general opinion was that Bob's stories were also just fantasies. They weren't of course, Bob had a larger than life history and he loved to relate it to whoever would listen. He knew that they were sceptical but he wasn't bothered because 'he' knew that it was the truth and he always had their full attention.

The next anecdote on this theme is not for the squeamish and I am only relating it because it is so tasteless it is hard to imagine. I worked beside a bloke who was in his twenties and was known throughout the factory as 'The Cacky Man'. (Cacky being a Geordie word for shit). One day I asked him how he had acquired this less than flattering nickname. He gave me a broad grin and enthusiastically told me the story as though it was a normal everyday event. It had taken place a couple of years earlier, soon after he had been married. It would seem that when they were in bed, he would think that it was highly amusing to press his bum against the leg of his new bride and fart, (And they say romance is dead). I was already wishing that I hadn't asked him but he pressed joyfully on with his disgusting tale. One night he was performing this woeful bonding ceremony after several beers and a vindaloo curry. The inevitable happened and he bathed her leg in a viscous bowel movement. He was racked with mirth as he told me that his new bride had got up, had a shower, got dressed and left. He had never seen her ever again, now that doesn't come as a surprise does it? I was dumbstruck and I could not believe that anyone would ever reveal something as grossly obscene as that to another soul. I think that he was a little bit disappointed by my un-amused reaction when I told him that he was a disgusting bastard. Still, you can't expect to make friends by telling a story like that, at least not with me.

******

CHAPTER 15

'H.M.S. LION'

Well enough of these nickname stories let us get back to my life in general. I had turned eighteen and to my delight I was at last transferred up to Swan Hunters to join the fitting out team. All of my mates from the erecting bay were already up there so it did not feel as though I was going into the unknown. I had to report to the Head Foreman, 'Archie Duncan' who was the brother of 'Billy Duncan' who had been my Foreman in the Brass-shop. Archie was a big amiable man just like his brother Billy and he always wore his white boiler suit. Unlike the other Foremen he never wore a hat and he was as bald as a coot. I don't think I ever saw him without his pipe in his mouth, except when he was pointing at something with its stem. He was well respected by all of the blokes and there was no aspect of marine engineering that he didn't know. In fact he was awarded the MBE for services to the industry while I worked there. He always had his boiler suit sleeves rolled up to his elbows, out of the way of his hands. I thought it looked great and so I began to emulate this habit, although my forearms weren't as impressive as Archie's. I still have to roll my sleeves up to the elbows 60 years later because I just don't feel comfortable if I don't. I have to admit that my forearms are still not as impressive as Archie's.

He took me onboard 'HMS Lion' a Royal Navy cruiser that had been built at the end of World War 2. She had never seen action and had been mothballed for years. Swan Hunters were going to update her, giving her steam turbine engines and Yarrow boilers a complete overhaul. She was also being fitted with the latest guns by 'Vickers Armstrong' Newcastle. Archie took me to the forward boiler room and introduced me to my latest fitter mentor, 'Arty Bainbridge'. I always seemed to get a good fitter to work with and Arty was no exception. He specialised in the boiler plant of whichever ship he was working on and he knew them inside and out. As with all good tradesmen, the more interest I took in the job the more Arty would show me. Sadly this was not always the case and some fitters were reluctant to hand their knowledge on to a new generation. Some of my mates told me that the blokes that they worked with would wait until the job was at an interesting or crucial part of its progress and then send them away on a message. By the time they had returned from this unnecessary task the job had been completed and the apprentice was left none the wiser, how mercenary is that?

Arty had another apprentice as well as me, a lad called 'Hughie' who was a bit of a nondescript sort of youth who didn't mix with the other apprentices at all. He was always smart and clean, wearing a spotless white shirt with a tie under his boiler suit and peering through horn-rimmed glasses. For someone who was nondescript, he comes out pretty well I have to admit. What I mean is, he was somewhat lacking on the personality front with little or no sense of humour. I always got on OK with Hughie but our attempts at discourse weren't exactly scintillating. He came from one of the better locations of that time 'Monkseaton' and he spoke very well. He didn't speak 'posh' but not broad 'Geordie' as the rest of us did. He was the only lad that I knew who got his Higher National Diploma at college. So, he was clever, clean and smart, spoke well and didn't like to get his hands dirty. It was obvious that he was destined for better things than the rest of us philistines. I was responsible for Hughie getting a junior engineers position on the ship that I was working on in my last year of training. It was the practice of Chief Engineer's on newly built ships to offer one of the last year apprentices the position of junior engineer on the ship. I got on well with the

Chief and so he approached me first with this prestigious offer. Although being a seagoing Engineer had been my driving force in my early apprenticeship, I knew now that it wasn't for me. There was simply no way that I could bring myself to leave my lovely Margaret, it was too much of a gamble. Hughie had told me that he would like to go to sea, so I pointed him out to the Chief explaining how clever Hughie was. Hughie duly sailed with the ship and after a few months I was delighted to receive a postcard from 'Rio De Janeiro' sent by him. (OK I may have been a bit envious but I knew that I had made the right choice).

Working in the boiler room was a bit of a traumatic experience for me due to the fact that the sound of hissing steam scares me. I got this phobia when I was very young and my dad had taken me up to the Newcastle central station to see the steam locomotives. I loved these beautiful, incredibly powerful machines and still do. When I heard the ticking of the hot expanding metal and the gurgling of the boiler and then inhaled the unforgettable smells I was captivated. Sadly, while I was inspecting the connecting rod from the piston to the massive driving wheels, the boiler safety valve released with a heart-stopping whoosh. I think I may have piddled myself with fright as my dad, the loco and the platform disappeared in a cloud of steam. I did not know what the evil screaming noise was and thought that it would never end. My dad found me and picked me up in his strong arms and cuddled me to his chest while I clung to him and sobbed. Dad explained to me what it was and why it had happened and I eventually calmed down but I still feel uncomfortable at the sound.

It's a bit of an enigma because I worked for a small company called 'Safety Valve Services' in North Shields for a while. My job was to remove the safety valves from ships, hospital and factory boilers, to service and repair and then refit them. When I had refitted them I would have to reset them to release when they exceeded a certain pressure. This would invariably require me to lie on top of the boiler waiting for an engineer to shout up that it had reached the optimum pressure. Then I would adjust the valve safety release mechanism until the steam blasted out through the escape pipe. It never stopped scaring me to the point of almost piddling my pants. Many times I wished for my dads strong arms to pick me up and give me a cuddle. Nobody knew of my phobia because it was during the insidious Margaret Thatcher era (Hoick, Spit) and jobs were too hard to find in those days.

Back in the forward boiler room of HMS Lion, my Fitter mate Arty didn't exactly help matters when he explained the dangers of super heated steam to Hughie and me. He told us to listen out for the distinctive screaming rather than just the usual hissing sound that steam makes. Boilers always have hissing steam leaks from valve glands or pipe flanges but super heated steam leaks needed to be dealt with immediately. Where you see a cloud of steam is not where the leak is coming from. It will be invisible for three or four feet before it turns to steam vapour and then condenses into water. While it is in the invisible state it will strip the flesh off your bones. Arty told us that he knew someone who had lost all of his fingers just by running his hand through a super heated leak. I don't know if this story was true or if Arty was just trying to make us more vigilant. Either way, it worked and I have always had the utmost respect of the dangers involved while working with steam. There were two engine rooms and two boiler rooms with a ratings mess above them filled with the steel frames of three tier bunk beds. Every morning the men and boys would gather here until the charge men or Foremen gave them their work for the day. They would also keep their toolboxes in the mess and congregate there for their tea breaks. Arty, Hughie and I could go straight to the forward boiler room because as I have said, it was Arties domain from beginning to end. If you wanted to 'skive' for a bit you could go up to the mess, open your toolbox and just sit and chat to who-ever else was getting tools or skiving. If a Foreman, Manager or charge hand came you simply rummaged in your toolbox, selected a spanner and returned to your job.

The only things that the 'Slipway' supplied to its apprentice workforce were a wooden toolbox, a padlock, a one and a half pound hammer and an eight-inch cold chisel. Every month a 'Rep' would come and show you a catalogue from which you could order tools and the payment was taken out of your wages weekly. At this time I had acquired a set of 'Britool' Whitworth ring-spanners, a set of 'Snail Brand' Whitworth open-ended spanners and an eight-inch 'Elora' shifting spanner. These were supplemented with tools that I had made myself, so I had plenty of stuff to rattle about if the Gaffa was watching. I still have many of my original tools in my garden shed along with a lot of other engineering paraphernalia. Most of which to be to be dumped unceremoniously when I am gone I would imagine.

Most of my pals were working in the forward boiler and engine rooms so it got a bit animated in the mess room during tea-breaks. We were allowed 20 minutes in the mornings that we usually stretched to 30 minutes if a Gaffa didn't come and roust us first. There was no official tea break in the afternoons, although we usually managed to have a quick coffee or tea covertly. A new ships Manager was assigned to the ship and none of the blokes, or for that matter the Gaffa's liked him. I can still remember his name but because this anecdote does not flatter him in any way, I will refer to him by his nickname, 'Speedy Gonzales'. He was named after the famous cartoon mouse because he ran about the ship and seemed to appear from nowhere. His sole purpose in life seemed to be to catch somebody doing something that he may not approve of. He never attempted to help anyone with anything and his only aim was to listen to his own voice berating someone. I soon discovered that the best way to get shot of him was to ask him a question about the job. He would bluster for a bit and then he would say that he would go and check it out, never to get back to me. One day, he came bursting into the mess about two minutes after the tea break should have ended. Men were hiding their sandwiches in their overalls and vacuum flasks were rolling about the deck, it was a complete farce. 'Speedy' was running about demonically, screaming for us to get back onto our jobs. I have always been of the mind that if you are caught with your trousers down there is no point in panicking. Try and save a bit of dignity and face up to whatever is coming your way. It was 'Speedy' who came my way on this occasion as I was putting my sandwiches back into my haversack in an orderly fashion. He became incensed because I wasn't running about like a headless chicken. It was then that he made the mistake of grabbing my arm to hasten my progress. I turned and took hold of his tie and shirt collar and pushed him against the bulkhead. He was shouting that he was going to sack me so I told him that I worked for the Slipway, not Swans and that he didn't have the authority to sack me, (I had no idea if this was true or not). I also told him that he had assaulted me by grabbing my arm and that I had plenty of witnesses. He stormed out of the mess room looking apoplectic and talking loudly to him-self.

The men all patted me on the back and the apprentices were chanting my name as I stoically awaited my fate. Eventually I saw Archie my Gaffa coming down the boiler room steps and when he spotted me he headed in my direction. My heart sank as he put his massive hand on my shoulder and said, "Are you the lad that had the run in with "Speedy". I nodded, looking at the floor plates as I related the sequence of events. When I had finished, Archie was silent for what seemed like minutes as he puffed on his pipe. Then he turned to me and said, "Keep out of his way in future son, he's a pain in the arse". He then walked away smiling, leaving me bewildered but relieved at his lenience and with the firm conviction that Archie was indeed a very wise man.

On the decks and bulkheads of the ship there were drawings of components done in white marker paint. Things like Fire Extinguisher, Hose Reel or Hammock, drawn to scale in dotted lines of the paint. Each depiction of a component was named such as 'Hammock Stowed' 'Hose Reel Stowed' inside the drawing. This was so that pipe work and electric cables could be routed around the drawings before the actual components were in place. I managed to borrow a pot of the marker paint with its brush and I drew a full size coffin in white dots on the mess room deck. Inside it I wrote, 'Speedy Stowed', (using his real name).

All of the blokes thought that it was hilarious but as was expected 'Speedy' was not amused, demonstrating to us that he was obviously an art critic as well as a pain in the arse. When he spotted my macabre masterpiece he screamed, "Who did this" and began to scrape his shoes back and forward over my dastardly depiction. It was a pointless effort because marker paint was designed not to scuff off easily when walked over. In the end he realised the futility of his farcical 'Irish Jig' and went to find a painter with some thinners to remove it. When he returned, the mess room was full of blokes supposedly getting tools out of their boxes and they were all laughing. 'Speedy' stood there flushed with impotent fury, watching the painter desecrate my sombre sketch. Had he been a more approachable man I would have felt sorry for the dilemma my joke had placed him in.

Everyone used to leave the ship at 11-50am, so that they could wash their hands for lunch at 12 Noon. 'Speedy' took it upon him self to stand at the top of the gangplank and stop them going ashore until the yard siren went at noon. Nothing was gained by his power trip because hundreds of people gathered there instead of leaving in dribs and drabs. When he stood aside it was just one mad rush down the gangplank and it was a miracle that no one got hurt in the stampede. This went on for a few days until an old Boilermaker walked past 'Speedy' saying, "I need to gan to the Netty", (lavatory). 'Speedy' smirked and replied in a sardonic manner, "Yes, of course you do, well you will just have to wait until the siren goes". At this the Boilermaker opened his overalls and trousers, dropped them to his ankles and then squatted on the deck. 'Speedy' started screaming, "You can't do that! You can't do that"! The old man smiled and said, "The ball is in your court son". One of the women cleaners shouted, "Go on Jackie, have a good shite". We were all in fits of laughter by this time and 'Speedy' told him that he could go ashore if he was in such great need. Everyone cheered him as he walked down the gangplank waving back at us. The following day, 'Speedy' was back on sentry duty to hold us back, not even smart enough to know when the battle was lost it would seem. Everybody just told him that they were desperate to go to the 'Netty' and he didn't have the nerve to call their bluff. He never showed up at the gangplank after that day.

The last anecdote I have involving 'Speedy is a bit scary. We were all having our tea break in the mess room when there was a crash bang wallop at the bottom of the stairs between the decks. When we looked, we saw that it was 'Speedy' who appeared to have fallen down the stairs. He was semi-conscious and moaning as he lay there in a crumpled heap. His leg looked like a badly formed Pretzel so someone ran ashore to get the first aid man. While we waited he regained consciousness and began screaming that somebody had tripped him on purpose at the top of the stairs. He could not remember seeing anyone but he was convinced that he had been deliberately tripped. We were all shocked by his apparent conviction as he was stretchered away that someone had tried to kill him. Was it just paranoia? God knows that there were plenty of things that he could have tripped over in the dim lighting, welding cables, air hoses, Etc! I sincerely hope that it was not a malicious act. He must have been given a job in an office when he recovered because I never saw him again.

✦✦✦✦✦✦

CHAPTER 16

Taking my driving tests

Meanwhile on the home front, my brother Bob had crashed his Sunbeam motorbike and hospitalised himself. He had hit a 1948 MG Magnette car and the ambulance crew had found him on the other side of a six-foot hedge in somebody's garden. He had been very lucky considering that he wasn't wearing a crash helmet and that he had been impeded in his flight by a tree. He had a couple of cracked ribs, facial abrasions and many contusions. Yes, he looked a mess but there was nothing life threatening about his injuries. I had already applied to take my motorcycle-driving test and it was due to take place very soon. Margaret and I had been thinking about buying our own bike and sharing the costs, (we have shared our money all of our lives without dispute). Bob's accident just hastened our decision, especially with my driving test being imminent.

Scooters were just beginning to be popular, with 'Vespa' and 'Lambretta' being the market leaders. My favourite was the Lambretta because it had a proper tubular steel frame under its skin, its engine was centrally mounted and it had a shaft drive. The Vespa on the other hand had a monocoque chassis with the engine mounted on the right hand side. This caused the rider to lean to his or her left to counterbalance it unless they had a spare wheel in the left hand compartment. It looked very ungainly.

We went up to 'Cowies Motorcycles' on Westgate Road in Newcastle to have a look at them. The new models had just come out, the LI 125 and the LI 150 and they were beautiful. I was a bit disappointed when they told me that they had changed the final drive from shaft over to chain but it didn't deter me. I ordered the LI 125 because it was more affordable and I still remember how much it cost because it was one Pound for every cubic centimetre of engine capacity, for example, £125 = 125cc.

Today you can't take your driving test on a motorcycle without sitting a written test first and practical riding course with an instructor. Back then, I just went up to 'Cowies' on a Saturday afternoon and collected my new bike. The bloke didn't ask me if I had a provisional licence, if I was insured, or even if I had ever ridden a bike before. He just pointed to the pedal on the right hand side of the footboard and said, "Back brake" then he pointed at the lever on the right handlebar and said, "Front brake". Then he pointed at the left hand side of the handlebar and said, "Clutch lever and twist-grip gear changer". After these comprehensive and in depth instructions, he wished me luck and went back into the shop. It's hard to believe how lax things were in those days when I think back.

I was excited as I rode down 'Westgate Hill', practicing my gear changing with the unfamiliar left hand twist grip. I made a few mistakes when it came to braking, feeling about with my left foot instead of my right. All British bikes had the rear break pedal on the left and the gears on the right but of course Lambretta is an Italian bike. Luckily for me, the front brake was in the usual place and quite efficient so I didn't have any close calls. Everything was going smoothly as I made my way through the City traffic until I reached City Road. The bike started to feel a bit sluggish for a while and then it began to chug and jerk. I pulled over to the side of the road and switched the engine off in trepidation. The man at the shop had assured me that there was a gallon of petrol in the tank but I shook the bike to confirm that I could hear it splashing about. I then did something that my wife Margaret will find hard to believe, I decided to read the Lambretta instruction manual that I had been given, (Yes, I am one of those blokes who only reads instruction manuals in desperation). Petrol starvation was still my first thought but on reading the manual it explained that the bike had a choke like a car. The bloke at the shop had turned on the petrol with the little switch on the right hand side of the engine housing and he must have turned the cold start switch (choke) on the left side at the same time. It advised in the book that the cold start lever should be turned off as soon as the engine had warmed up. It warned that the engine would begin to misfire if it was left on for too long. Sure enough, it was confirmed for me when I looked at the position of the switch I had ridden a couple of miles with the cold start on. I turned it off and after a couple of kicks of the kick-start the motor sprang back into life. I never had another moment of bother from the bike after that day. Sadly, it still has to be an act of desperation for me to read an instruction manual, some people just never learn it would seem.

At least I had the sense to get crash helmets for Margaret and myself, or perhaps it would be more accurate to say 'Margaret' had the sense. We bought matching white Gino's, which were considered to be one of the best helmets on the market at the time. They were made of steel and weighed a ton, compared to the more popular Kangol's which were a leather covered cork shell and known in fact as 'Corkers'.

✴✴✴✴✴✴

THE SAME MODEL NORTON THAT BOB PAINTED BLUE AND ALLOWED ME TO RIDE WHEN I WAS UNDER AGE.

THE SAME MODEL SUNBEAM S.8. THAT BOB LET ME LEARN HOW TO RIDE LEGALLY ON.

THE SAME MODEL `1959 LAMBRETTA L.1
AS MINE

THE FIRST BIKE THAT I
OWNED AND THE ONE THAT
I PASSED MY TEST ON.

The law at the time was the same as it is now in as much as a learner rider wasn't allowed to carry a pillion passenger unless they were a qualified rider. It shouldn't take a genius to work out what I did with regards to this inconvenient law. I simply took the plastic learner plates off the bike whenever I had Margaret on the back. We had a good scoot about, discovering our lovely county of Northumberland long before I had past my motorcycle-driving test.

I had asked the driving test authority if I could have a cancellation test, which meant that if someone cancelled their test, I would jump the queue into their place. It happened sooner than I expected and I got my test date for only two weeks after I had bought the Lambretta. To make it worse, cancellation tests by there nature could be anywhere in the Northumberland area and not just in your own. Mine was to be in 'Blyth' and although it isn't very far up the coast, I had never been there before in my life so it would all be strange to me. I went early so that I could familiarise myself with the area and then I went into the office to let them know that I was there. I was told to go outside where I would see a man with a clipboard conducting a test on someone. I was to introduce myself and then follow his instructions while he conducted a test on me too. I spoke to the man with the clipboard and he pointed out a lad on a Vespa scooter at the far side of a large grassy area. He told me that he was testing the Vespa rider and that I should follow the lad around the green expanse so that he could test us both at the same time. I was to stop as soon as I had completed the circuit so that he could give me further instructions. Lambretta and Vespa riders were always rivals and I shot off like a Bat out of hell, I honestly thought that the examiner would be impressed if I could beat the Vespa around the square. I arrived back beside him well ahead of the other lad and feeling smug, awaiting further instructions.

The examiner asked me to take my helmet off so that he could have a word with me. I did as he asked and he said,

"Who do you think you are son, 'Geoff Duke' (Famous TT racing motorcyclist). I was at a loss for words because I could see that he had not been impressed with my performance and I thought I had been great. "You rode that scooter like a maniac, throwing it into corners like a motorbike", he said. Going onto the defensive I told him that up until two weeks ago I had been learning to ride on a 500cc Sunbeam. He replied, "Well you're on a scooter with small wheels now and I think you should go away and learn how to ride it before you apply again". I was mortified because it had not even occurred to me that I might fail my test. What was I going to say to Margaret how could I face my brothers.

As I rode home along the seafront at 'Seaton Sluice' the tears filled my eyes and I was forced to stop in a lay-by next to the sand dunes. I felt that I had been badly done by and treated unfairly by the authorities. After a bit of deep thinking I realised that I had not failed my test, I had thrown it away. You can't go on feeling sorry for yourself when you know that you have brought the negativity to your own door. So I decided to go home, face the derision and stop whining. If I am given time to ponder things I usually come to the right conclusion and the best course of action. This does not stop me from making the same mistakes time and time again. It just means that I don't have to ponder for as long to come to the same conclusions.

As expected, Margaret was her loving and supportive self, just like she always has been throughout our lives, bless her. My brother Alan had a good laugh but said, "Better luck next time son". My brother Bob also had a good laugh but went on to say, "The examiner was right, you do throw the scooter about like a motorbike and I do the same when I ride it, so practice riding it more sedately before your next test". So, my humiliation was a fraction of what I had been expecting and I had come to the same conclusion about riding more sedately.

When I turned eighteen in the January of 1959 I started taking driving lessons in a 1949 Morris Minor with the 'Wallsend school of motoring' High Street East'. It was a one-man set up and the owner/instructor was a man called 'Mr Logan' who charged five Shillings a lesson. I was able to go once a week due to being subsidized by my lovely Margaret. Although the car was ten years old, it was in immaculate condition and had dual controls. Mr Logan was an excellent instructor and although he was impressed by my initial driving ability he told me that I had acquired many bad habits that would have to be addressed. And so, I took my car-driving test at Osborne Road test centre in Newcastle almost immediately after failing my motorbike test. As we sat in the examiners waiting room Mr Logan told me not to make small talk with the examiner and under no circumstances was I to blow the horn at anybody.

A tall, bald man who reminded me of my dad came into the room and called my name. As I left with the examiner I looked back at my instructor and he gave me a smile and the thumbs up. I was confident at the end of my test because in my eyes my driving had been impeccable. The examiner turned to me and said, "I'm sorry but on this occasion I will have to give you a fail certificate and the reasons are on this form". At this he got out of the car and left me dumbstruck once again. On the form I had past every part of the test but at the very end in the 'other comments' box he had written 'Lack of courtesy to pedestrians'. I knew exactly what he had been referring to and I could have kicked myself for my stupidity. I had been doing my hill start on a small hump back bridge in 'Jesmond' Newcastle. Just as I pulled away from the kerb four women met each other in the middle of the road and started to have a chat. I remembered what Mr Logan had said about not blowing the horn, so I stopped and applied the handbrake. I revved the engine a little bit to attract their attention and one of the women turned and looked at me. Instead of urging the other women onto the footpath she just looked me up and down. Her face could have stopped a clock and she looked as though she had just trod on a dogs egg in her bare feet. It seemed like an age as I sat there waiting for the narrow road to clear. I have never been very patient and so I remembered muttering, "Daft old bag", under my breath. It must have been more audible than I had intended because I also remembered him writing something down. Thus, I facilitated yet another failed driving test due to my own stupidity.

I applied for both my car and motorbike re- tests straight away and asked to be considered for any cancellations that became available. My bike test came first and I was to sit it at North Shields, at least it was somewhere that I knew this time. It was a lovely July day and I rode that Lambretta like a big girlie. (Yes, I know that was a chauvinistic remark, 'so', I am not Mr Perfect) but It did help me to passed my test.

My car test came through for August at Long Benton test centre in Newcastle. This time as we sat in the waiting room, my instructor Mr Logan said. "They are all nice examiners here except the only female examiner they have". Apparently because she was a big lass and a hard liner on the tests, she was known as 'Fatilla the Hun' among the instructors. Yes, you have guessed where this is leading. The door opened and there stood a large lady holding a clipboard and calling out my name, my heart sank as I left the room. One of the other instructors whispered to me as I passed him. "Don't open the car door for her, she doesn't like it".

We were out on the test for the full hour driving about the city of Newcastle and I was sweating like a pig on a spit in the August sun. Luckily, hand signals were still a required part of the driving test in those days and my door window was open. Needless to say, air conditioning or even air ducts were not the things that British car manufacturers thought of as necessary back then. Like true 'Brits' we stout heartedly froze in the winter and roasted in the summer. We can lay the blame on the Japanese for turning us into sissy motorists. Many is the time I have had to scrape a square of ice off the 'inside' of the windscreen as well as the 'outside' to see where I was going. 'Ah' Halcyon days.

Where was I, oh yes, the driving test. At one point I thought I had blown it again when I was overtaking a Trolley Bus that was standing at a bus stop. I was half way past when the Bus just shot away, leaving me in the middle of the road. When we got back to the test centre I fully expected to get another fail. She turned to me smiling and said. "I'm happy to inform you that your driving has met with my requirements and here is your pass certificate". Once again I was dumb struck but this time for happier reasons. As she was climbing out of the car she stopped and turned to me. "In future, be careful when you overtake a Trolley Bus because they have incredible acceleration as you found out today". I could have kissed her lovely chubby face.

Was it my skill behind the steering wheel, or was she smitten by my charm and boyish good looks. That's the trouble, when I have dealings with the fair sex I'm never sure whether they have judged me on my merit or are blinded by my striking countenance. (Yes, I know that you are sneering. 'SCEPTICS').

CHAPTER 17

My 'Rolls Royce' era

When my brother Bob's Sunbeam was fixed, he fitted it with a sidecar but he never got used to the way it handled. I only rode it once as a motorcycle sidecar combination and I too thought that it was dreadful. I have tried several three wheeled vehicles over the years and I still find that they are unstable to drive. So I have always stuck to multiples of two wheels for my own transport. Bob sold the combination and bought himself a three-ton 'Ford Thames Trader' ex-army truck to become a scrap metal dealer. He bought it at an auction and it had a closed canvas loading area with a hydraulic tipping mechanism. He brought it home and had a look in the dashboard glove box out of natural curiosity. He was surprised to find about a dozen logbooks for motorcycles. He went to the back of the truck and opened the canvas doors. Sure enough, there were all of these bikes standing in a row, tied to the floor. It was just as well he hadn't tried the tipping gear before he looked in the glove box. When he checked his receipt from the auctioneers it confirmed that he had bought the truck plus its load without realising. After he had sold all of the ex-army bikes, the cost of the truck had been covered and he was still into pocket with the excess cash.

I loved the Thames Trader because he used to let me take my mam in it when she visited anyone or went to the Bingo, then I would go and pick her up again later. Knowing Bob, it probably wasn't insured for him to drive it let alone me, I never asked and I was still three years too young to drive a truck anyway.

My brother Alan was now working as a milkman for Close's dairy on Station Road in Wallsend. Every Saturday and Sunday he would call into Union Street for half an hour to have a cup of tea with our mam. While he was there, he would let me borrow his electric milk float laden with crates of milk to drive along to see my darling Margaret. As I have said, acting in a responsible manner has never been an obvious first choice for my brothers or me. When I returned, I would then help Alan to deliver his milk and he would let me do all of the driving.

One of the lads that I worked with told me about a job that he had on Saturdays driving 'Rolls Royce' cars for a firm called, T. Howe + Co., in Newcastle. I was green with envy and begged him to take me up to see the Boss. The following Saturday I went up with him for the start of his shift. My pal put on a bottle green trench coat and a peaked chauffeur's hat then drove out of the garage in a short convoy of gleaming black Rolls Royce sedans. I was almost salivating as I watched him drive this beautiful vintage machine past me. I presented myself at the Boss' office and asked him if he needed another Saturday driver. I'd had the sense to wear a shirt and tie and he looked me up and down in appraisal. He took my name and address and said he would get in touch if he needed anyone. I thanked him and turned to leave the office feeling disappointed. "Just a minute son", he said, "I might as well take you out for a test drive while you're here". I was elated that he was actually going to let me drive a Rolls Royce. He went through the start up procedure with me and it was like an aeroplane. There were about four switches that had to be turned to different positions in the correct order. There was an advance and retard lever in the centre of the steering wheel that had to be set, similar to old motorcycles. On the other side of the steering wheel there was another lever that controlled how hard or soft the suspension was. When I had completed this procedure I pressed the silver start button on the dashboard. The muted growl of the massive engine was like music to me as a shiver ran down my spine. We left the garage and he directed me around the area for about fifteen minutes. I think that driving Alan and Bob's trucks had stood me in good stead because the huge 1930's 'Roller' was like a luxurious truck. The gear stick was on the right hand side of the driver's seat next to the door, which was a bit strange at first. The steering wheel must have been two feet in diameter, so the steering was quite light. The big black bonnet over the engine stuck out about eight feet in front of me, flanked by the beautiful curves of the front mudguards. In front of these were mounted two immense chrome headlamps. The famous Rolls Royce radiator adorned with the lovely 'Spirit of Ecstasy' was the icing on the cake.

When we returned to the garage he told me that he was happy with my driving and would call me if he needed a driver in the future. His phone was ringing so I said goodbye and walked away with a big smile on my face. I was about 50 yards down the street when he shouted after me. He asked me if I knew where Forrest Road was in 'Walkerville'. I told him that I did because my old school stood on the corner of Forrest Road and West Street. He said that one of the cars had broken down and I could start immediately if I wanted to. I eagerly agreed and he got me one of the bottle green trench coats and a chauffeur's hat. Giving me the address he told me to take the car that he had tested me in. When I arrived at the house there were two other cars parked outside. For some reason I had assumed that it was a wedding but when the door opened to reveal the sombre face of an undertaker it wiped the daft smile off mine.

I helped the elderly passengers into my car and followed the other two cars up to Jesmond Road Cemetery. As the car in front of me drove through the cemetery gates, he stopped suddenly for some reason. I over reacted, stamping hard on my own break pedal. The car stopped in a split second as the huge brake drums locked the wheels. In another split second I heard a thump on the glass partition between the passenger and driver compartments. I looked around in time to see an old lady's face pressed against the glass and sliding down like a clip from a 'Carry On' film. I jumped out of the car in shock and rushed to see how she was.

When I opened the back door, the other passengers were helping her up. The poor old soul was apologising to me, saying that she had been trying to get up too soon. Everyone assured me that she was OK and that it wasn't my fault. I still felt that it had been my fault and I was shaken up more than the old girl seemed to be. I think that it made me more considerate of my passengers after that incident.

When we returned to the garage, the Boss thanked me for standing in at short notice. He told me to phone in every Friday to confirm that I was available because I was now one of his drivers. The pay was five shillings (25 new pence) for the Saturday whether you did one run or four runs. Sometimes I would be finished for the day by 11-am and on other occasions it would be after 3-pm but either way, the pay was still five shillings. In truth, I would have done it for the joy alone.

On top of the pay, there were a few perks. At weddings the Best man would usually give you a tip that often exceeded the pay. At funerals you could earn another five shillings by being a pallbearer and help to carry the coffin. I've seen some of the older drivers having heated debates as to who should get the chance to carry the box for the extra five bob. It all seemed a bit macabre to me, not carrying the coffin but the arguing about who was going to get the extra cash. I was a pallbearer for a burial at a cemetery in Gateshead over the Tyne from Newcastle. The grave was at the top of a steep hill and the Hearse could not get up the narrow path. The trouble was it was covered with hard packed snow and treacherous to walk on even without a coffin on your shoulders. I had visions of us dropping the box and watching the dearly departed Tobogganing down the hill and out of the gate. It took us about fifteen minutes to inch our way up to the grave. On a few occasions the coffin was on its end or its side on the path as one or other of the pallbearers lost their traction. There were Ooo's and Ahh's from the mourners but they were having trouble themselves staying upright. By the time the poor cadaver was laid to rest it must have looked like

'Muhammad Ali's' sparring partner.

I had an upsetting experience at a funeral in 'Westerhope' Newcastle. I had to go upstairs to a small bedroom to collect the floral tributes and wreaths from around the coffin before it was conveyed to the hearse. The coffin was in the corner of the room and still open for people to pay their last respects. In these circumstances I always looked into the coffin and acknowledged the deceased. There was nothing morbid about this I just felt that it was disrespectful to ignore a person just because they were dead. On this day though, as I looked down I was shocked to the core. Lying there was a beautiful young girl who must have only been about eighteen years old when she died. It had never occurred to me that young people died, my own life had always been so secure I had become insulated. It made me think of my lovely Margaret and the fragility of our tenuous existence. For a long time after that I would look at Margaret and worry myself sick that something could happen to her.

I learned to rationalise these morbid thoughts because I had to. We are sentient beings and because of this we are aware of our own mortality. The down side of this unique ability is that it would be easy to become obsessed with dying or our loved ones dying. The plus side of this gift is that we treasure what we have, while we have it. I had my treasure and I wanted to cherish it for as long as had been allotted to me.

I was a driver for T. Howe + Co., for about three years and I loved every minute. Between jobs I was allowed on occasion to go home in my Rolls Royce for my lunch. I would take my mam up to the shops on Wallsend high Street and she would sit in the back like the Queen she was. The neighbours would bow and doff their caps as I drove out of the back lane and mam would smile and give the royal wave from the rear window. She loved it.

This is one of those memories that are so beautiful to recall that it hurts.

✶✶✶✶✶✶

THE SUPERB 1930^s ROLLS ROYCE
CAR'S THAT I HAD THE PRIVILEGE
OF DRIVING WHEN I WAS 18 YRS. OLD,
FOR T. HOWE & CO., NEWCASTLE.

THE BEAUTIFUL 'H.M.S. LION'

JUST AFTER BEING RE-COMMISSIONED

CHAPTER 18

Sea-Trials With H.M.S.LION

Let us return now to my apprenticeship for a while in Swan Hunter's shipyard. The forward boiler room was coming along well and we were testing the boilers. The foreman Archie Duncan asked me to bring my shifting spanner and follow him. We climbed up to the top of the starboard boiler, which was as high as a two- storey house. We then walked along the catwalk between the two boilers to the back. To say that I was apprehensive is an understatement, with the boilers seething, hissing and shuddering like living things beneath my feet. As we neared the back the hissing grew louder and the steam all but engulfed us. At last we were on the catwalk between the bulkhead and the rear of the boiler. I was trying my best to look composed as Archie started shouting something to me. I couldn't hear him over the sound of escaping steam so I put my ear next to his mouth. On a Yarrow boiler top at the back, the water tubes form an apex like a triangular cave. This formation is large enough for a man to walk inside of if he is stooped over. Archie was pointing into this steam filled cave and shouting, "Go in there with your spanner and tighten the leaking gland on the valve at the back". Whatever pretence of composure I had mustered disappeared in a flash. "Do I look daft or what?" I shouted back, "I'm not going in there". Archie started to laugh, then shouted, "Give me the spanner then you soft shite". I was only too happy to oblige.

He went into the hellish cave and completely disappeared from sight in the loud hissing steam. He was in there for ages and

I was getting worried. The heat was almost unbearable and I was soaked with sweat and steam. After a few minutes I knew that I would have to go in because it was no good shouting for help with all of the noise. Also, it would take me too long to climb back down from the boiler top to seek assistance so I steeled myself and walked into the cave. I found Archie thank 'God', standing with spanner at the ready. I went and stood beside him and he turned to me and smiled. It was surreal because he still had his pipe in his mouth. He gave the bolts on the gland a couple of nips with the spanner and the hissing began to abate.

When the steam dissipated and the noise dropped to a dull roar, he winked at me and shouted "I knew that you would follow me when I called you a soft shite". We both laughed and made our way down off the boiler. The joviality was short lived because when Archie reached the boiler room floor, he hit his baldhead on the corner of an air vent. I don't know why but the outlets of every air vent on the ship had sharp corners and were always set at head level. I'm sure the blokes who put the ventilation ducting up did it on purpose for a laugh. Archie didn't say a word but there was a deep right-angled cut on the top of his scalp. The blood started slowly and then became heavy, running down his face. He turned to me and asked if my toolbox was handy, I said that it was and he asked me to fetch him a hammer. He took the hammer and proceeded to knock all of the protruding corners over on the vent. He then went around the boiler room, top to bottom and did the same to every vent. He returned my hammer and thanked me, saying that he was off to get himself cleaned up. By now his head and face was just a mask of blood and I can still picture him climbing the stairs out of the boiler room, still puffing away at his unlit pipe. He was a man among men was Archie Duncan.

✶✶✶✶✶✶

Another anecdote that I like recalling from my days in the boiler room of H.M.S. Lion is so over the top, that you will think it is a fabrication. It does sound like an excerpt from a 'Laurel and

Hardy' film but I swear that it really did happen to me just as I am telling it.

The ship was nearing completion and the Admiralty were sending a delegation for an inspection. We were told what time they were to visit the boiler room and we had it spick and span. Arty Bainbridge my fitter mate stood me in front of the port boiler and went through the procedure for demonstrating the new Slipway oil fuel burner. He told me to look casually confident while the big brass did there tour, cleaning the glass in the pressure gauges Etc!

On the dot, like all military men, an Admiral and three other officers came down the stairs. Arty met them and began their tour of inspection. After a while, they began to approach my position and in an attempt to look super cool, I lifted my left leg and stood it on the nearest raised object. Unfortunately, it turned out to be a fire extinguisher and my weight on the trigger set it off. There was a whoosh and rancid smelling yellow foam squirted all over the Admiral and his entourage. I picked up the extinguisher in a blind panic and looked for a way to turn it off. They are not meant to be turned off and will simply spew their noxious gunk until they are empty. In my maniacal and futile struggle I was squirting this stuff all over the boiler room. Over the sounds of the boilers and the whoosh of the extinguisher came the Admirals voice, "Throw it down the bilge you bloody idiot".

I did as I was bid and tossed it under the floor plates into the bilge. I then made a hasty retreat from this farcical scene and the boiler room. I was convinced that I would get the sack this time and I actually hid for two days. After that, if I saw the foreman or manager coming I would hide until they had gone. Miraculously, these feeble tactics seemed to have worked because nobody ever mentioned the incident to me, at least not on an official level. I wasn't very popular with the cleaners though I recall.

✦✦✦✦✦✦

H.M.S. Lion had to undergo sea trials to the satisfaction of the Royal Navy before she could be re-commissioned. Hughie, the other apprentice and I were chosen to sail with her and assist Arty in his running of the boiler room. Although the Royal Navy had their own engineer artificers on the ship, they were only allowed to observe us. The ship was still the property of Swan Hunters until it was handed over at the completion of the sea trials. This meant that the entire crew were the civilian workmen who had created her.

✦✦✦✦✦✦

The first trial was the tilting trial. For this, the ship was towed across the Tyne to the 'Jarrow slacks'. This was a wider part of the river and meant that we would not impede the passage of other ships, of which there were many, until Margaret Thatcher (HOICK SPIT!) Once in position, cables were attached to the starboard side of the ship and she was pulled over to a 45-degree tilt. The idea of this was to see if she would function at full steam with this amount of list. The trial lasted 24 hours to starboard and then 24 hours to port. You should try working, eating, sleeping and using the lavatory with your world tilted to 45-degrees, it's a nightmare. I had a splitting headache for the entire 48 hours of the trial. Even sleeping was hard because I had to lie in the 'V' shaped notch where the bunk met the bulkhead one way and then dangle between the two retaining straps when it tilted the other way. I would have been more comfortable in a hammock but they hadn't been deployed. It was a very strange and unpleasant experience all round.

The sea trials 'proper' were a different kettle of fish and I loved every minute of it. The first one was the speed trials on the measured mile off the coast of Northumberland. There were two white pylons one mile apart on the shoreline. Then about half a mile directly behind each of these pylons was another white pylon. The ship would sail at full steam along the coast and as it passed the first two pylons, an observer would register on a stopwatch the moment that the two pylons lined up. The ship would continue up the coast at full speed until it passed the second pair of pylons. Once again the observer would register when they lined up. He would then be able to calculate the speed of the ship over the measured mile. We did this exercise over and over again for a full day. Then from all of his calculations, a mean average speed was registered for the ship. I know that on one run she exceeded 40 knots but I can't remember what her final average was. I do remember how breath taking it was to be standing on a vessel of that size and weight hurtling through the sea in excess of 40 mph. When she was flat out like this she would shake and judder as she sliced through the waves. In the boiler room, I fully expected to see the pipe work breaking free from its hangers.

The next trials were really exciting we were to look for bad weather conditions to test her seaworthiness. We steamed up the east coast and around the top of Britain. We found the bad weather that we were looking for between the Shetland Islands and the north coast of Scotland. A gale was blowing and we were ploughing through mountainous waves. The men on the bridge put the 'Lion' through some hair-raising manoeuvres. Full ahead, hard to port, hard to starboard, that sort of thing, simulating battle tactics. The ship heaved and bucked and you could feel her four propellers race as her stern lifted out of the water. Her bow would rise on a giant wave and then crash down again cutting into the next one. It must have been awesome looking out from the bridge. Everyone clung to whatever handhold they could find as they were flung about as though they were Rag-dolls. Sometimes the deck would fall away from you leaving you in a state of weightlessness, or it would heave upwards jarring your knees. We learned to stand and walk with our knees slightly bent to act like shock absorbers. The effect of this was to make us all look like 'extras' on the 'Planet of the apes' movie.

When we were in the mess having our meals, we would look out of the porthole at blue sky one moment and under the sea the next. Some of the lads found this a bit disconcerting and a lot of regurgitating ensued. I did not succumb to seasickness myself thank God but a lot of the lads did. It looked like a malady that I would rather not experience. They would be hanging onto the handrails and puking over the side of the ship. What with the roll of the ship and the wind, most of the vomit spattered themselves and their puking neighbours. The small latrines on the ship were reeking with the smell. When I needed to pee, I would just go to the leeward side of the ship and piddle into the sea. Unfortunately, after a couple of days I became desperate to use the lavatory. When I opened the oval steel door, the smell almost knocked me over. There was vomit two inches deep, rolling in wavelets around the deck with the movement of the ship. As I have said I was desperate but not desperate enough to go and hang my arse over the side of a warships gunwale in this weather. I took my boiler suit off, rolled my trouser legs up to my knees and stepped over the six-inch door ledge. Taking a deep breath I waded through the shallow cauldron of rancid broth. My fear was that I would slip and fall full length into this evil morass. Having got myself ensconced in a lavatory booth I sat down and held onto the grab handle provided for just such conditions, my other hand clutched my trousers. I had held my breath for what must have been a world record but I eventually had to breathe out and inhale the putrid air. As I watched the vomit sloshing over my boots, it occurred to me that I had never seen so many peas and diced carrots in one place in my life. If I had been going to be sick, it would have been then because I was gagging. It must also have been a world record for the fastest ever expulsion of excreta.

✹✹✹✹✹✹

We completed our rough weather manoeuvres and sailed down the east coast of Scotland back to Northumberland. The sea became progressively calmer until it was like a millpond in the lovely autumn sunshine. The 'Lion' was slipping through the water at about 30 knots like a knife through butter. I had come up on deck after finishing my four hours on watch in the boiler room. It was such a lovely day that I decided to have myself a promenade around the ship. It was decidedly breezy at this speed but I found it refreshing after the heat of the boiler room. I thought I would give the stern a looking at and made my way aft. As I cleared the superstructure, the view aft was stunning with the stern wave produced by the four propellers 20 feet higher than the afterdeck. The ginger beer and white churning water trailed back as far as you could see in the still blue of the North Sea. I began to walk down the aft deck towards the ensign on its flagpole. When I had reached halfway, the thirty-knot wind coming down both sides of the ship met in the middle. I felt myself being pushed faster and faster towards the stern and I was obliged once again to ponder the wisdom of my judgment. I was in full gallop when I hit the flagpole and clung on for dear life. Davy Jones' locker came to mind and I had no desire to peek inside.

I soon began to feel more secure, hanging onto my sturdy flagpole and I decided to enjoy my wonderful predicament. The ship was zipping along like a speedboat, the sun was shining and the wind was blowing through my hair, (Yes, I had hair then). I was just contemplating getting to my hands and knees and crawling back towards safety when the ships 'Tannoy' boomed into life. An angry voice shouted, "Send a squad of marines to retrieve that 'Bloody Idiot' from the stern rail". As I was the only person taking the air in this vicinity I concluded that it must be me he was alluding to. It also crossed my mind that either the general opinion of the Royal Navy was that I was a 'Bloody Idiot', or it was the same bloke I squirted with gunk who possessed a limited vocabulary.

I realised that their opinions on both occasions had been more or less proven, so I chose not to be captured by over zealous marines whose card game I had just ruined. I went into a low crouch and made my way back along the port handrail to the sanctuary of my waiting bunk. As I reached the aft superstructure I saw the marines coming from behind the starboard side and heading aft. Once again I had escaped humiliation and possible retribution, I'm sure I have a guardian angel.

★★★★★★

The last trial was the gun trials in which we just cruised off the coast while the guns were fired. The fore and aft twin six inch guns were completely automated and radar controlled. They were a 'Vickers Armstrong' patent and built in their factory on Scotswood Road in Newcastle. They had the fastest delivery of any six inch guns and the 'Lion could out gun any ship in the world at that time. It was said that they were so fast that they would completely empty the ships magazines in twenty minutes. Of course nobody could know that they would be obsolete in a couple of years with the adoption of rocket launchers and self-guiding missiles.

It was only a one day trial and the ship was going to head off for Gibraltar immediately afterwards. Her Majesty's Ship 'Lion' had been re-commissioned into the Royal Navy with the usual 'pomp' and ceremony and this trial was also the hand over from Swan Hunters to the ships crew. We returned to the mouth of the Tyne and were met by a Tug just outside of the piers. There was a strong wind that was causing a heavy swell on the sea and the captain was reluctant to bring his newly acquired warship into the river for fear of the 'Black Middens'. (Dangerous rocks just inside of the piers). You couldn't blame him, they were notorious and it would have been like collecting a new car for your boss and then crashing it into the showroom doors.

The Tug came alongside and a rope ladder was hung over the side of the ship. The swell was making the Tug rise and fall about ten feet and crashing it against the side of the ship. In one of these collisions the Tug's Radar dish flew off into the sea. The Tug pulled away from the ship and we could see its captain shouting what we assumed were obscenities into a microphone.

Eventually he calmed down and pulled alongside again. The Tyne river pilot was the first one down the rope ladder to show us how to do it, after all this was a daily requirement for him. He told us that the way to successfully transfer to another vessel was to wait until the other boat was at the top of its rise and then jump the gap onto its deck. He then demonstrated as he shouted back his advice, timing was the key to success. With his coaxing, we all made the transfer safely. A few years later, one of the Tyne river pilot's missed the jump and was lost between the ship he had been piloting and his recovery vessel, very sad.

The Tug took us into the river and dropped us off on the North Shields ferry landing. I never saw H.M.S. Lion again after she steamed away but she will always be indelibly imprinted in my mind.

✴✴✴✴✴✴

CHAPTER 19

Life outside of the shipyards

OK, returning to my life outside of the shipyards. My courting of the lovely Margaret Rose Magee was going well, even though I was as green as grass. There were no instruction manuals on the art of love in those days. I knew that I had acquired the female equivalent of a 'Stradivarious' violin and I also knew that I wanted to play her like the maestro 'Yehudi Menuhin'. Luckily, I have always had an imaginative and inventive mind and I swear to you that I honestly believed that I had invented everything with regards to lovemaking. Most of our courtship took place at my sister Joan's house and we used to go there most nights. Margaret had to be home by 11 pm even after we were engaged and should we be a little late her big brother Henry would walk up the road to meet us. He would just say to her, "Home, now", he would then turn and walk a few steps ahead of us. I didn't resent this in fact I thought it was a big brothers duty to protect his little sister from my dastardly clutches. A trifle late you may think. (Who's to say?).

We also did our courting at the home of Margaret's eldest brother George and his wife Kitty. We baby sat Margaret's nephew and niece 'Michael and Margaret' Magee while George and Kitty went to the workingmen's club. This was the only time that Margaret was allowed to be out after 11 pm. This was because their home was a flat above a bank in the village of 'Lemington' twelve miles up the river from Wallsend. The club didn't close until 10-30 pm so it was impossible to get home for the 11 pm curfew even on my Lambretta. I believe that they lived in the flat rent free, in exchange for Kitty cleaning the bank when the staff had left at night. At first I was intrigued and when they left to go to the club I would get the keys to the door that connected the flat with the bank and have a snoop about. This is before closed circuit cameras or laser-beam security systems but you would think that a wooden door with no alarm from an adjoining flat was a bit lax. I was impressed with the huge vault door though and every time that I see one in a movie, it takes me back to this time. I would scout about looking in drawers and cupboards in the hope of finding overlooked cash.

At Georges we had hours to our selves and no Television to distract me, so a lot of mutual face sucking ensued. It is amazing how much kissing you can do if that is all you are going to get. Thus, I honed my already legendary prowess in this department to the equivalent of a degree level in fine arts. (Scoff if you must). I still maintain that kissing is the most erotic and arousing form of contact between a man and a woman.

★★★★★★

One night we were riding home from Lemington on the Lambretta along Scotswood Road, Newcastle. As we passed Vickers-Armstrong factory, a police car passed us and pulled us over. I had forgotten to take the plastic 'learner' plates off the bike and this was before I had passed my test. He asked me if my pillion passenger was a qualified motorcyclist and if not why was I carrying her with 'L' plates on the bike. I said the first thing that I could think of to get me off the hook. "This is my brothers bike that I've borrowed and I have a full licence". The copper looked me up and down then said, "OK, what is your name and address". I told him that my name was Robert Blevins then my address and as a bonus I added five years to my age telling him that I was 23 years old. He told me to ride carefully and bid us both good night. When he had gone, Margaret was furious with me for telling a policeman lies but I was feeling smug thinking of how I had pulled the wool over his eyes. A couple of days later I was at home alone when there was a loud knocking on the front door. This was unusual because nobody ever came to the front door in Union Street apart from the Doctor. I opened the door and almost had apoplexy at the sight of the same policeman who had stopped me. "Hello Bob" he said, "Is it OK for me to come in for a minute". I stammered that it was and led him in. He sat smiling at me for what seemed like ages and then he said, "You're not Robert, your William aren't you". Spluttering, I confessed that yes I was. I rambled on about not being able to get Margaret home from her brothers at a reasonable time by bus. He sat patiently listening to this lame drivel until my whinging petered out. "Is your brother Bob insured to ride your bike", he asked. "No," I replied. "Then it was an even more stupid lie because you would have still been breaking the law by allowing him to borrow it," he said bemusedly. I admitted that I was obviously not the sharpest tool in the box but I had been in a corner at the time. This seemed to amuse him and he stood up smiling, "I won't be taking this any further this time", he said. "We will be keeping an eye on you though". Thank God for coppers with a sense of humour. When he left the house I vowed to myself that I would be good henceforth and be more responsible. (This was manifested by my always remembering to remove the 'L' plates in the future).

⁂ ⁂ ⁂

At the back end of July 1959 Margaret and I became engaged and we went to the 'Northern Goldsmiths' in Newcastle to choose the ring. She chose a lovely solitaire diamond and I remember that it cost £34, which was about seven weeks wages to me so it was quite a substantial amount at the time. The last time we had it valued it was worth well over £500 and that was years ago. It just doesn't seem right that a ring can go up in value like that when an organ donor clinic would probably refuse to have me for free. As we were returning to Margaret's house on Gerald

Street, her dad was just on his way out. I asked him if he could wait a moment because I wanted to ask him something. He must have guessed what it was because he adopted a more serious demeanour. Once inside, I formally asked for his daughter's hand in marriage. He looked at me for a few moments with a solemn and thoughtful expression. He then began asking me searching questions about what my true feelings were for his daughter. He wanted to know if I would be able to keep her in the manner to which she was accustomed Etc. Realising that it was all tongue in cheek I relaxed, entering into the spirit of it and we both enjoyed the mock formality of the occasion. He was a true gentleman Patrick Henry Magee.

✴✴✴✴✴✴

We used to visit Margaret's friend Nancy in 'Seaton Sluice', a coastal village between Whitley Bay and Blythe, up the coast north of the Tyne. Nancy Curran and Margaret had been best friends since their schooldays and in fact they still are. She had married a lad called Reg Forster who I liked immediately because he had a genuine kindness about him. He had been in the Royal Air Force for his national service and was more mature than me but he never talked down to me like the twerp I obviously was. Reg was in the engineering drawing office at Vickers-Armstrong's and was working on the guns of H.M.S. Lion, so we had that in common. We all still go out for meals together regularly and I have to say that he is still more mature than me. I soon discovered that we both have the same dreadful line in wisecracks.

On one winters night we were riding home from Nancy and Reg's house on the winding country lane between Seaton Sluice and St Mary's lighthouse. I enjoyed weaving the Lambretta around the bends on the narrow lane. It was a moonless night and there were no streetlights on the lane at that time. I was doing about 50 mph as I weaved, watching the road ahead lit by the main beam on my headlight. I liked riding at night (and still do) because you can see the lights of the oncoming traffic even when there are high hedges. On this occasion, just as I had begun to take a left hand bend, my headlights went off and we were in total darkness. I knew that if I braked hard I could lose control on the narrow lane and wind up going through a hedge or fence. In my mind I could still see the left hand curve of the lane so I kept the bike on this imaginary trajectory while I braked gently and changed down through the gears. Eventually after what seemed like an age, we came to a stop. I took off my gauntlet and felt for the light switch. It was in the 'off' position, so I must have caught it with the thumb of my heavy leather glove as I was changing gears on the bend. It was a relief when I switched it on and the darkness disappeared like a miracle, "Let there be light" said the Lord. I was amazed to find that I was still on my own side of the road, so my mental projection had been perfect. It gave me a scare but I was secretly pleased with myself for not panicking and staying in control. The lane has been widened now and there is street lighting.

****

Winter set in and we had our first snowfall of the season, it must have been six inches deep. We were going up to my sister Joan's house as usual but Margaret was reluctant to get on the bike. I was even more reluctant to walk and I eventually talked her into getting on. We set out intrepidly and managed to get about five yards before we fell off into the soft snow with the rear wheel of the scooter spinning aimlessly. With only my ego damaged I amazingly talked Margaret into getting back on the bike. By the time we had reached the top of the back lane, we had been off about four times with our legs in the air. Margaret lost patience and refused to remount our trusty if unstable steed, (no sense of adventure). We undoubtedly reached Joan's house quicker by walking on that day and I realised that the small scooter wheels had serious disadvantages. So, the bike wasn't used much over the winter and I sold it the following spring to a friend of

Margaret called 'Margaret Wafer'. She bought it on the promise that I would teach her to ride it. It was a hair-raising experience teaching her to ride it while I was on the pillion seat behind her. I have to give credit where it is due though, she past her test on the first occasion, which is more than I can claim for myself.

I worked with her brother 'Geordie Wafer' and he was a bit of a character. He was a part time Taxi driver and was killed in a crash in North Shields. The 'Evening Chronicle' printed a transcript of his inquest. Apparently his passenger told the Coroner of the court that just before the impact that killed him, Geordie said of the other driver, "Look at this stupid bastard". His timely observations were hailed as truly great 'last words' by me and his other workmates.

CHAPTER 20

Apprenticeship continued

Well, the 'Lion' was gone and I was transferred to a merchant ship being built on the stocks. It was either the 'M.V. Amadu Bellu' or the 'M.V. Nnanamdi Azique' I believe. I was on both of these sister ships being built for the 'Nigerian National' shipping company but I can't remember which was first. When a ship is built on the stocks its keel is lain down at an angle so that they will slide into the water when the chocks are removed after the launching ceremony. This angle is exact from the keel of the ship to the top of the mast. When lining up machinery, pumps, electric motors Etc., it requires the use of special instruments and gauges to compensate for the deviation from the horizontal. I found this a bit perplexing after having just learned how to do it on a level plane.

We had lots of time to ourselves, waiting for components or other trades finishing work that barred our access. This meant that apprentices could have an hour or two to amuse their-selves (not always a wise thing).

One day we were at a loose end when Len Button and I found the paddle for a canoe washed up on the shore. We decided that it would be a good idea to build ourselves a raft. There was always plenty of driftwood and lengths of rope lying about, so we set about the task with enthusiasm. When we were almost finished, another one of the lads asked us if he could come on the maiden voyage. I think it was Bill Davidson (the one who only built up one arm using dynamic tension). We told him that

CHAPTER 20

he could and gingerly pushed ourselves away from the shore. We were teetering a bit and the raft was really low in the water, with the river lapping over the sides. We took turns to paddle, with Len on one side and then passing the paddle over to me. Bill was shouting that he wanted a turn at paddling and pulling at our overalls. We told him that it was our project and that he was just a passenger. He kept grabbing at the paddle and eventually he lost his balance and fell into the river.

Bill was a big lad and his untimely swim caused the raft to immediately become more stable and higher in the water. We were about 30 feet from the shore so we told him to swim for it. He begged us to pull him back onboard and we felt sorry for him so we decided to be magnanimous. Unfortunately, when we had him halfway onto the raft, we were compelled to change our minds. Hanging out of the front of his boiler suit was the biggest 'turd' we had ever seen. A Canadian lumberjack could have log rolled on it, a south American native could have hollowed it out for a canoe, if someone had painted it white 'Captain Ahab' would have harpooned it, it could have done more damage to the Titanic than the iceberg did, a Palaeontologist would have named it 'Craposauris Gigantus', the anal sphincter that had held this monolith in check was on a par with the river Thames flood barrier.

I have just written six inane one-liners to describe a piece of human excrement, think yourselves lucky I could have kept it up all day.

We couldn't chance swamping our vessel with Bill and his chocolate caber, so we were obliged to throw him back into the river out of expediency. We paddled back to the shore, selflessly giving him verbal encouragement as he floundered with his new found friend. Was he grateful for our concern? Not in the slightest, his tirade of abuse was harsh and explicit. His suggestions to us were not only unhygienic they were also humanly impossible. He then had the audacity to plead with us to help him out of his sodden boiler suit. He was afraid that he might have to manhandle this bloated bowel movement. Both Len and I remembered something urgent that we had to do and left him to wrestle with the putrid Python on his own. He wouldn't speak to us for about two weeks and this is why I think that it was Bill Davidson. If you recall, I told you earlier that Bill had a tendency to be 'huffy' at times.

✾✾✾✾✾✾

I was in the engine room workshop cage having my morning tea break with the other blokes when in came 'Tossa' Thompson, the belligerent baby faced apprentice that I have described earlier. He was in a particularly antagonistic mood and was upsetting everyone young and old. (You had to know Tossa to understand his unique personality). I didn't normally rise to the bait due to him being cherubic and harmless but this day for some reason I had had enough of his ceaseless badgering of people and disturbing our tea break. So I jumped up, grabbed him by the front of his boiler suit and told him that I was going to turn his head around like a doorknob if he didn't shut his hole. I'm not proud of this 'macho' display it was like threatening a garden gnome. Everybody in the workshop was shouting, "Go on Bill, stick one on the cheeky little swine". There was never any chance that I would ever have hit him, as I have said before, I liked the perverse little toe rag. Unfortunately, the charge-hand fitter came in just in time to witness the whole scenario. "Right you" he said to me, "I've got just the punishment for you". Tossa was trying to defend me by swearing that we were only fooling about. The charge-hand who was a smashing old bloke just laughed, "I don't care, I was going to have to pick one of you for something but William here has just made it easy for me". He turned to me and said smiling, "You are now the apprentice to the handrail mechanic, good luck". With this he started laughing and left the engine room. He knew that none of the apprentice fitters wanted the job because it wasn't deemed as 'real' engineering. I had made it easy for him by having my little tantrum. The so-called handrail mechanic was an old fitter whose name I can't for the life of me remember. I was gutted but I had no choice in the matter, so I went in search of my new mentor. When I introduced myself he told me that he knew that none of us fancied being his apprentice but that I would soon change my concept of the job. He was a nice old bloke and I decided that I should make the best of things. His job was to make and install all of the handrails in the engine room and the boiler room. The Platers used to put up the chequer plate walkways, decking and stairs. We would follow them and attach the cast iron uprights and tubular steel handrails. It was a lot more complicated than any of us had thought. There were no drawings and my fitter had to assess the job in hand and take accurate measurements. We would then go ashore to the workshop and make sections of handrail. The tubular steel had to be shaped on a bending machine into all sorts of convolutions, to follow the lines of walkway and around any obstacles in its path.

I was amazed when we took our first sections of twisted tubing and iron uprights onto the ship. It was like a three-dimensional jigsaw puzzle the way it slotted together perfectly. Where two bits of tubing came together we would slide each end into a steel ferrule, drill through the ferrule and tube and secure them with tapered cotter pins. Then after cutting off the excess of cotter pin, we would give the entire section of handrail a good polishing with emery cloth. I was truly impressed and I decided to embrace this new skill. I worked alongside my new mentor for a couple of weeks and then he asked me if I would like to do a section of handrail on the other side of the engine room on my own. I was delighted because I was nineteen now and nobody had ever let me do a job from start to finish. I can't say that it was perfect, I had a few discrepancies in my tube bending, ends didn't always meet together to accept the ferrules Etc. With a bit of tweaking and a considerable amount of time I have to admit, I completed the job to my fitter's satisfaction. After that, I more or less worked on my own and thoroughly enjoyed it. A plus side of this job was that I got more money than all of the other apprentices my age. There was a bonus system in which the men working on the main engine received more money than if they were working on auxiliary plant. For some reason, the handrail mechanic was paid main engine bonus all of the time. I presume that it was an incentive to get a fitter to volunteer to concentrate on the one task.

When the handrails were finished we moved onto quick release gear. The fitter had a list of vital valves that had to be closed in an emergency. The idea was that if the engine or boiler rooms had to be abandoned for any reason, everything could be shut down from the deck and all in one place. The valves had a trip switch built into them that activated a spring mechanism that closed the valve instantly when triggered. We had to plot our way from each valve to a designated point on the open deck of the ship. Then we welded pulley wheels to the decks and bulkheads up and out of the engine or boiler rooms, avoiding any obstacles. We then attached a steel cable to the trigger on the valve and it would meander its way via the pulley wheels until it reached the open deck. On the deck we fitted a row of pull handles and each cable was attached to one and labelled as to which valve it was attached to. In an emergency, the engineer would be able to come up on deck and close every vital valve taking only seconds. The less important valves were connected to the open deck via spindles attached to the valve hand wheel. This was a similar procedure except that instead of steel cables you had spindles that changed direction using universal joints or crown wheels and pinions. Instead of a row of pull handles, there was a row of hand wheels. Thus you could open or close the valve in the normal manner by turning the wheel, albeit from a distance. The advantage of this system was that the engineer would not have to risk his life scrambling around the engine or boiler rooms looking for the valves because they were all together in relative safety.

Please note, the reason that I keep giving you these long-winded descriptions is because they may be of interest to some future engineer. I am aware that everything would be shut down electronically from the ships bridge these days while the engineer drank his coffee. I still tend to put more trust in something purely mechanical than electronic. I have found that computers have a penchant to mislead us humans from time to time, or perhaps they have developed a sardonic sense of humour, like me.

******

I was in the workshop operating the big radial arm drilling-machine one day and I had just set up a component to drill four holes in it. A young fitter who had only been a fully-fledged tradesman for a couple of years approached me, I think his name was Reggie but he was a bit unsociable so I had never had much to do with him. "You will have to take that job off the drilling machine because I want to use it", he demanded. "I have only got four holes to drill and the machine is all set up for it" I replied. "Never mind about that mate, you are just an apprentice and I am a time served fitter so just move it now, "he ordered". There were two other fitters who were nearby and they witnessed his obnoxious behaviour and shouted over "Let the lad drill his holes you miserable sod". He then took his shifting spanner and began to loosen the bolts holding my job. So I grabbed him by the back of his collar and the backside of his boiler suit and threw him up the workshop. He went sprawling face down on the dirty, greasy floor to the mirth of all of the lads and men in the shop. He jumped up red faced and said that he was going to get me sacked. He left the shop and I carried on drilling my holes. I had just finished when he returned with one of the foremen. "Is it true that you just hit this man" the foreman asked me. Before I could speak, one of the older men said, "I can tell you what happened gaffa, he wanted this lad to take his job out of the machine and we told him to let the lad finish. So he stormed off in a huff, tripped and fell making himself appear like the prat that he is".

The gaffa turned to Reggie and said, "Is that what happened"? "No, he grabbed me and threw me up the shop", yelled Reggie in frustration. Another one of the blokes spoke up, "I can confirm it, he tripped and fell nobody touched him, I think he was having a tantrum". The gaffa went mad at Reggie for wasting his time and as they left the shop I could hear Reggie protesting that he hadn't tripped. I thanked the blokes for defending me and one of them said, "That's OK son, he was an obnoxious little shit when he was an apprentice and he still is".

******

They say that revenge is sweet and Reggie got his revenge on me many years later. We will jump through time for about 20 years so that I can explain how he managed to attain his retribution on me. I was working at George Angus &Company as a 'Die Fitter' and had been there for many years. It was a large factory and there must have been over a thousand people employed there. I knew that Reggie was working there somewhere too because we had nodded to each other in passing from time to time. Neither of us had made any attempt at conversing, lets face it we were never going to be bosom pals were we. A better job with more money and staff status came up on the notice board. It was in department five, known as MI5 among the rest of the workforce because it was the only department in the factory that wasn't open plan. It had a twelve-foot wall all of the way around it and the Manager had his office on stilts so that he could look down on the entire department. The reason for all of this cloak and dagger stuff was because they made and operated experimental machinery for producing oil seals. I knew a few of the lads in the department and it sounded very appealing to me. Apart from the extra money it was the fact that you could be innovative in your work, thinking of new ways to achieve a goal. Also, although it was production work there was no bonus or piecework scheme. So you didn't have to work your nuts off. Because it was experimental work it could not be accurately timed so everyone got paid the same money. This was substantially more than I was earning inclusive of piecework bonuses.

So, no hard graft and more money, a no brainer you could say. I applied for the job and was asked to go to an interview with the department Manager John Mathews. The interview went really well and John more or less told me that it was in the bag for me because I was miles ahead of all of the other applicants. The following day I got a memo from the personnel office telling me that I had been unsuccessful on this occasion. I was curious at this after such a glowing interview so I went up to John's office to ask where I had failed. John was sitting with the obnoxious Reggie when I was invited in. I had been told that he was a regular visitor to John's office, so they may have been pals, I don't know. I asked John why I had been rejected after his earlier enthusiasm about my suitability. He looked a bit sheepish and went onto the defensive, "You know that I am not obliged to give reasons for my decisions Bill", he said. "I'm not trying to embarrass you John but we've known each other for a long time and I thought you may be able to point out any flaws for future interviews", I put to him. He looked apologetic and said, well Bill I was told by someone that with your strong personality, you could clash with my other four Fitters". I looked across at Reggie who was looking anywhere but at me and said, "Well John, I go for a drink every Friday night with three of them one of whom is my best friend and one of them is Joe Magee, my brother-in-law". John looked at Reggie hoping for some sort of input I presumed but there was no chance of that, he wouldn't even make eye contact. I got up to leave the office and said to John while looking at Reggie "We both know who advised you against me John. I suggest that you ask Reggie here if it was because I was obliged to chastise him when I was nineteen and he was twenty three because of 'his' bolshie attitude and this is his spineless revenge". I left the office with John glowering at Reggie, who still had not spoken or looked at either of us.

I still did not get the job and Reggie had achieved his

retribution so you have to admire his patience, it paid off in the end. (God moves in mysterious ways). I had never had much contact with Reggie after the drilling machine incident in Swan Hunters and didn't miss it. After I had helped him on his way to the exit, I don't think that he wanted to kiss and make up.

✦✦✦✦✦✦

The charge-hand often gave us jobs to do on our own after we had turned nineteen if they were not too complicated. I say on our own but I mean that he would pair us off with another apprentice. I was often paired with a lad called 'Ken Robson' who was heavy set with a face like a pugilist and short ginger hair. He looked like somebody you would find working as a bouncer on the door of a nightclub. Looks can be deceiving as we all know and Ken was a smashing easy-going lad. It turned out that we were both fans of 'The Everly Brothers' the best harmony group who have ever lived. Not only that but he had a good singing voice too. (As you probably expected to hear, I too have a have a good singing voice. Sorry). Every time that we worked together we would harmonise our way through the entire 'Everly' repertoire. The other blokes would actually ask us to do requests for them. (Not always to do with singing I have to admit).

I worked on several more ships being built at Swan Hunter's including another Royal Navy ship, 'HMS Falmouth'. She was nothing like HMS Lion whose hull was made of three inch steel with six inch amour plating running along both sides where the engine and boiler rooms were located. The Falmouth was an anti-submarine frigate and to us she looked like an anorexic greyhound that had suffered dysentery. She was built for speed and when you looked at her being built on the stocks you could see the frame of her structure through the steel plates of her hull. To compare her to the mighty HMS Lion would be like comparing 'Mahatma Gandhi' to 'Arnold Schwarzenegger'. I also worked on 'HMS London' a destroyer and she too was built looking severely malnourished, at least in my eyes. Although I helped to build these warships, I didn't get to go on sea trials with them. I did go out with a few merchant ships and although it was very enjoyable, it was never as exciting as HMS Lion.

✴✴✴✴✴✴

On nice days during slack periods, some of us would congregate at the east side of the shipyard. It was known as the 'Klondike' and was a large area used for storing logs and wooden sleepers. The wood was used as props for shoring up the ships being built on the stocks so I suppose the name was in reference to shoring up the tunnels in the goldmines. It was easy to hide from the Gaffa's among the piles of wood and our fitters would know where to find us if we were needed. Making our way between the piles it was easy to find open areas like fortified campsites. Here we could sunbathe, chat, play games and generally waste our time while being paid for it. Happy days. The smell of the tar-impregnated wood on a hot day was nostalgic for me. It reminded me of being a little boy and watching the men repairing the roads. They would have a glowing brazier full of coke, with a cauldron of boiling tar on top of it. When they had used some of the hot tar they would replenish the cauldron with lumps of black pitch. I remember that we used to get small pieces of pitch off the men and chew it like chewing gum. They told us that it would clean our teeth and that it was full of minerals that were good for us. Apparently, this is true and at least it didn't contain sugar. There is no doubt about the fact that it cleaned your teeth, I can attest to that claim. I loved the taste and the smell and I still get nostalgic if I pass a road repair or a roof being re-felted.

We were in our Klondike fortress one day when one of the lads took a twelve- inch round file from his rule pocket and took the wooden handle off. He then began throwing it like a throwing knife at a wooden sleeper lying on the ground. This developed into a game and we would all take our own round files to the Klondike. We had to throw them at wood lying on the ground because if you threw them at something vertical and missed, your file would disappear into the pile of logs forever. After a while we all started buying cheap sheath knives instead of using round files. They only cost 2/6 (12-5 new pence) at 'Hills' hardware shop on Wallsend High Street. They always had Tartan painted tin handgrips that inevitably flew off after about a dozen throws. Eventually I went to a sports shop in Newcastle and bought myself a proper throwing knife. It was 8 inches long overall, flat with a short rudimentary handgrip and a heavy blade. It was excellent for throwing and I became highly proficient with it. On occasion I even managed to hit fly's that landed on the log. I know that this may sound as though it was just a fluke but I usually managed to hit one or two fly's every session. I think this warrants a belief that there was a touch of skill involved. I tried my skill at upright targets but although I could stick my knife in the vicinity of the target it was never very accurate or even consistent. Then, one day I missed the plank that I had stood against a pile of logs and my lovely little throwing knife was lost to me forever.

✦✦✦✦✦✦

A few years later, when I was in the Army reserves I was able to impress the other squadies with my knife throwing skills. We were camped in some woods near to 'Aldershot' in Hampshire and we were all a bit bored. I took my bayonet out and said to one of the lads, "Point a fallen leaf out to me". He pointed to a Maple leaf about 10 feet away from us and I threw my bayonet pinning it to the ground. "My God" he shouted, "That was a lucky shot, I bet you can't do that again". Feeling brave I told him to point out something else. He did and luck was with me as I split the twig that he had suggested as the second target. By now, all of the lads were taking notice and before long they all had their bayonets out and it became a competition. I must have been on form that day because I rarely missed what I was aiming at and even then by fractions of an inch. The other blokes who were from all different parts of the country were impressed and gave me the title of 'The Geordie Jim Bowie'. Someone suggested that I should have joined the SAS and I joked that I had but that they had been jealous of me and kicked me out.

I didn't have the heart to tell them that if the targets had been enemy soldiers, they would have all had to lie down first for me to be able to kill them.

✶✶✶✶✶✶

CHAPTER 21

Shy bairns get nowt

Having read my worthy 'Opus' up to this point, (Assuming that you have), I am about to tell you an incredible thing about myself. I am shy, 'YES' shy. I told you that it was incredible but never the less it is true. As a child I would never go to any birthday parties being held for my pals and refused to have one of my own. I had to be coerced into visiting any of my parent's friends. You may remember that I told you that I was a good swimmer well the teacher could not persuade me to enter the local swimming 'gala' even using bribery or threats. I knew that I could have thrashed most of the lads from the other local schools from seeing them perform in Wallsend swimming baths. Basically, I was just an insecure pain in the bum when it came to public appearances. I have no idea why I was like this, or I should say 'am' like this. I have always mixed well and been popular with most people (to my knowledge). It just seemed to be social events that I found (find) difficult to cope with.

This dysfunctional side to my demeanour was the only fly in the ointment during my courtship years. Margaret was a good dancer and went to 'Hamils' school of dancing in Willington Quay, Wallsend. She went every Friday and Saturday to dance and being a callow youth, I was jealous of the time that she wasn't with me. The obvious thing for me to do would have been to join Hamils myself and go with her and in my heart I really wanted to. As it was, I couldn't summon up the courage to do it, pathetic I know. Sadly after a lot of whinging from me no doubt,

Margaret stopped going to the dances. I regret this dismal bit of my history because Margaret loves dancing and she gave it up for me. What could have been more romantic than the two of us learning together? Later in life, I did go to dancing lessons in preparation for a works staff dance at the 'Mayfair' ballroom in Newcastle. I took tuition in the Waltz, Foxtrot, Quickstep, Tango and Cha-Cha-Cha. I suspect that this was a bit too ambitious in the half dozen or so lessons that I had.

We attended the staff dance in all of our finery and Margaret looked like the princess that she is. I had a white shirt with a ruched frilly front and black buttons with a black bow tie, I felt like James Bond. I swept her onto the dance floor like Fred Astair and then I proceeded to step all over her lovely little feet, roughly in time to the music. Verbally she was magnanimous about my newly acquired skills facially she was a tortured soul. No it was never going to be a show stopping performance, the gap was too wide in our dancing abilities. I decided to take her back to our table before hospital treatment became necessary. Luckily my brother Bob was there and he was a good dancer. I was green with envy as I watched them gliding across the floor but I knew that I only had myself to blame. My sisters Joan and Hilda had taught him to dance at the Memorial Hall as soon as he was big enough. They had tried to get me to go and be taught when I was big enough but my shy side wouldn't let me.

Another phobia was going into a café' I just would not do it. This is strange considering that I used to go into the 'Jackdaw' and the 'Luxor' coffee bars with my mates. I think I must have considered them 'hangouts', where as Café's were refined and respectable. On one memorable occasion Margaret and I went to 'Durham' city for the day and after looking around the Cathedral and the old town, we got hungry. I would have settled for fish and chips but Margaret fancied going into a lovely little tearoom she had seen. I steeled myself and entered with her, full of inane trepidation. The place was full of people happily chatting and enjoying their tea and scones. The waitress led us to the back of the room and pointed at two vacant seats at a table occupied by two smiling ladies. This became too much for my delicate sensibilities and I mumbled something like, "We won't bother thank you". Then I fled the tearoom with my tail between my legs, leaving Margaret deeply embarrassed and apologetic. Needless to say she was furious with me and rightly so. If you are not shy yourself it's difficult to explain the suffocating symptoms that you feel.

I have no idea how she didn't bin me after that pathetic debacle but thank God she must have seen something in me that was worth keeping. I have photographs taken of us in a rowing boat on the river in Durham later in the afternoon. She looks like she is chewing a wasp and I look like I am remorseful and walking a thin line.

Another manifestation of my shyness was when we were invited to the engagement of Margaret's cousin 'Micky Rider' and his then future wife 'Norma McConnel'. I knew them both very well and they were a lovely couple, in fact Micky was an apprentice like me at the Wallsend Slipway. The trouble was, I didn't think I would know anybody that was there and I simply didn't want to go. We had bought them a present and Margaret insisted that we should at least go along and deliver it personally. We still had the scooter at the time so the plan was that we would take the gift along to the party for them and then make our excuses and scoot off. (I still find it painful to see how stultified I was when I read this). We went along to Micky's parent's home in 'Point Pleasant' at the east end of Wallsend and were warmly ushered in. I had no doubt hoped to congratulate them both on the doorstep, bung them their present and then leave.

We were shown to two chairs in a room full of faces, with loud music playing and louder voices. I could feel the icy grip of what I can only describe as a growing panic squeezing my heart. I still can't understand my feeling like this because I was always so gregarious in my dealings with people in general. Micky came up and stuck a pint of beer in my hand and something for

Margaret to drink. "I have a keg of Newcastle Exhibition Ale, so get that down your neck", he told me. I had never tasted beer in my life due to my being too shy to go into a public bar. I thought OK, I'll drink this and then we will make our excuses and slip away. The beer tasted dreadful and I couldn't think why anybody would buy it. As I finished the pint Micky appeared and stuck another one in my hand, "Plenty more where that came from" he said. The second pint was less of a struggle and the third was like mothers milk. I began to recognise faces from work and felt more at ease with myself. After that I began to get my own pints from the keg. I think that I had seven pints of Exhibition Ale all told. I enjoyed the evening and the socializing and was indeed very drunk for the first time in my life. At least I had the sense to abandon my Lambretta and walk home at the end of the evening. Or what is more likely, Margaret had the sense. On the way home I had the opportunity to try out my new drunken status. I was loud, I sang, I climbed every lamppost and I became gushingly affectionate. All the while, Margaret did her best to contain my alcohol induced, or at least enhanced exuberance. She was firm but patient with me and we survived the trek home.

When I finally arrived home to Union Street I was a lot later than I had ever been out before. My mam was waiting up for me, obviously worried about me being so late and on my scooter. As I walked through the door, before I could say a word she said, "You silly lad, you're drunk". I was amazed that she could tell that I was drunk because like drunks the world over, I was being meticulous in my posture and demeanour. She sat me down and I was telling her how sorry I was while wearing a stupid grin. My sister Alma and my brother-in-law Jimmy were living with us at the time, as were my brother Bob and sister-in-law Mary. This was the usual arrangement in those days, newly weds would live with their parents until they found a home of their own. Alma and Jimmy had the bed-settee in the front sitting room and Bob and Mary had the big front bedroom. At nineteen years of age I was sharing the small back bedroom with my mam. I was always asleep by the time my mam came to bed because she would be washing and ironing till the early hours, God love her.

When Alma and Jimmy heard the commotion they got up to investigate. They were both as astute as my mam and proclaimed in unison, "He's drunk". Amazing powers of deduction I remember thinking, it must run in the family. Jimmy was laughing and went to the foot of the stairs to shout the news up to Bob and Mary. They came down stairs and it was like a circus in our little kitchen. Bob asked me where the scooter was and seemed relieved that I had left it behind. I had to slur my way through an account of my evening for them, much to their amusement and then Bob got a bucket for me and took me upstairs to my bed. I don't think that I was actually sick but I remember the room spinning every time I closed my eyes. It didn't stop me from drinking alcohol, the way that smoking the five 'Woodbines' stopped me from taking up smoking. It did stop me from getting drunk too often though and Newcastle Exhibition Ale is still my favourite beer. I do get a bit 'tipsy' now and then but I know when to stop and go onto tomato juice. I prefer to be in charge of my faculties and I also know that I am a lightweight among my drinking friends.

After reading this chapter through, I am aware that I don't come out of it in too good a light. I will let you know how I dealt with the debilitating affliction of shyness later in this chronicle and deal with it I certainly have. I hope that it will raise the pathetic image that I have portrayed of myself if that is possible.

✷✷✷✷✷✷

THE FORCED SMILE
OF A LESS THAN
HAPPY MARGARET
AGED 18.

'ME' KNOWING
WHEN TO KEEP
MY MOUTH
SHUT.

DURHAM.
1959.

THE GINGER TOM-BOY

HILDA BLEVINS
1926 — 2011

MY SISTER HILDA
1926 — 2011

STILL A BONNY LASS AT THE END
WHEN SHE WAS EIGHTY FIVE

CHAPTER 22

My sister Hilda

I now have the awful task of telling you that my sister Hilda has just died and I want to say a few words about her.

She and my sister Joan have been in and out of hospital several times of late due to not eating and drinking enough. Joan was the first to get her-self dehydrated through self-neglect and it was simply because it was too much effort for her. At 87 years old she is unsteady on her feet and prone to falling over. I told you at the beginning of this journal that my three sisters all lived in the same sheltered accommodation for the elderly. I also joked that they took it in turns to fall over. This was a light-hearted statement of the facts. Of course it's not a joke and they often hurt themselves in the process. It is a 'Blevins' trait to find humour in the face of adversity and I don't apologise for it, it's as good a way as any to cope with what life throws at you. All of my sisters would joke about it to everyone, wondering who would be next. This does not mean that we don't care it's just a way of getting through it.

After a few spells in hospital for dehydration, Joan finally admitted that she wasn't coping. Her children found her a place in a nice nursing home in North Shields. Happily she loves it and I haven't seen her looking so well for a long time. She says that the food is lovely and she can't get over the way the care-staff are looking after her, cleaning her room, making sure that she takes her medication, taking her for a bath Etc. She has had a hard life and it's lovely to see her being pampered for a change.

The carers all seem to think the world of Joan because she makes them laugh with the many stories she tells them. They take her down to the communal lounge for her morning coffee and cake and to have a natter with the other guests. Then she has her lunch, after which she goes back to her room and sits in the huge bay window to watch the world going by beneath her. Or she will read a book or watch the afternoon 'Soaps' on T.V. We are all relieved to see her settle in so well and embrace being looked after for a change.

At the same time my other sister Alma and her husband Jimmy were given the chance to move to an old people's bungalow. It is in the same street as their son Ian and daughter-in-law Alison at 'Seaton Delaval' near to the coast. It's a lovely little bungalow and Alison takes all of her meals up for her and Jimmy. She also keeps the place spotlessly clean for them and their grandchildren and great-grandchildren are always popping in to see them. Needless to say, Alma has no regrets about leaving sheltered accommodation at 'Iona Court'.

Sadly, this meant that Hilda was the only one left in the court and she took it badly. Even though they had argued most of the time they were always in each other's flats. In fact Joan had spent more of her time at Hilda's than she spent in her own place. Hilda's decline was quite rapid after their departure and she stopped looking after herself. She couldn't be bothered to cook or make herself a cup of tea. She had chronic back pain and I believe her bones were starting to crumble. For some reason she was never prescribed anything stronger than 'Paracetamol' and because of this she started to have a glass of Whiskey before she went to bed to help ease the pain. As time went by, the measures of Whiskey got larger and then when Joan and Alma left she became depressed and began taking the bottle of Whiskey into the bedroom. She would no doubt wake up with the pain in her back and have another drink. She too was taken into hospital several times after falls and found to be severely dehydrated. They would build her up and send her home again after she had promised to take better care of herself. Her daughter Valerie and grandchildren all live on the other side of the River Tyne which sometimes made it very difficult to reach her in an emergency. Valerie works in a care home for the elderly and wanted her to move there to be looked after properly. She would not entertain the idea, saying that she could look after herself and refusing to even go and have a look at the accommodation. I must point out that Hilda always did have a stubborn streak and as the saying goes, "You can lead a horse to water but you can't make it drink".

Three weeks ago Valerie got a phone call from Hilda asking for help because she felt so ill. Valerie rushed to her side and phoned for an ambulance. This time, the hospital said that she was so dehydrated that her kidneys, liver and lungs were starting to fail and that she was in a bad way. During that night Hilda pulled all of the tubes and pipes out of her self and tried to climb out of bed. She fell, hitting her head on the hard floor. They got her back into bed but she began to act as though she was having a stroke. After a head scan they discovered that her brain was bleeding and causing a build up of pressure and they had to operate on her. The operation was a complete success and she was transferred over to the Queen Elisabeth Hospital in Gateshead to be nearer to her family. Sadly, her other organs were still failing and she lapsed in and out of consciousness for the next couple of weeks.

On Tuesday the 24 May 2011, I got a call from Valerie telling me that the doctors didn't think that she would last the day. I rushed to the hospital and sat with her from 10am until 5pm when Hilda left us. As I sat there, I couldn't believe that anyone could stay alive with such shallow breaths, they were tiny. Every now and then she would take a deep breath and then resume the tiny ones. At about 5pm the breaths became further apart and we knew that it was almost her time. Valerie was holding her hand and I was stroking her head when she finally let go of her tenuous grip on life. Her grandson Barry and his partner Elaine were at the end of the bed, so at least she was with people that she loved at the end. We all wept and said our goodbyes to her and then I went and opened the window, this is an old custom to let the departing soul leave the room.

I have too many memories of my ginger haired tomboy sister Hilda to list here. I had her in my life for the whole of my seventy years after all. When I was small she used to make me lovely little jackets and shirts with her being a Tailor by trade. She also used me as a mannequin when she was making little bridesmaid dresses for friends and family weddings. She often told me that she had a tantrum when I was born because she wanted another sister, no doubt due to the tormenting antics of my two brothers. When she took me to the shops or for a walk she would set my flaxen hair into waves and curls, making me look even cuter than I was. It's a wonder I didn't grow up doubting my gender or even batting for the other team. Perhaps it is due to Hilda that I grew up so macho, in protest to her endeavours to feminise me. She always claimed this honour whenever I told the story to anyone.

Ironically, during one of her more lucid moments in hospital she told Valerie that she realised that she wasn't coping on her own and that she did need help. It is clear that it was too late but I prefer to think that in the end she got her own way and didn't have to go into a care home.

CHAPTER 23

Back to my youth

Margaret and I had planned on getting married when we were 21 years old and I was finished serving my apprenticeship. This would have made our wedding day some time after 27 January 1962. These plans were scuppered one night during a 'loving' liaison. Margaret wanted to bring the wedding forward and it was obvious that she wanted to abuse my innocent but willing body on a more regular basis. I ceded to her lust fuelled demands due to the exquisite torture she was subjecting me to (we all have moments of weakness). I don't know how we put the idea to our families but it was accepted thank God. The wedding was brought forward to 7 October 1961.

I had just purchased another bike, only this time it was a real motorbike not a scooter. This was because a pal of mine at work, 'Brian Curry' had bought a brand new 500cc Triumph Tiger 100. I asked him if I could have a go on it and to my amazement he said that I could. I was nearly peeing myself with excitement at the prospect when he took me up to the Coast Road and handed it over. He said that he would just sit in the grass until I returned, a very wise thing to do I would say.

Today, the Coast Road is a six-lane dual carriageway but back in 1960 it was just a two-way ordinary road. My riding was very sedate at first, while I got the hang of the gear change because the Triumph gear change was, first gear one click down and then, second, third, and forth three clicks up. This was the opposite of all other British bikes. I felt that I had the hang of it by the time I got to 'Wills' cigarette factory so I turned right just past the factory. I positioned myself to come back onto the Coast Road during the first lull in the traffic for my speed run back to Station Road Wallsend. I was determined to reach the Ton (100mph) before I passed Brian sitting there in the grass. I sat well back on the dual seat, lying over the petrol tank so as to be more streamlined. I pressed the gear lever down into first, waited for a gap in the traffic and shot off straight down the centre of the road. I remembered that I had to lift the gear lever with my toe into second and felt the breath taking acceleration as the bike shot up to 70mph in a couple of seconds. Once again I remembered to lift the lever with my toe up into third and blasted the bike up to 80mph. Sadly the euphoria of the occasion must have addled my brain because when I went to change up into forth gear I pressed down on the gear lever instead of up. This meant of course that instead of the transition being from third to forth gear it was third back down to second gear. When I let the clutch out it was like someone had slammed on the brakes by remote control. At 80mph this is not the sort of surprise you want to happen to you. I shot up the petrol tank and my head and shoulders went over the handlebars with my head just inches off the front wheel. The engine was screaming like it was about to explode. I must have dipped the clutch instinctively because the screaming stopped and the bike ceased its sudden deceleration, allowing me to shuffle backwards and back into the saddle. When I looked at the speedometer I was still doing 60mph but I think the oscillation of my sphincter muscle was well in excess of that. It was like the reed of a Clarinet playing the 'William Tell' overture. My anus was so puckered it could have whistled in the ultrasonic range.

I cruised sedately past my mate Brian and turned left up Station Road. This was a quiet road then, although it is a main road now between the Coast Road and the Old Coast Road. I figured that this was my last chance to achieve 100mph so I may as well give it a shot. I achieved it both going up and coming back down Station Road thus elevating me into the 'Ton Up' club. Brian was blissfully unaware of the drama that had unfolded while he sat in the grass. I couldn't see the need to burden him with the fact that I had almost destroyed his bike and possibly myself. So, to save him any angst I kept it to myself, that's me, selfless to the end. He had the Triumph until we finished our apprenticeship and he never had any bother with it, so it must have had a well-made engine and gearbox.

Riding Brian's Triumph had given me the urge to have another bike. I couldn't afford a 'Tiger 100' even second hand, so I set my sights on a 'Triumph Tiger Cub'. They had a second hand 'Cub' at the 'Dene Motorcycle Company' in the Haymarket at Newcastle. Tiger Cubs were reputed to be the fastest 200cc road bikes of the time, so the appeal was instant. It was within my price range too, which swung it for me. It was a bonny little thing with plenty of chrome and light blue metallic paintwork, come to think of it all Tiger Cubs were in light blue metallic paint. The Saturday morning that I went to collect it was lovely and sunny so I was dressed only in my jeans, short sleeved shirt and sandshoes, plus my helmet of course. As I left the shop, there was a crash of thunder and the heavens opened up into a deluge of torrential rain. I shot away up the Haymarket like a mad man, wanting to get the bike home and covered with a tarpaulin. I could hardly see with the rain hitting my face like bullets. Before I realised it there was a policeman standing with his back to me with his arm outstretched, signifying that I should stop. He was on point duty at the crossroads at the top of the Haymarket directing the traffic across from Claremont Road over to Sandyford Road. It is now all changed since the New Town Hall was built and the new urban motorways but back then it was just an ordinary crossroads with a policeman directing the traffic. I realised that I was going too fast to stop quickly on the wet road so I accelerated and ducked under his raised arm. Luckily the traffic crossing my path was well spaced out so it wasn't too difficult to weave my way in between them. I could hear the copper shouting after me and I was hoping that he was finding it as hard as I was to see through the pounding rain.

I slowed my pace and by the time I got home I was like a drowned rat, freezing cold and feeling sorry for myself. I got the bike into the backyard but I didn't bother to cover it with the tarpaulin. It was still lashing down with rain and it would be a pointless exercise covering it if I couldn't dry it off first. So I sulked for the rest of the day, watching the incessant precipitation and imagining all of the lovely chrome rusting before my eyes. I also had the prospects of a visit from the police about my reckless riding. No police came, he must have been as blinded by the rain as I was and unable to read my number plate. The next day was sunny again, so I decided to take Margaret for her first ride on it. Our first two stops would be at my two brother's houses in 'Howdon'. This was always a bit of a tradition with us, if one of us got a new car or bike the other two had to have a shot of it at the first opportunity. The 'Cub' lived up to its reputation of being a fast little bike and I whizzed down 'Church Bank' and up 'Rose Hill' at the other side. To be more accurate, I whizzed half way up Rose Hill because there was a loud bang and the engine stopped. I coasted to a halt and as we stood there in silence I could hear bits falling down into the crankcase. I can only assume that the piston rings had disintegrated.

My brother Bob was working for a wholesale grocery suppliers called 'Nesbits' in Byker and he had the use of a large van. We loaded the Tiger Cub onto the van and took it back to the Dene Motorcycle Company. Bob managed to convey his utter disappointment at them in, let us say, a colourful manner for selling his little brother, "A heap of shite that didn't even last for two days". They were obviously taken by the eloquence of his verbal denunciation. So they vowed to refund my money or allow me to choose another bike in the same price range. The only bike that I fancied was a brand new 'Francis Barnet Falcon' 200cc. It cost about £30 more than the Tiger cub did (a months wages to me then). Bob convinced them that it would be an act of good will on their part to let me have it for the same price. I was over the moon, a brand new bike instead of a used and obviously abused one. The Dene had offered to fix the Triumph for me if I preferred but the shine had gone off it for me. When I rode the Francis Barnet home I was delighted at how much more comfortable it was and how well it handled. OK, so it wasn't as fast but it was far more substantial and the build quality was vastly superior. Mam was over the moon with it and loved me to take her to visit my brothers and sisters on it.

✸✸✸✸✸✸✸

Back at Swan Hunters a few of us were sent on loan up to the 'Neptune' shipyard for a few weeks to perform some repair. I can't remember the name of the ship except that it was the 'Port something or other' This lapse in my memory is probably due to the fact that we apprentices were off exploring a lot of the time with it being new and strange territory. We found a place that offered us endless entertainment and amusement. It was a really old toilet facility down on the jetty. It was simply a long shed containing about ten toilet cubicles. Along the wall at the back of the cubicles was a trough of running water flowing the full length of the shed, the trough was covered by a wooden plank. The men would sit over holes in the plank to defecate into the water much like the roman soldiers did 2000 years earlier. Their excrement would then be carried by the running water out of the shed to cascade into the river below. Apart that is, from the morsels being caught in mid flight by the hovering seagulls. This is why all shipyard men refer to seagulls as 'shitehawks'. Every sewage outlet on the river had its colony of seagulls queuing up to dine.

Now for the questionable amusement that we derived from these antiquated toilets. We would wait until the cubicle at the inlet end of the trough became free and then one of us would set fire to a screwed up ball of newspaper and drop it into the flowing water. As it floated under each of the occupied stalls there would be a scream of pain varying in tone from baritone to falsetto. This I would assume, depended on how hairy a posterior the recipient had, or should I say 'victim'. You can imagine that someone who was particularly hirsute in this area of their body could smoulder for ages. As I said, it was endless entertainment, plus it was educational, with the chance of us learning new profanities.

✦✦✦✦✦✦

When we returned to Swan Hunters I was sent to work on the first 'Super tanker' to be built there. It was called the 'Solent' and had a displacement of 65,000 tons. She was so big they had to knock down the huge sheds that the ships had previously been built under. The sheds had been a landmark on the River Tyne and home to thousands of Starlings since the previous century. Every evening the Starlings would take to the sky and as-one they would form vast undulating avian clouds, it was truly spectacular. I haven't witnessed this phenomenon at anything like this scale since that time, except on T.V nature programs.

Just getting on board the Solent was tiring enough, climbing up a tower of scaffold tubes via dozens of flights of stairs. Then you had to make your way aft over pipes, cables and ducting for the extractor fans to reach the superstructure. Then you had to go down the many stairwells to reach the engine and boiler rooms at the bottom of the ship. All of this while carrying your toolbox and a sack containing nuts, bolts and the various components that you may need for the job in hand. If you required anything else, you had to repeat this trip for as many times as was necessary. It's no other wonder that I'm knackered now.

One day a few of us were walking along the riverside mooring jetty when we came across one of the 'Foy Boatmen's' rowing boats tied to a post. It was almost time to clock off and he must have had another job lined up here for the next day. It would be easier for him to catch the ferry to the south side where they all seemed to live than to scull back over the river. I say 'scull' because the Foy boatmen only ever used one oar. They would stand at the back of the boat with the oar in the single rowlock on the rear. They moved the blade in a figure of eight fashion like the Gondoliers in Venice. It had always fascinated me and here was my chance to have a go at it. I climbed down to the boat and positioned myself with the oar in the rowlock until one of the lads untied the line and gave me a push off. I was clumsy at first but I eventually got the hang of it. Turning the boat was just like using a rudder, pushing the oar to the left and keeping up the figure of eight movement to turn right and the opposite for left. I was having a great time sculling about when one of the lads shouted that it was time to clock off. I turned the boat and started to scull back but I wasn't making any headway. The tide had turned and it was pushing me the wrong way. A couple of the lads tried to help by throwing bits of old rope but they couldn't find a bit long enough to reach. Before long, the call of home got too great for them so they bid me farewell and good luck which I thought was unusually considerate of them.

I battled on for some time but I was starting to run out of steam and the tide was getting stronger. I could see the ladder to safety dwindling into the distance and realised that it would be better to go with the tide and steer myself toward the Wallsend Ferry landing. I managed to do so and hauled myself up onto the floating pontoon holding the rope of the rowing boat. I tethered the boat to a bollard and then I realised that I was outside of the shipyard but my coat and haversack were still inside and I hadn't clocked out. I have no idea what excuse I gave to the timekeeper the next morning but I'm sure that it was ingenious.

****

CHAPTER 24

My mother:
Hilda May Blevins

I have dreaded reaching this part of my story because it concerns the loss of my beautiful, incomparable mother.

OK, here goes. Margaret and I had our wedding all arranged, or at least Margaret and the rest of the women in our families had. The only input that I made was to arrange the wedding cars from T.Howe & Co., my part time employers and to hire a car for our honeymoon. We were to be married at St Johns Church of England on Station Road, Wallsend. This was a bit controversial because Margaret was a Roman Catholic. I was quite happy to marry in a Catholic church due to my liberal beliefs with regards to religion. The choice was made when the local priest came to have a talk with us at the Magee house after we got engaged. It was all very amicable except that he didn't address me very much and tended to preach to Margaret rather than talk. At some point during a lull in his diatribe, I asked him what difference it made as to which church we were married in if we both believed in the same God. He turned to me and said in his strong Irish accent, "You wouldn't understand", as he waved his hand at me in a dismissive manner. Margaret jumped to my defence bless her and said, "I don't understand either, could you explain it to me"? The old priest turned to Margaret's brother Henry, who was the only regular churchgoer in the house and said, "Tell them what you think Henry". To our astonishment, Henry looked up and answered, "If two people love each other, it doesn't make any difference as to where they get married". The priest looked apoplectic, he raised his hands above his head and then looking at the ceiling he shouted in his Irish brogue, "LORD! WHAT KIND OF HOUSE HAVE I COME TO", it was like a comedy version of the 'Exorcist'.

At this he stood and walked to the door, telling Margaret that he wanted to see her on her own at St Columba's for a talk one evening. She didn't want to go but I told her that she should because it was important to her. She dutifully went to the church as requested but said that all he did was to show her all of the vestments and he still could not tell her the difference between her and me. Being the strong-minded woman that she is, this episode made her decide that she wanted to marry me in a Protestant Church of England. I thought that this decision may cause dissent in the Magee household but thankfully I was wrong. Mrs Magee, 'Mary Ann' was Church of England herself and Mr Magee, 'Patrick Henry' was what they called a lapsed Catholic. When he returned shell shocked from World war one, none of his parish priest's ever visited him and he never forgave them. They had never missed coming to see him on paydays for a donation before the war he told us. The Magee's had dutifully raised their seven children as Catholics but they were by no means staunch.

Margaret chose St Johns church on Station Road because it was the newest Church of England in Wallsend. And so, all of the arrangements were made for us to be married by the vicar of St John's, Reverend C.W.Stromberg on 7 October 1961. Our wedding reception was to be held in the church hall and we were going away in our hired car for the honeymoon. There was only my mam and I living at Union Street now so as tradition and lack of money dictated, we were going to live there until we had enough points with the council to be offered a council house. My sister Hilda was making the wedding dress and bridesmaid dresses. It was decided that myself, Margaret's dad and the best man my brother Alan would hire morning suits. Everything it would seem was running like clockwork, until an unimaginable and life changing event happened.

✳✳✳✳✳✳✳

On July the 28th 1961, just over two months before our wedding day my lovely mam died. I had been along at Margaret's house and was returning home at about eleven-o-clock at night. As I rode my motorbike into the back lane I saw our neighbour Mrs Wynne waiting for me. She told me that my mam had collapsed hurrying to catch a bus home from the Bingo hall up Station Road. They had taken her in the ambulance to Preston Hospital in North Shields. I rode straight over to my brother Bob's flat in 'Willington Square' as it was on the way to Preston Hospital. They were already in bed, so I knocked them up and told them the news. Bob told me that he would follow me down as soon as he was dressed. I reached the Hospital and went into reception to ask where mam was. It was dimly lit due to the late hour but there was a nurse on duty at the desk. She asked for the name of the person I was looking for and I told her. She ran her finger down a list of names and then said, "Oh yes, Hilda May Blevins was taken straight to the morgue". Her words were like a sledgehammer hitting me in the chest. I remember walking backwards until I came against the wall. I had no words to say, the grief was instant and overwhelming. The nurse must have realised what she had done with her crass statement of fact. She came from behind the desk apologising for her stupidity and sat me down in a chair. She asked me if I would like a cup of tea, (the English panacea), I shook my head still unable to speak. She then said that she would send for a porter who would take me to my mam. I sat in this dimly lit brown painted corridor sobbing into my hands and I have never felt so alone, then or since. In my sheltered world, mam's weren't supposed to die and leave you. The possibility had never crossed my mind and I wasn't prepared for the pain. I heard the main doors open and when I looked up my brother Bob was standing beside me. He knew the situation immediately when he saw the state that I was in and put his arm around my shoulders. The relief that I felt on seeing my big brother was heaven sent. I don't know how I would have coped being taken down to see my mam on my own.

The porter came and led the way down to the windowless white tiled morgue. He took us to our mam lying on a table and covered with a white sheet. It felt as though none of this was real and I would soon wake up after having a bad dream. It wasn't a dream and I knew it as I looked down on her lovely peaceful face framed by the salt and pepper curls of her hair. I realised then that I would have to grow up now.

There was a droplet of saliva at the corner of her mouth and Bob took his hankie and wiped it away. I remember thinking how loving a gesture this was and how I wished that it had been me that had done it. We said our tearful goodbyes and reluctantly left her in this cold place. Bob said that he would break the news to our brother Alan and sisters Joan and Alma. I said that I would call in to our other sister Hilda on the way home. It must have been after one-o-clock in the morning when I knocked on Hilda's door and the first words that she said on answering were, "My mam is dead isn't she". I was taken aback at this and she told me that she had told her husband Val in bed that she had dreamt it minutes before I knocked. Val confirmed the story when he came down stairs. My mam and Hilda both had these premonitions from time to time it was uncanny. In fact it had only been a few days earlier that my mam told me that she had been dreaming about my dad during an afternoon nap. He had smiled and told her that he had come to fetch her. She had told him that she wasn't quite ready to go and he had smiled again and disappeared. I swear to you that this is true and I am not just writing it to enhance the poignancy of the memory. All I can say is that I am glad that I don't seem to have inherited this particular gene.

And so I was to set out into my life as an adult and I was aware of the maturity that had been thrust upon me. I went home to a house that had never felt so empty but I can't recall if I went to bed or not. In the morning I went along to Margaret's house and had to live again the raw grief as I told them the news. My next stop was Swans shipyard because I had volunteered to work during the summer two weeks holiday break. This was so that I could have the two weeks off later for my honeymoon. There were only about a dozen men working the holidays and I made my way across the yard to the S.S. Solent. I found the other men where I expected them to be, fitting the huge propeller shaft into its bearings. I explained why I hadn't turned up for work to the old charge-hand and he looked genuinely concerned for me. All of the men expressed their condolences to me and the charge-hand told me that he would see to it that I still got my time off in October for my honeymoon. As I walked back through the shipyard I realised that I had not given a thought to the possible consequences with regards to our wedding. First things first, I had my mam's funeral to sort out and I was determined to do it myself as the man of the house. I got the death certificate from the doctor to register her death and I had to go to 'Morpeth' to get a copy of her birth certificate. The little office of the registrar of births and deaths was on Station Road, in Wallsend, just up from the railway station. I sorted out her life insurance policy and arranged for an undertaker to look after my mam's body. Once again I hired the Rolls Royce cars from my part time employer T. Howe & Co. I asked the boss if I could drive my mam in the hearse but he wisely refused, saying that I would be too emotional to concentrate on my driving.

I never asked for help from my two brothers because I wanted my mam to be proud of me and I think that they could see my resolve to cope. As was still the tradition, the undertaker brought my mam home on the day before the funeral. Her coffin was in the front room on trestles under the window. She genuinely looked as though she was just asleep as a long line of family and friends passed her in silence. When everyone had left Bob and me for the night we stood and looked down at the woman who had carried us and nurtured us and we ached at our loss. We kissed her goodnight and with mutual silent agreement we left off the little embroidered cloth that was supposed to cover her lovely face.

The funeral went off without a hitch and when we got back to Union Street, Margaret's mam Mary Ann had the tea and sandwiches etc., all organised for our return. Mary had watched over me like a mother hen since my mam died, even though we had always clashed. This friction was due not only to my having too much to say for myself but also the fact that I was obviously harbouring aspirations of violating her daughter. In the end though, we developed a mutual love and respect for each other. She always turned to me throughout her life and I knew that when the chips were down I could rely on her just as I had at this awful time.

****

Here are a few of my thoughts about my mother Hilda May Blevins. She was the most-gentle woman I have ever known. She never raised her voice in anger and the harshest thing she ever said to me was, "You silly lad" and this usually while she was giving me a cuddle. She never smacked me and God knows I must have deserved a good smacking from time to time. I never heard her say a bad thing about another person. She never complained about anything and always seemed to be smiling and seeing the bright side. She worked from dawn till dusk and sometimes even after the rest of us had all gone to bed and yet she was always singing. She came in one night really upset because some young lad had opened his coat and flashed at her at the top of the street. Bob and I ran out of the house like a pair of rabid Rottweiler dogs to try and find him. We hadn't even asked what he looked like or what he was wearing. Luckily there were no young lads to be seen in the area or I think that we could have killed them, innocent or not, like a lynch mob. Our mam was worried sick when we eventually returned frustrated at our impotence. Typically, she was afraid that we might have hurt the poor lad, (her actual words). We were spluttering about what we were going to do to him had we caught him. So she made us sit down while she told us what had happened.

She had been coming into the top of our street under the dim glow of the gas streetlight when this young lad had exposed himself. Again typically, she calmly told him what a silly lad he was and asked him why he would show himself to a woman, especially at her age. The lad had started to cry, so she sat him down on a doorstep and had a good talk to him. He told her that he was really sorry and she told him to go home and not be so silly again. He promised that he would change and ran off up the road. Bob and I were still incensed and still wanted to damage him, especially in the area that he had flashed. My mam just said that he must have been really unhappy to do such a thing and that we should feel sorry for him. As I have said, she always saw the good in people.

She had this serenity about her and she was always calm and never startled by sudden events. One night we came home late and as we entered the dark back yard, 'Felix' our cat jumped off the scullery roof and onto her shoulder. This sudden and unexpected event scared the life (and other things) out of me. She just reached up and stroked the cat saying, "It's only Felix, don't be scared".

I could go on telling wonderful stories about my mam but I will tell you the last thing that sticks in my mind and leave it at that. I had come home late at night just before she died and she was sitting in her chair and still wearing her pinny beside a lovely coal fire. She had no doubt just made me something delicious for my bait (packed work lunch). It was often something exotic, like stuffed sheep's heart or a piece of belly pork. Even my sandwiches were made with crusty home baked bread with home cooked ham and peas pudding, that sort of thing. I was the envy of all of the blokes at lunchtimes. I once had my bait stolen out of my haversack and the thief left me a note saying, "Thank your mam for the bait, it was delicious". It was a while before I saw the humour in this but I had to admire his audacity. The other blokes were highly amused but they all made sure that I had something to eat, i.e. meat paste sandwich, cheese sandwich, not my usual repast.

Normally, if it was this late I would have just kissed my mam goodnight and went straight up to bed. On this night, I took my coat off and sat on the clippie mat in front of the fire, leaning against her legs. She reached down and began to caress my head and twirl my hair, just as she had done when I was little. We sat like this in silence for ages as I regressed into my idyllic childhood. After more than 50 years this memory is still vivid and needless to say poignant to me. I love you mam and you deserved more than I was ever able to give you and more than your 59 years.

CHAPTER 25

My wisest achievement

As it always does life goes on, I knew that there were changes of plans to be made and not a lot of time to do it in. I had informed the landlord of 3.Union Street and because my mam's name was on the rental agreement I was told that I couldn't stay on as a tenant. They had decided to sell the house rather than rent it out again. To be fare they did offer it to me for £300 if I could get a mortgage, which was highly unlikely at 20 years old. To be honest I had no desire to live there anymore, neither renting nor buying. It didn't feel like home anymore without my mother being there so I refused the offer.

My brother bob had recently moved into his new council flat 14 Tiverton Close Willington Square and he had a spare room, so he and my sister-in-law Mary kindly took me in. Bob was still working as a driver for 'Nesbits' the wholesale grocer at the time and to say that we lived well as a result of this is an understatement. Bob would slip the lad that loaded his truck a couple of quid (British pound note) and the lad would load an extra couple of cases of tinned food or trays of bread. Bob knew a couple of corner shops and travelling shops that were happy to buy the stuff at knock down prices. You the reader may think that this was stealing but in that money strapped world I prefer to think that he was engaged in lucrative recycling.

What he didn't sell he stored in the flat like a squirrel with its nuts. Cases of food were on every shelf, in every cupboard, under the beds, on top of every wardrobe. You couldn't walk across a room without zigzagging around cases of canned food, you name it we had it. Any extra perishable foods such as bread, cheese, eggs Etc, were distributed among the family. Even Margaret's mam Mary was grateful for the odd delivery from Bob. I think he always thought of himself as a 'Robin Hood' figure taking from the rich and giving to the poor. Eventually and inevitably, probably after a stock take, the losses were noticed and the depot manager called Bob into his office. The lad from the loading bay was already there and looking guilty and terrified. The manager told them that they had been watched and that their illegal enterprise was over. He gave them the choice of resigning with a decent reference from him or getting the police involved. Not wishing to look a gift horse in the mouth Bob and his accomplice, or should I say Robin and his merry man, wrote their letters of resignation immediately. Why? I ask myself was the manager so magnanimous under the circumstances. Well, the cynical part of me suspects that he didn't want the police snooping about in case they uncovered a scam that he was involved with himself. Or he may just have been a kind-hearted bloke with a forgiving nature. Either- way Bob and the lad were grateful for their good fortunate on this occasion.

The final consignment of contraband goodies was to be six cases of 'Tyne Brand' mince & onions. Tyne Brand was a small canning company at the end of North Shields fish quay. I have to say that their mince & onions was delicious and I had plenty of opportunity to arrive at this conclusion. Mary wanted to have some more floor space in the flat, a reasonable aspiration I'm sure you'll agree. So we had mince & onions for every meal during the next two weeks. We had mince stew, mince with dumplings, Bolognese and if we fancied a snack, mince on toast. I have to give full credit to Tyne Brand because I can honestly say that I never got sick of it. The rest of Bob's cache of foodstuff must have lasted them a year.

✝✝✝✝✝✝

Meanwhile I still had our wedding rapidly approaching and things to sort out. I asked my eldest sister Joan and my brother in law Alby if they would stand in for my mam and dad at the wedding. They were both pleased to be asked and proud to represent our parents. I also had to find somewhere for us to live after we were married. I was reluctant to move in with Margaret's parents knowing that Mary Ann and I had this propensity to rub each other the wrong way. I loved and respected her and I know that she had grown to love and 'tolerate' me. I also knew that she saw me as a predator with unsavoury plans for her angelic daughter, (true), plus in her eyes, I was still a gobshite, (also true).

With this in mind I decided to go to the town hall to see if I could be bumped up the list for a council house. They were very sympathetic but were unable to help with regards to a council house. The girl behind the desk was kind enough to tell me about a flat that had just become available in the private sector. It was an upstairs flat at the west end of Wallsend, on Cresswell Road, just off the High Street. I went to see the landlord who was a lovely old bloke who lived with his wife in the flat below. He and his wife were moved by my predicament and told me that we could move in as soon as we wanted to. We were over the moon it was a lovely little flat with two bedrooms, a sitting room, a kitchen and a first for us, a bathroom and inside toilet. The rent was two pounds and ten shillings, (£2-5o new money). This was about double the rent of a council flat but we were glad of the chance to be on our own. The thought of having hot water on tap was a luxury to us. I had had a couple of months with hot water while I was living with Bob and Mary but Margaret had lived her whole life with one cold tap and an outside toilet the same as I had previously. An added bonus was that it had a lock up garage attached to it to keep my motorbike in. This was pretty posh because I didn't know anyone whose house had a garage.

The flat was in good decorative order but because we were no longer going to be living with my mam we needed furniture. We had Margaret's bed and a double wardrobe from Gerald Street but we had to get up to the eyes in debt at 'Callers' furniture store in Newcastle. We bought a black and grey tartan effect sofa and two armchairs plus a 'G-Plan' dining room suite, chest of drawers and dressing table. When everything was delivered and in place it seemed like we were in our own little heaven. I lived there on my own for a couple of weeks before the wedding but I ached to have my woman with me.

✴✴✴✴✴✴

At last, the 7th October arrived and to be honest I can't remember very much about it. I remember that I told myself that the ceremony had to go off perfectly if nothing else did, to my mind at least, I think that it did. I saw this tiny Goddess standing next to me in her beautiful white dress and I wanted her more than I wanted to breathe. I think that I looked at her throughout the ceremony and I can't remember making any mistakes. All that I can recall after that is that it was very windy while the photographs were being taken. The reception is almost a complete blur to me and I can't recall my father-in-law's speech, or my best man's speech. I must have been sitting there in a blind panic waiting for it to be my turn. I remember standing up and then making strange noises. I swear to you that I am not joking, I can't remember anything vaguely coherent coming out of my mouth. I must have been close to a meltdown on the shy- boy front and I think Margaret sat me down. After that it was just a sea of white blobs presumably the faces of our wedding guests. I may have regained a vestige of vocal ability after I sat down, I truly can't remember. My only conscious thought was to get Margaret and myself into the Ford Anglia rental car and escape.

Our escape was delayed due to my brother Bob deciding to go for a little spin in the car. My brother Alan glibly lied in Bob's defence saying that he had an important message and that he would not be very long. We had said our goodbyes to everyone and our little entourage stood about for about 30 minutes becoming more and more embarrassed and agitated.

He returned saying that he had decided to go back home for something and forgot the time. I was thinking that he must have went home via Morpeth and it was confirmed when I saw that the petrol tank was now only three quarters full instead of full. I wanted to kill him on the spot but I wanted to escape even more. We jumped into the little Ford, waved goodbye one last time and drove away, literally into the setting Sun. After the chaos of the day I can honestly say that I absolutely loved the ceremony.

✶✶✶✶✶✶

I had given no thought what so ever to our Honeymoon and just headed west, as I said, into the Sunset. I had been to the lake-district before and I knew that it was beautiful. I hadn't even booked a hotel for our first night assuming that because it was October we would have our pick. Fortunately, I was correct in my assumption. We drove along the old A69 military road that follows Hadrian's Wall the new A69 dual carriageway had not been built yet. The rain got more and more torrential and it was getting foggy and dark so I was relieved when we reached 'Carlisle' in 'Cumberland' (before the name was changed to 'Cumbria'). I stopped at the first hotel that we came to, 'The Viaduct' and rented a room for one night. I can't remember us having anything to eat perhaps we were still full of ham and peas pudding salad, the traditional wedding fair of the working classes in our region at that time. We stayed up quite late under the circumstances watching Coronation Street on the television in the hotel lounge. After such a harrowing day, 8pm seemed like a decent hour to retire to our room. I am not going to describe our first night of marital bliss except to say that it was a night of marital bliss. After more than 50 years together we still seem to be able to press all of the right buttons, (perhaps not as often).

I said in an earlier chapter ('Shy bairns get nowt') and that I would tell you how I dealt with my crippling shyness, well this is how my Dragon was finally slain. I knew that I would have no option but to dine in public places while we were away. I had determined that I would not spoil the Honeymoon for Margaret and embarrass her like I had in that café in Durham city. We came down to breakfast in the dining room of the hotel and I was steeling myself against another meltdown. The room was by no means full but it was still a daunting prospect for me. We sat down at our table and ordered our breakfasts full English, a first time for both of us. As we ate, probably in silence, I looked around the room at the other guests. Some were reading newspapers, some were smoking one lady had her elbows on the table and was reading a paperback book. These were all of the things that I had been taught were bad manners and not to be done in strange company. I listened to the voices of people and some of them were really well spoken and yet they flouted good manners. I began to realise that 'so called' good manners were for more formal occasions and these people were just acting in a relaxed manner as they would if they were at home. This does not in any way condone bad manners but being relaxed in what for all intents and purposes is a home away from home can only be a good thing.

It came to me in a flash that I wasn't centre stage and I wasn't the focus of everyone's attention. From that moment on, my shyness was ninety nine per cent eradicated. The remaining one per cent is because if I am caught by surprise it tries to rear its ugly head again but I am now able to dispense with it in a nanosecond. I am never awestruck by anyone and would be comfortable in the Queen's company. I respect well-earned status but never become blinded by celebrity. After all, we are all born as equals and we leave nothing but other peoples memories of us when we die. I am willing to bet that even the Royal Family have farted in the bath on occasion. In other words we are all no more or less than human beings. I have found that if I find myself in strange company, it helps if I engage them in conversation no matter what their background is. They are usually happy for someone to break the ice and I have had some really interesting chats. Yes, it can sometimes be boring but it doesn't matter because it's still social intercourse and who among you doesn't enjoy intercourse.

And so, my honeymoon changed me for the better although some may say that I have gone too far the other way. The moral of this story is, don't allow phobias to rule your life, it's too short for us to create our own constraints. After breakfast Margaret and the 'new-me' set off on the rest of our honeymoon. The sun had come out for us and the drive down to 'Keswick' was lovely. After looking around the picturesque little town we walked down to look at the beautiful lake 'Derwent Water'. I have been around the world several times now and I still think that it would take a lot to beat the English Lake District. It's not only the lakes themselves but also the lovely way that they construct the houses and public buildings with the use of loosely stacked local shale. There is no sign of cement so I have no idea how they are still standing they certainly have a unique beauty.

The sun was still shining so I hired a little motorboat and we set off intrepidly to circumnavigate the lake. At least that was our intentions until the heavens opened up again when we were at the far side. Anyone that has been to the lake-district will know that when it rains it 'really' rains. We putt-putted our way back over to Keswick getting soaked to the skin and the little boat was gradually filling with water. By the time I moored the boat at the hire company jetty our feet were underwater. We found a hotel near to the lake and booked in for the night. I can't remember what it was called but it had a large dining room with windows wall-to-wall on two sides, a bit like a conservatory. We were glad to get out of our wet clothes and we were freezing. I can't remember what we did to get warm, (well that's my story anyway). I can honestly say that I don't remember any relapses with my shyness for the rest of our honeymoon, or since then I'm glad to say. I have become an avid restaurant and café goer now and I will sit and talk with anyone, I am probably unbearable.

On the Monday we headed south but the torrential rain never ceased. The clouds have to dump their load to rise over the

'Penine Chain' of mountains and the lakes and lush countryside are the results of this so it would be churlish to complain. When it's nice in the lake district its unbeatable. I drove south and then East in the hope of finding the sun again and it was dark and still raining when we reached Manchester. I was in a strange city with the windscreen wipers struggling to clear the water from the screen. I could hardly see over the bonnet of the car and when I saw the blurred red sign for the Grosvenor Hotel it was like a beacon to a sailor lost at sea. This was by far the poshest place that I had ever seen the inside of, with a chandelier, oak panelling plush carpets. It was very impressive to a pair of naïve, outside nettie types like us. The tariff for one night's stay was also impressive, 'FIVE POUNDS'. You have to remember that this was equal to two weeks rent for our flat. I had to bite the bullet and pay up because we couldn't face going out into that incessant deluge. We walked through the lobby passing the potted palm trees and into the huge ornate lift like two film stars, albeit damp film stars. When we stepped out of the lift onto our floor the elusion ended. We were in a dingy, badly lit corridor with faded threadbare carpets and flaking paintwork. We made our way to our designated room and found it to be just as dilapidated. The furniture looked as though it had been salvaged from an abandoned Gypsy camp before world war one by someone with myopia. I had thought that this was going to be the jewel in the crown as far as our hotels were concerned but in fact it was the worst, in spite of the fact that it cost twice as much. This could be why it took us half a century before we visited Manchester again, perhaps a bit unfairly.

It was still raining when we left the 'Grosvenor' and I decided to keep heading east in search of some better weather. It was a lovely drive across the country and we eventually arrived at the seaside town of 'Skegness'. It was Autumn now and the bustling holiday makers were long gone. I drove along the deserted promenade and chose one of the many hotels to stay the night. Once again I can't recall the name only that it faced the sea and

I think that it was painted white. The desk clerk told us that we were the only guests and that he would give us his best room in the new annex. True to his word he showed us to a modern, beautifully furnished room with a huge picture window facing the North Sea. As he had told us the place was deserted, we could have done somersaults on the bed and nobody would have heard a thing, (perhaps we did).

The weather was better now and we headed north following the coastline, stopping at various places along the way. The little Ford Anglia was running sweetly and I loved driving my woman to places that we hadn't been, very alpha male stuff. It was the same model Anglia that could fly in one of the Harry Potter films. When we got to 'Whitby', Captain Cook's birthplace, we decided to stop for the night and have a good look around the lovely little harbour town the following day. We chose a nice hotel high up on the cliffs facing the sea, once again the name of it eludes me. For a change we decided to go to the pictures at a little cinema we had seen in the town. I have checked the inter-net (even though I'm a technophobe) and I found that the name of the cinema at Whitby in 1961 was the 'Colosseum'. Unfortunately I couldn't find the name of the film that was showing but the main actor was 'Richard Jaeckle'. He was never a big star but he was an excellent bit part actor and usually a baddie or a tough guy. I enjoyed his performance in the film in question and so I have always associated him with our honeymoon whenever I have seen him. After having a good look around the town and harbour we climbed the steps to the top of the cliffs to see the old Abby. Whitby is where 'Dracula' came ashore in 'Bram Stoker's' famous vampire book. The Abby is the place that the toothy Count bit his first English throat, (come to think of it, I was doing a bit of neck biting myself at the time).

When we left Whitby we continued to drive north up the east coast of Yorkshire and Durham. It's a lovely coastline and we stopped at a couple of places on the way. We were headed for home because we were running out of money and there was no such thing as credit cards or ATM machines in those days. The exorbitant cost of our night at the Grosvenor in Manchester had robbed us of one night of our honeymoon. We did not know that Bed & Breakfast places existed, that is how unworldly we were and I always just looked for Hotels. Bed & Breakfast establishments would only have charged about £1, per night in those halcyon days. Our meagre stash of cash would have gone a lot further if we had known.

As it was we drove back into Wallsend with ten shillings (50 new pence) left of our spending money. This was in fact every penny that we possessed in the world. We had nothing in the bank and no wages due for another two weeks. The light at the end of this budgetary tunnel was the knowledge that I would get the £10, deposit back when I returned the hire car on Saturday morning. It was dark, it was raining and the streetlights were dazzling. Yes, these are just a few of the fatuous reasons that I came up with when I drove out of a junction onto the High Street and into the path of a motorbike. He was travelling slowly due to the bad weather and the fact that he was a learner rider. Thus, the impact to my driver's door was minimal and the bike rider didn't even fall over. I made sure that the rider was OK and apart from being shaken up, he was fine. His bike was unmarked it had just been the front tyre that had come into contact with my door. It had left a dent in the panel but I couldn't see how bad it was in the poor light conditions. He was happy to just go merrily on his way and not involve the police or insurance companies. This suited me too because I had lied about my age to the car rental bloke.

You were required to be twenty-one years old or over to hire a self-drive car and I was only twenty. I know now of course that this meant that I had been driving around the country in atrocious weather without insurance. I know that ignorance is no defence but I honestly believed that I had just pulled a fast one on the car hire bloke. I suppose that he was as much to blame as me for not asking for proof of my age. I realise now that I was still dangerously wet behind the ears. My brother Bob had a pal, 'Stuart Jackson' who had his own car body repair business, so we took it up on the Friday to see if he could fix it. He told me that if it had just been a dent, he could have just pushed it out from the inside without charge. Unfortunately it had creased and so it would have to be filled and then painted. He pointed out that this would cost more than the ten quid deposit I would lose if I just left it as it was. I took the car home and washed and polished it to within an inch of its life in the hope of distracting the bloke when he examined it. On the Saturday morning I returned the gleaming Anglia back to the hire shop in Whitley Bay. I stood with a gormless smile on my face as the bloke walked around the car. Within seconds he pointed at the damage and said, "That wasn't there when you picked it up". I wiped the stupid smile off my face and feigned surprise and incredulity at his discovery. He produced the drawing of the car with the known marks depicted that I had signed when I had collected it. And so I magnanimously conceded that the dent must be a new feature on the car. As expected, he withheld the ten Pounds deposit. I went home as poor as a church mouse with a gambling addiction, having just been mugged, who has a shopaholic wife. I can only assume that we mooched our food for the next week or so by visiting our many relatives at meal times. I don't think that we cared because we were in our own flat and blissfully happy.

And so, my life as a single entity was over and I embraced the concept of being a couple. I have never once had doubts about getting married to Margaret then or since and if she has harboured any regrets they have escaped my notice. We've lasted more than half a century up to now so I'll keep my fingers crossed shall I. It may just work out for us.

✦✦✦✦✦✦

7. OCTOBER. 1961.

ALBY ASHBURNER AND WIFE JOAN, MY ELDEST SISTER

LUCKY SWINE 'ME' + MARGARET

MARY ANN AND HARRY MAGEE. BRIDES PARENTS.

JOAN AND ALBY WERE STANDING IN FOR MY MAM AND DAD. JOAN IS STILL BLIND AT THIS TIME, BLESS HER.

THE SAME MODEL 'FORD ANGLIA' THAT
I HIRED FOR OUR HONEYMOON.

THE SAME MODEL 'FRANCIS BARNET FALCON'
THAT I OWNED AT THAT TIME.

CHAPTER 26

Finishing my apprenticeship

I had another three months to go to finish serving my apprenticeship and I was still working on the super tanker 'The Solent'. Once again I was asked to go on sea trials with her and I jumped at the chance. As she lay alongside the wharf she still had the launching stays welded to her hull on both sides at the bow and stern of the ship. These were huge steel girder frames that came against immense wooden blocks bolted to the ground. These would stop a ship from sliding down the slipway into the river until it was launched officially. At the launch these chocks were removed and hydraulic rams would push on the other side of the stays. This would start the ship sliding on the freshly applied tallow down the slope of the slipway and into the river. Then there would be a tremendous roar that sounded like a football stadium crowd after a winning goal. This was the noise of the tons of drag chain that was attached to the ship being hauled behind it to check its momentum otherwise it would crash into the other side of the river. The Tugs would then position themselves to push and pull it straight into a dock to have its launching stays removed and the hull repainted. On this occasion due to her colossal size and weight, the wash from Solent's entry into the water caused a 'tsunami' of river water. It swept over the crowd of people that were watching the launch from the opposite bank of the Tyne. It also flooded the houses near the riverside with filthy river water and hundreds of mangy river rats. I promise you that these rats are the size of cats and that is not an exaggeration. The steep hill, 'Ellison Street' that leads up from the river into the town of 'Hebburn' was black with these scuttling rodents. People were scrambling up the old ballast hill to escape them.

This time the tugs were unable to put her into dry dock because we didn't have one that could accommodate her. She was berthed alongside the wharf and we proceeded to finish getting her ready for her sea trials. It had been arranged for us to sail her south to the Royal Naval Dockyards at 'Falmouth' in Cornwall. We were to conduct the sea trials on the hundreds of miles voyage around the coast via the North Sea and the English Channel. We sailed her out of the Tyne and into the North Sea just to see how she handled with these somewhat less than streamlined launching stays still attached to her flanks. As expected she wallowed about like a harpooned whale. It wasn't deemed to be safe to make the journey with encumbrances like these so we returned to our berth at Swans. It was decided to hire divers to burn them off under water as she lay alongside the wharf. It was fascinating to watch them go about their business. The diver's were a father and son team who were self employed and did small diving jobs up and down the river. They had a floating platform with an air pump and a generator attached to it. It was a bitterly cold winters day as I watched them getting set up. It was snowing lightly and there were half-inch thick slabs of ice floating down the river on the ebbing tide and brushing past their platform. I watched the older man don his canvas suit over his thick trousers and fisherman's sweater. He was no doubt wearing thick woollen Long Johns under his outer garments. The younger man placed the big copper helmet over his dad's head and fastened it into place. They were talking to each other through the open faceplate as the younger man fastened on the weighted belt. Lastly the young man screwed the faceplate into place and his dad winked at him through the glass. The diver walked to the steel ladder at the end of the platform, his lead boots making him lurch like the Frankenstien Monster.

He climbed down the steel ladders and stepped over onto the launching stay framework. There was only about one foot of the stay above the surface of the water so he was now submerged apart from his helmet. The son lit an acetylene torch and handed it down to his dad who then began to climb down the frame to start his cutting at the bottom. We couldn't see the diver through the murky water of the Tyne but we could see his bubbles and the yellow bubbles of his burning torch.

After about fifteen minutes he came up and climbed laboriously back onto the platform. The son removed his helmet and gave him a mug of hot tea or coffee from a flask. He sat on a stool holding his cup with both hands and something occurred to me, I couldn't remember him wearing blue gloves when he entered the water. I then realised that he wasn't wearing gloves his hands were blue with the cold. This was why he could only stay under the water for short periods. Thinking of the pain he must have had to endure took all of the imagined romance out of being a deep-sea diver for me. He continued doing these short dives all morning and then his son took over the task in the afternoon.

When the stay was almost free of the ship a crane was attached to it and the diver was able to make his last cuts from above the waterline. When it broke free it was lifted up onto the jetty by the crane. The diver had not burned through the stay too close to the hull because of the bad visibility under the murky water. He had left stubs of the framework sticking out about four to six inches from the hull of the ship. This wasn't expected to alter the handling of the ship so after all of the stays had been removed we were on our way. The North Sea was a bit rough as we made our way south and the ship was heaving about a bit. She would have handled a lot better if her cargo tanks had been full but as it was she was bobbing about like a giant cork. It was hard to sleep when we were off watch because every time she climbed over the apex of a big wave her huge propeller lifted out of the water and it was like an earthquake. When we turned west into the English Channel everything changed and it was like a millpond. We made our way around to Falmouth and she was as smooth as silk. As soon as we docked, the dock burners set about burning off the stubs of the stays. The hull was then made ready for the dock painters who were to give the entire lower hull a fresh coat of paint. This was going to take a couple of weeks so they gave us all jobs for the first couple of days. We were fixing faults and making adjustments to things that had caused concern on our voyage down. One of the propeller shaft bearings had been running a little bit warm so I was given the job of checking that the oil channels weren't obstructed in the white metal liners and feed pipes.

We had been told that before we could start work a union shop steward would have to assess the job. After a considerable wait the shop steward turned up. He reckoned that I would require a plumber to strip off the pipe work, a labourer to set up the chain blocks to lift off the top bearing and a cleaner to clean up any oil spillage. I had another interminable wait until he had gathered this team before I could make a start. I loosened the top bearing cover bolts and stood back, everything else was done for me until I could inspect the oil channels Etc. A sliver of white metal had been obstructing one of the channels so I removed it with a small round file. When I had done, the reassembly was all done for me again until it was time for me to bolt down the top bearing cover. This was union solidarity gone mad, when you consider that I would have done the whole job on my own back home on Tyneside.

✴✴✴✴✴✴

I don't blame the lads for looking after their jobs it just annoys me that the sub-human Margaret Thatcher (hoick spit) used to accuse us in the north-east of the very same thing. I can categorically tell you that although I am ashamed to say it, the men in the northeast would sell their granny's to work a weekend and two half shifts. Solidarity with their workmates is only given lip service when they are talking in the pubs. Thatcher shut the northeast down and yet she kept the Falmouth dockyard and most of the southern dockyards open. Tell me that this wasn't political expedience because of our lack of support for the conservatives. It may be a consequence of the famous 'Jarrow Crusade' when the men marched from Tyneside to London trying to get some work sent to the Northeast without too much success. It may have caused them to lose their 'Mojo' and the fear of unemployment is now bred into us to the point that most of us have lost the spirit to fight for our rights.

I have worked in most of the shipyards and docks on the river as well as several factories and I have always come to the same conclusion about our lack of solidarity as I have just expounded. I worked at a factory in Wallsend called 'Victor Products' who made flameproof lighting for mining and petrochemical installations. I was the new boy in the assembly shop when the engineer's union shop steward called a meeting of the assembly fitters. We gathered together in the canteen and he told us that the management wanted to start two more fitters because we were very busy. I was delighted because it meant that my new job was looking safe. One of the men raised his hand and said, "I suppose that means that the gaffa will be cancelling the mealies", (A mealy is when you work for half an hour of your lunch break but are paid for the full hour). The shop steward replied, "Well I suppose it's possible". I honestly thought that they were joking but the rest of the blokes started shouting that it wasn't right that they should lose their overtime. The shop steward said, "OK, I'll let the management know how you feel, meeting closed". I was furious so I put my hand up and shouted with my usual diplomacy. "You greedy bastards, you would rather see two lads struggling to raise a family on dole money than lose your half hour per day overtime, how the hell do you live with yourselves". The shop steward just reiterated, "The meeting is closed". I was still furious as we all made our way back to our jobs, a couple of the blokes sidled up to me and said quietly that they agreed with me and thought that it was disgusting. I just told them that if they were so disgusted they should have backed me up instead of just standing with their fingers up their arses. That same afternoon a friend of the family 'Mandy Millbanks' who was a secretary in the offices came down to see me. She told me to be careful because she had heard the management talking about me and said that they had been told that I was a troublemaker. I don't know if it was the shop steward or one of my spineless workmates who couldn't wait to stick the knife in but it proves my point.

I was a shop steward myself for a while when I worked at George Angus & co. There were only six fitters in my department and I still couldn't get them to stand together for anything. They would all have a genuine grievance about something and would vehemently ask me to approach the Foreman about it. I would talk to the Foreman 'Sid Dixon' and he would come and talk to them. This I can tell you happened on several occasions I swear to you. Sid would ask them individually what their grievance was and they would all lower their eyes and say that everything was fine. Even when I told them what a spineless shower of shit they were for asking me to speak on their behalf and wasting my time, it didn't encourage them or even embarrass them it would seem. This has been the same wherever I have worked. The men around here would rather roll over and have their belly tickled than stand up for themselves with the management. I hasten to add that it is not that way with the women and I would rather represent them anytime, in fact if anything they can be a bit on the 'Bolshie' side.

Thatcher (Hoick, spit) closed the Northeast down like a corner shop, like the one that she was spawned in. She decimated our industries, Shipbuilding, Coalmining, Steel making, all for political reasons. The unions were ten times more militant down south and yet it was us who were destroyed. Being traditionally Labour voters we were of no use to her Machiavellian despotic ambitions. I am not a militant Labour supporter or union man as this tirade may have you believe. All I would ask for is a fare and frank discussion between all of those concerned and a fare outcome. You may have become aware that I am not a Conservative supporter and this is true. This conviction has only been enhanced by the less than comic duo that we have running the country as I write this, Cameron and Clegg. As much as I despise the abhorrent Thatcher, (Hoick, spit) she was at least decisive whether she was wrong or WRONG. These two odious 'Eton' regurgitations couldn't hit their-own boots in a pissing competition. Cameron will say anything that he thinks you want to hear and Clegg is his voiceless lapdog. I must concede that they are all that we deserve. It was the short memories of the great British public that inflicted them onto us. God, it felt good getting that bile off my chest. Sorry for my over-indulgence. You may also have come to the conclusion that I hate Margaret Thatcher this is not true. I hate what she did to my country and the long-term consequences of her actions but I am sure that she could be a charming woman, in a reptilian sort of way. My vitriolic rhetoric is in my eyes a purgative way of venting my spleen and also fun to do.

******

Once again I have digressed, so now it's back to the story about the good ship 'Solent'. As I have said we did a few minor repairs and adjustments and then we got the train back home until the Falmouth dockyard had finished their work on the hull. We were being paid for twenty-four hours when we were living on the ship so it was cheaper to bring us home and then return us when the ship was finished. When we returned later the ship was back to her pristine self. We then took her out into the English Channel to finish off her sea trials. When they were completed she was officially handed over to the shipping company and we got the train back to Newcastle. I never got the chance to see anything of Falmouth and sadly I've never been back there as yet.

******

Just before the Solent was handed over the charge-hand approached me and said that he had been asked by the management to recommend a last year apprentice to be given the job as a charge-hand in the apprentice training school at the 'Slipway' yard. He had thought of me for the position because I had always seemed to show interest in what I was doing. I was good with tools and machinery and he had been given good reports from all of the fitters that I had worked with. (So, I wasn't the moron that I had suspected I was). The thought of being stuck in a small workshop full of gobby, spotty faced sixteen year olds didn't ring my chimes, (Been there, done that). I told him that I was flattered to be asked but I just didn't fancy it. He was flabbergasted and told me that because the sixteen year olds couldn't work overtime I would be getting paid the yards average overtime money without working any. He stressed how cushy a number it was (Easy work) and told me to think again. I still answered in the negative so he pointed out that all of the last year apprentices would be finished when they reached the end of their training. This was the custom at the time, when you had served the five year apprenticeship they let you go. This is how the term 'journeyman' came about you had made the journey and were now an 'Artisan' of your trade. I told him that I didn't mind making the journey because it would be an adventure. You must realise that jobs were plentiful at that time and men would even resign from a company and move next door if they had more overtime on offer. The charge-hand shook his head and said he would have to ask someone else. I told him that the lad that I was working with 'Hudson Morgan' might be interested and that he was a good lad. Hudson was duly asked and he accepted, obviously having more foresight than me it would seem. The Foreman in the apprentice school either retired or died shortly after Hudson's appointment, so Hudson became the Foreman. Then sometime in the future a management position became available and he successfully applied for it. I quite often see Hudson in Wallsend that is how I know of his progress in life.

I am happy the way things worked out for him he was a smashing lad and he seems to have turned out to be a really nice bloke.

Do I regret that I didn't take the job instead of Hudson? Well strangely no. I wouldn't have necessarily taken the same promotion opportunities as Hudson and I have had a diverse and interesting working life. (What a mug, I hear you say).

✶✶✶✶✶✶

Eventually, the other lads and I from my year group were told of our coming dismissal. On the Friday afternoon we said our goodbyes to the blokes and went up for our severance pay thirty minutes early as requested. This was before redundancy payments were implemented so it was just our week's wages and our week lying on, about £16. I don't know what we expected but the reality was a bit disappointing to say the least. We were handed envelopes containing our wages, our indenture papers, (Contract with the firm) and a note that simply said, "Your services will no longer be required as of this date". No congratulations for completing our apprenticeship or wishing us good luck for the future, nothing. I don't know if it was because we were working at Swans and not in our home yard of the Slipway & co., ltd. Regardless, it was a bit of an anti-climax for all of us. At the time of course we all made jokes about it as we walked up Swans bank as journeymen. (God bless the British stiff upper lip).

✶✶✶✶✶✶

During my last few weeks at Swan Hunters I had enjoyed the feeling of being married. Living in our own home, sleeping with my woman (or not) and waking up in the mornings next to her. Kissing her goodbye as she handed me my haversack with my 'bait', (Not as diversified as my mam's but you can't have everything can you?). Being seen off to work by my wife made me feel as though I had grown up at last. This marital bliss thing didn't last very long I'm afraid. The trouble was, Margaret didn't really have to get up for her own work until 7-30am and I had to leave the house at 7-15am. She had insisted that she wanted to get up with me at 6-30am and make my breakfast like a good little wife should. This was all very sweet and romantic you may have concluded, well you can think again. I would turn on my new KB radio as soon as I reached the living room and sing or whistle until it was time to leave for work. This very soon began to get on her nerves and with a face that only she can produce she would ask, "Do you really need the radio on", or, "Do you have to sing and whistle all of the time". It didn't take long for me to realise that while I was a morning person, Margaret wasn't. So, the only way that our marriage could possibly survive was for us to be segregated in the mornings. I persuaded her to stay in bed and as I left for work I would go into our bedroom where only the top of her head could be seen protruding from her cocoon. I would pull the blankets down revealing her lovely little face and kiss her awake. Another thing that possibly saved our marriage was when I stopped her from putting 'Echo' margarine on my sandwiches. She had been raised on this rancid stuff and she loved it. I had been raised on butter and to me Echo was a poor substitute for axle grease. The proof is in the pudding I suppose, I'm the one who has had six heart by-passes and Margaret is virtually bullet proof. With both of these hiccups resolved our marriage has stood the test of time, (So far).

Talking about walking up Swans bank for the last time as an apprentice made me think of one of the infantile jokes that I used to pull regularly. I would get three lengths of very thin wire and twist them into a tripod with a stem. I would then sharpen the legs and bend the ends into little inward turning hooks. I would then make a little flag for the stem saying, 'I AM DAFT' or something equally inane. Then as we all walked up the bank from Swans gates I would walk up behind somebody and gently stand the tripod with its flag on top his cloth cap. The little hooks on the feet always held it in place as he walked on. Just about everybody wore cloth caps then so there was no shortage of victims. We would then follow him all of the way up to the High Street and it was always a bonus if he got onto a bus. Shockingly, nobody ever told them about their adornments. 'Hilarious stuff or what'?

⋆⋆⋆⋆⋆⋆

CHAPTER 27

Buses and tunnel

I had decided that I fancied a complete change of career for a while due I am sure to both of my brothers having been bus drivers for short periods. Being in charge of a big double-decker bus full of people seemed in some way to be an exciting job and I had always fancied it. I went down to the 'Tynemouth Bus Company' depot on Norham Road, North Shields where both Bob and Alan had worked previously. The depot Manager asked the driver training bloke to take me out in a bus to see if I had the potential. I drove the bus in a big circuit of the area under the direction of the trainer and back to the depot. He told the Manager that I was good enough to start training for my 'public service vehicle' licence (PSV) on the following Monday. That is how easy it was to get a job in those days.

Normally it would be four weeks training before you were ready to take the PSV driving test but on the day that I started the instructor dropped the bombshell on me. Unfortunately he was off on his holidays from the coming Friday night for two weeks. The good news he hastily added was that he had been able to book my test for the Friday afternoon. I was aghast at the prospects of having four weeks training condensed into four and a half days. He just laughed and said that he wouldn't have got me a start if he hadn't thought I could do it, (No pressure then).

I was really glad of my felonious truck driving experiences with my two brothers. My instructor really put me through my paces that week and we were both confident that I would be successful. The bus that we used throughout the week was an old 'Leyland' but it had synchromesh gears and was nice to drive. It was the old fashioned sort of bus where the driver sat in his own little compartment over the front wheels and was completely cut off from the passengers. If the conductor or in this case the examiner wanted to communicate with him, they had to talk through a small sliding window behind the drivers head. At the start of my test the examiner told me that I was to perform the compulsory skid test before we left the depot. There was a long narrow lane just wide enough for a bus that ran the full length of the sheds between them and the wall of the 'Ronson' cigarette lighter factory. It led to a large open square between the bus sheds and the bus workshops. They had hosed water all over the square to facilitate a skid. I drove the bus down the lane, reaching a speed of about 30 mph (50 kph). When I reached the open square I steered to the left to move away from Ronson's wall then I put a full left hand lock on to throw the bus into a skid. When the back of the bus swung out to the right I had to turn the wheels back into the direction of the skid to get the vehicle back under control and come to a halt.

I looked over my shoulder and my instructor gave me the thumbs up. The examiner told me to leave the depot to begin my road testing. I left the depot full of confidence after this because although it was exciting and great fun to throw an eight-ton double-decker bus into a skid I was glad to have gotten it over with.

I handled the rest of the test with great aplomb and when the examiner told me to make my way back to the depot I was relaxed and happy with my performance. As I looked into the left hand mirror I could see my instructor smiling and I felt good. There were no other vehicles to be seen as I happily cruised along 'Waterville Road at just under 30mph when, as I should have expected, I burst my own bubble. Just before you enter 'The Ridges' housing estate, (now named 'Meadow Well'), the railway line crosses the road via a stone bridge at an angle. Because the bridge runs obliquely, there is a slight chicane in the road. I was sailing along euphorically and didn't even slow the bus down, passing under the bridge in a gentle serpentine manoeuvre. Of course if you drive a double-decker bus the upper deck sways dramatically in these circumstances and any passengers that were up there would be shaken up a bit. I was oblivious of this until we got back to the depot and was told that I had failed my test. My instructor said that I had passed easily until I had blown it going through the bridge. He knew himself from that point that I would fail, from the way that the bus had swayed. I certainly could not blame anyone else for it, it was just my own cockiness again and now I had failed yet another first test. You would have thought that I was out to get the world record for first time failures. The instructor told me that I would get one week's wages and if I came back after his two weeks holiday he would get me a start again. I don't think that I felt the need to burden my two brothers with the news of my latest failure. After all, it had all taken place within five working days and I hadn't seen them to tell them that I had started. They could well have hurt themselves laughing as hard as they would have so I was thinking of their welfare really.

✹✹✹✹✹✹

My brother Bob was working as a tunnel miner for a company called 'Nuttals' who had the contract to dig the first road tunnel under the River Tyne from Wallsend to Jarrow. I asked him to enquire on my behalf if they needed a maintenance fitter. He did but they didn't need one at the time. They did however offer me a miner's job the same as Bob until a maintenance fitter job came up. I was to start on the following Monday morning on the same shift as bob. It sounded promising to me so at 5-45am on the Monday Bob picked me up in his old 'Austin Somerset' car and took me into work with him. The hours were barbaric twelve-hour shifts six till six with Sunday off alternating weekly dayshifts and nightshifts. There were two ten-minute breaks and one twenty-minute break. None of which were to be taken away from where you were working on the tunnel face. On the plus side, you didn't have to take a flask with you because they brought a big urn of milky sweet tea down to the face. (That was sarcasm in case you hadn't realised). The money was good, three times what I had been earning but I can promise you that it wasn't worth it. We were in the main tunnel and about a third of the way under the river towards Jarrow. Another team of men were tunnelling from the Jarrow side to meet us in the middle. Bob had been one of the men who had dug the pilot tunnel and he had a photograph of himself shaking hands with one of the Jarrow team when they met in the middle. The pilot tunnel had to be dug in short pressurised sections to keep the river water out. When they finished their shift the men had to go into a decompression chamber like deep-sea divers before they could go home. Often, Bob would get the bends, (bubbles of nitrogen in the blood). The ambulance would have to take him back to the tunnel because they had the only decompression chamber in the area. They would then pressurise him as far as they could go and then bring the pressure down really slowly. This would dissipate the nitrogen bubbles and he would be OK. It sometimes didn't work straight away and he would be in the chamber all night. When he had the bends he would turn ash pale and be in agony with cramps in all of his muscles. Luckily for me the main tunnel didn't need to be under pressure thank God. The river still leaked in but it was such a big space the pumps sucked it away before it became a problem. Apart from this though, the working conditions were still absolutely abysmal. On my first day I was issued with an orange boiler suit, a hard hat, a pair of Wellington boots and a locker for my clothes in the work cabin. We stripped down to nothing but our underpants and put on our boiler suits, hard hats and Wellingtons. Then we began the trudge through the viscous mud leading down the half-mile or so into the tunnel. I was freezing and I asked Bob why we couldn't have kept our trousers and T-shirts on at least. He laughed and said,

"You won't be cold in about fifteen minutes". As we trudged, the mud was getting deeper and deeper the further we descended into the tunnel, we had to walk in the deep tyre ruts of the earth moving machines. If you had to step aside to let one of them past you found yourself up to your thighs in mud. You inevitably lost one or both of your wellies so I was glad now that I had left my socks off. When we reached the work face there was a huge circular open gantry with two platforms. This was the shift that we were to relieve and they were still working, the noise was deafening. There were men working at the semi-circular base and on the two platforms above them. They were digging with what looked to me like pneumatic road drills. They started with them held shoulder high and cut their way down the tunnel face. A man that looked like a Silverback Gorilla came up to me and started shouting something to me above the noise of the hammer drills. It was in the broadest Irish accent that I have ever heard and I couldn't understand a word of it. I looked at Bob and he translated for me, "This is Paddy the shift Foreman and he wants me to show you what's expected of you".

I then began my training as a tunnel miner under the instructions of my brother Bob. I had been assigned to work on the top platform, which suited me because I had been watching the clods of clay falling from the men working on the upper platforms. It was missing the men working on the bottom OK but what I hadn't realised was that the men working on the tunnel face staggered their work positions for this very reason. The pneumatic impact diggers were in fact only half the size of the road drilling variety but they were still pretty heavy. They had a spade attachment instead of a drill bit and Bob and I worked together for a couple of hours. He showed me the best way to use the machine, lifting it up to shoulder height and then bringing the spade down the face as far as you could reach. After we had dug out about two feet (61 centimetres) into the tunnel face the roof had to be shored up with wood before we could proceed. He showed me the technique for cutting and erecting the shoring and then he left me on my own on the top platform, a fully trained tunnel miner. It was the longest twelve hours of my life and also one of the hardest. Bob had been right when he said that I wouldn't be complaining about the cold for long and I was sweating like a pig on a spit. The icy river water was seeping through the roof in places and at first I was avoiding it but after a while I was deliberately standing under it to cool down. It had been filtered through about sixty feet of earth so it wasn't filthy or smelly and it even looked drinkable, I hasten to add that I still didn't drink any of it. At first I didn't even drink from the standpipe that was attached to the gantry because it looked a bit cloudy and brown. My reluctance didn't last for long because I was becoming a bit de-hydrated and in the end I was guzzling it down.

And so I slaved away at this backbreaking work and I didn't try to skive or sit about because I knew that it would reflect on my brother Bob. I couldn't even escape from it in my sleep because I used to dream about it all night and every night. I thought that I had died and gone to Hell and the Devil was a huge Irish bloke who spoke in tongues. During my second week we were fitting the large cast iron segments that bolted together to form the rings of the tunnel wall like giant curved 'Leggo' bricks. The JCB had lifted one of these heavy segments and was lowering it into position when the wire sling snapped. The segment landed correctly inline with the other completed rings but it was half way up the curved wall of the tunnel. It then slid down the muddy slope but it did not make the loud clang that I was expecting when it met the bottom segment. I looked down to see what had stopped it and to my horror, there stood the Irish Foreman with one of his legs between the two segments. As I watched, the blood began frothing over the top of his Wellington boot like a glass of freshly poured 'Guiness'. He didn't scream or even say OUCH! He just began giving orders in his incomprehensible Irish brogue and point at his leg. Luckily there were enough people who could understand him and he kept on giving them instructions until they had freed him. He was carried out of the tunnel and taken to hospital but he was still shouting orders until his voice was out of earshot. I had left the job long before he was able to return to work and my brother Bob was given his job until he was fit enough to come back. After a couple more hellish weeks had passed the job came to a standstill because we had come up against some large rocks. We were told not to come in for our shift on the following day while they blasted them out with Dynamite.

This was a heaven sent opportunity for me to seek a more agreeable way to earn a living before I expired in subterraneous circumstances. At that time you could walk into shipyards and docks without much hassle if you were seeking employment. Eventually I found myself in the fitting shop of 'Palmers Dock' at Hebburn on the south side of the River Tyne. The Foreman told me that there weren't any vacancies at that time but that he would take my name and address for future reference. As I was spelling my name for him he stopped writing and looking at me more closely he asked, "Are you any relation to Archie Blevins". When I told him that I was Archie's youngest son he grabbed my hand and shook it delightedly. Apparently he had worked beside my dad in several shipyards on the Tyne and they had been good pals. He told me that my dad had been the best boilermaker he had ever worked with.

I was over the moon to hear someone praising my dad like this and I was even happier when he told me that I could start work on the following Monday nightshift if I wanted to. It was wonderful to think that my dad's influence had got me a job ten years after his death, 'thanks dad'. I went straight back to Nuttals and handed in my notice with a happy heart. I still had a few days hard labour to do but at least now I could see the light at the end of the tunnel, (I thought that was a clever pun).

I was a bit worried that Bob would be annoyed with me for leaving the job so soon after I had started but he was pleased that I had been able to get a job back at my trade. He knew the score when it came to changing job's, he had dozens of different and varying occupations in his lifetime.

✶✶✶✶✶✶

CHAPTER 28

Palmers Dock

My debut as a ship repair fitter instead of a shipbuilding fitter was a shock to my system I have to admit. Instead of creating something new to exacting but well documented information, I now had to strip components down to repair or replace breakages or adjust them for wear. Mostly this had to be achieved without blueprints and dock fitters relied on their accumulated experience. At this point in my young life I was almost totally devoid of this kind of experience and I felt that I had bitten off more than I could chew. On my first night I reported to the charge hand in the ships boiler room and he introduced me to an old labourer telling me that we would be working together. We were to take the soot-blowers out of the boiler and strip them down for cleaning and adjustment. I nodded with sham confidence, opened my toolbox and began rummaging around through my tools while my labourer prepared the chain blocks and slings.

Soot-blowers are exactly what their name suggests, a devise that blows off the soot that accumulates on the water tubes in the boiler with blasts of steam. They always reminded me of anti-aircraft guns, 'Ack Ack' or 'Pom Pom' that sort of thing. I had fitted them before on a couple of ships during my apprenticeship so I was confident that I could safely extract them from the boiler. I was at a loss however about how to strip them down to their component pieces. They seemed a bit more complicated than you would think considering their mundane purpose. All I could remember being told about them was to be careful if I was removing some part or another because they were tricky, I am ashamed to tell you that I took as long as was humanly possible to remove them from the boiler and lower them to the boiler room deck. After that I killed as much time as I could messing around in my toolbox and then I feigned having chronic Diarrhoea to enable me to go ashore several times and waste even more time.

When I left the ship to go home in the morning the soot-blowers were still lying at the foot of the boiler but completely untouched. I went to bed but I didn't sleep because I was so ashamed of myself. I returned to work that night dreading the thought of seeing them still lying there. I was relieved to see that the dayshift squad had finished them and they were back in place in the boiler. The charge hand took me to a two-cylinder transfer pump and told me that the crankshaft bearings needed to be replaced. He pointed out a box filled with the replacement parts that I would require. I was delighted because I knew that this was a job that I had had experience of.

While we were working, the old labourer said, "You weren't sure how to strip those soot-blowers down last night were you son". I blushed scarlet but I admitted that I didn't have a clue and explained that I had never worked on repair work before. He told me that I should never be too proud to ask people for help. He said that he had been a boiler room labourer for twenty years and had assisted countless fitters with their work. Although he wasn't a tradesman there wasn't much that he didn't know about boilers and their ancillary plant. This was a major breakthrough in my way of thinking and if you are unsure of something there is no shame in asking someone for help. Nobody can know everything but they may know something that will make your life easier. If you are sent to repair a machine in a factory it's always wise to ask the machine operator if it is a recurring fault and if he has witnessed it being repaired. This can save hours of fault-finding work and people like to be asked for their help or opinion. Beware of those among us who think that they are always right they are usually politicians. I don't know if I have always been lucky, as with the old labourer or if I just remember the good ones.

I enjoyed my three months or so at Palmers Dock and I grew a bit more capable as a fitter into the bargain. I also augmented my tool collection somewhat from the engine room tool store. The engine room workshop was inside a large wire cage containing a lathe, a milling machine, a radial arm drilling machine and a pin driller. There would also be workbenches with vices along the bulkhead and best of all a wonderful array of hand tools hanging around the walls. It looked like the cave of 'Aladin' to me, with its treasure being the leading brand equipment on display. On dayshift these cages were open because there was always a junior ships engineer on watch there. On nightshift however they were always locked up to keep the nimble fingered out. This became a challenge to me and I studied the cage for its weak spots. I noticed that pipes and electric cables went into the cage, leaving a small gap around them of about one inch (25mm). I devised a convoluted fishing rod from some thin copper tube and put a hook on the end. It was made in a way that allowed me to guide it around obstacles while I supported its length from below with another length of tube cut into a 'V' shape on the end.

During the meal break between 1 am and 2 am while most of the blokes were having a nap I would go fishing. I managed to hook myself quite an impressive collection of tools and they served me well for the rest of my working life. I knew that everything that I purloined would be replaced during the pre-sailing inventory and I can't honestly say that I was wracked with guilt at the time. Most of them are still hanging in my garden shed so I suppose I must still be a bad lad. I promise you that if the Conservatives ever open up the shipyards and docks again I will return them and confess. Then, between falsely claiming expenses for houses they don't own, giving well-paid non-existing jobs to their families, they can think of some suitable punishment for me, (Should I lose any sleep at the prospect of this do you think)? The best acquisition that I was able to hook was a shifting spanner that was made in the USA. I can't remember the name on it but it was almost certainly made by the company 'Snap on'. This American company do make the most superb hand tools I have to say. This shifting spanner was a thing of great beauty and it made my mouth water when I saw it hanging there. I had made friends with another young fitter and he was with me when I landed this exotic hand tool on one of my fishing trips. He openly coveted my spanner and one night I generously allowed him to borrow it. That morning as we walked along the deck to go home I told him not to forget to give my spanner back to me. He was just saying that he wouldn't forget as he stepped over a small open hole in the deck. There was a loud whoosh and he screamed and fell to the deck clutching his throat. They were shot blasting the insides of the ships cargo tanks and someone had forgotten to put a blank on this pipe hole. As luck would have it, he had stepped over the hole just as the shot blaster had swept his gun over that area. It had caught him just under his chin and it looked like he had been shot with a shotgun. The underside of his chin and the sides of his face were like chopped liver but luckily his eyes and the front of his face were untouched. We got him to the first aid room and he was taken to the hospital. A week later, Palmers dock had a payoff and I was once again on the dole. Hence, I never saw my lovely shifting spanner ever again, I hope that he had many good years work out of it and perhaps it's still hanging in his garden shed.

Getting home in the mornings from Palmers was a bit frustrating because the gate to the dock was about half a mile from the ferry that would take me back to Wallsend. No matter how fast I ran I always missed my ferry, this meant that I would have to wait for half an hour for the next one. While running down Ellison Street one morning I noticed that men were leaving the 'Hawthorn Leslie' shipyard by a small side door near to the bottom of the hill a mere hundred yards from the ferry landing. That night during my meal break I reconnoitred the wall between Palmers dock and Hawthorn Leslies shipyard. At its lowest point down by the river I found that I could easily scale it. I went under the two ships that were being built on the stocks and found my way to the little side door out onto Ellison Street. That morning I clocked out in Palmers fitting shop and hurried over the dock gates to the dividing wall. I climbed the wall and made my way across to Hawthorns side gate and left the yard with the other men. I couldn't believe it when I saw the ferry leaving the landing because I thought I had made good time. I raced down the hill and the gang- plank to the landing stage judging the gap to be about three yards (2-74 metres) I leapt across the churning river water and grabbed the handrail of the ferry. The men on the ferry grabbed me and pulled me over the rail and onto the deck. They were all laughing and cheering and I thought that it was because I had made it. My smug look soon changed when one of the blokes pointed to the landing stage and said, "We were coming in not leaving you daft young bugger". They were still laughing as they disembarked and climbed the gangplank. I'm glad that I was successful in my jump because if I had not been squashed between the ferry and the landing pontoon I could have been poisoned in the filthy river. At least now I knew that my short cut through Hawthorns was a success, all's well that ends well as they say.

I had sold my motorbike because with our rent to pay and the hire purchase on the furniture things were a bit tight. The fact that I took the ferry to and from work every day meant that the bike wasn't being made use of.

CHAPTER 29

Back to the buses

By now we were aware that Margaret was pregnant to our mutual delight. She must have conceived on our honeymoon because the birth was almost exactly nine months after the wedding. I could imagine my ma-in-law Mary Ann counting off the days. Margaret was a bit worried about having to bring our imminent progeny home to our flat because we had discovered that the bedroom was cold and damp. This was due to the bay window leaking when it rained and we were reluctant to complain to our landlords downstairs because they had been so nice to us. Anyway, we had realised that we wouldn't be able to afford the rent when Margaret left work. So we decided that it would be a good idea to accept my in-laws invitation to live with them for a while. My sister-in-law Connie helped me to decorate the big front room and she even managed to paper the ceiling on her own. I have no idea how she did this except that she told me that she had used two long handled brooms. All I know is that you couldn't pay me enough to even attempt it. She made a beautiful job of it and I can still remember the paper she used. It was dark blue with constellations of stars all over it. Margaret and I used to lie on our settee in front of a big roaring fire and look up at our very own 'Starry night' like the Vincent Van Gogh painting. Perfect. Mam and dad Magee moved into Margaret's old bedroom and we had the larger back bedroom for when the baby came.

✿✿✿✿✿✿✿

I still had the urge to become a bus driver so I went up to the 'Newcastle corporation transport' depot on Shields Road in Byker. They took me out in an ancient AEC bus from the early forties with a crash gearbox. This meant that to change gears you had to double de-clutch between each one. I had learned how to do it while driving trucks with my brothers but this thing was antiquated to say the least. It was OK changing up the gears but it was a nightmare changing down because the engine revs were so slow in coming down I could have knitted a sweater while I was waiting. (I may be exaggerating). Most of the time I mistimed the change and there was a horrible crunching of gear cogs. I thought that I had blown my chances of a job but the instructor told me that I had handled the bus well considering what an old mangle it was. He got into the driving seat and said that he would show me how to change gear in these old vehicles. The procedure was to count six seconds after you had moved the stick into neutral and then dip the clutch again and gently push the stick into the next gear. You had to feel for the cogs to mesh on their own when they had matched their speeds. He told me not to dip my clutch pedal to the floor but to feel for the teeth of the cogs rubbing together without making them crunch and then select the gear. I had been pressing the pedal too far and missing this natural marriage of cogs as they synchronised speeds.

He put me back in the driving seat and I drove the way he had told me. I couldn't believe how smooth the gear changing became and true enough I could feel the cogs through the pedal without making them crunch. He told me that I could start driver training on the Monday and that in the meantime I could practice on my own in the old bus, as long as I didn't leave the depot yard. I drove around the depot having a great time, reversing between buses, doing emergency stops, it was all good fun and I grew to love driving the older buses. I was the only trainee again so after two weeks of one to one training I passed my driving test and got my public service vehicle (PSV) licence.

The best thing about Newcastle Corporation Transport buses

was the variation. They had old 'Leyland' and 'AEC' with crash gearboxes and they had more up to date versions of each with synchromesh boxes. They also had old 'AEC' and 'Daimler' buses with pre-select gearboxes. Newcastle transport were also the first company to get the semi-automatic 'Leyland Atlantian' buses with the little gear lever on the steering column and an automatic clutch. I would normally change buses three times during a shift so it made life more interesting for me.

★ ★ ★ ★ ★ ★ ★

I'll try to recall a few of the more amusing incidents from my bus driving days. As you can imagine, dealing with the public on a daily basis is fraught with confrontational possibilities. Especially if you're like me and have a sardonic sense of humour and don't suffer fools gladly, biting my tongue has never been my forte.

The first one that comes to mind was when I was driving my Leyland Atlantian along City Road in walker and I stopped to pick up a passenger. On an Atlantian bus the passengers got on at the front next to where I was sitting in the open drivers cab. I knew his face from somewhere but I couldn't place him. He was irate and shouting that I was late getting to this stop. I apologised to him and explained that I had been held up at some road works in Byker. He would have none of this and said that he would report me for being late. I explained to him that I couldn't get into trouble for being late because that was in Gods hands. I then told him that if I was ever to leave a bus stop too soon it would be down to me and he would be within his rights to report me. (I may have said this in a sardonic manner, who can say?). At this he became even more irate and shouted these immortal words, "Do you know who I am" (Pause for effect), "I am 'Tony Gish' of Tyne Tees Television and you have made me late for a very important meeting". That's where I knew his face from he was a 'sometimes' presenter on the local TV station. Laughing at his Diva type posturing I said in a loud voice, "Do you know who I am" (my own pause for effect), "I am the driver who is going to throw you off his bus and make you even more late". I started to get up but he jumped off without my assistance, shouting that he was going to report me. I couldn't wipe the smile off my face and the passengers and my conductor all had a good laugh. When I got back to the depot the inspector was waiting for me, saying that there had been a complaint. I explained the whole incident to him and he too started to laugh saying, "Aye, he looks like a snotty little sod" and that was that.

✶✶✶✶✶✶

Another time I was on the last run to the 'Stack Hotel' in Walker, I was almost finished my shift and I was ready for my bed. I stopped on Shields Road in Byker and a load of drunks got on to go home in Walker. The bus filled up and there were about eight drunken blokes standing on the platform beside me. I wasn't allowed by law to have people standing on the platform and I asked them to get off. They all refused and slurred in unison that they wanted to go home. Trying to appeal to there better nature I explained that I could lose my licence if I allowed them to stand there while the bus was in motion. As one, they told me which orifice I could stick my licence in should I be so disposed. I declined their suggestion and switched off the bus engine, "I can sit here all night if I have to" I informed them. "So can we mate" was their harmonic, if petulant reply. They then began to sing a medley of old songs from their no doubt extensive repertoire and the rest of the passengers joined in. After sitting there for a few minutes I realised that my bluff had been called and this was rapidly turning into a party. You know how irritated you can get when you are the only sober person at a party and I'm ashamed to say that I lost my temper. Taking the fluted brass fire extinguisher out of its bracket from behind the driver's seat, I stood up and shouted, "I'm going to knock all of your teeth out with this if you don't get off". They all looked shocked and one of them said, "Al reet bonnie lad, divn't get ya knickers in a twist man, tha woz nee need ti get nasty like". 'Translation' - ("I say young chap, I hope our revelry has not caused you displeasure in any way, your demeanour seems a trifle fraught"). At this they all got off the bus and bid me goodnight. I was guilt ridden as I continued the journey after all they had just wanted to get home the same as I had.

🔭🔭🔭🔭🔭🔭

Another incident happened late at night as I drove down 'Stamfordham Road' into Newcastle, It was the last run of a long shift and I had a bit of a headache. I hated this run because it always picked up a full load of drunks from the 'Jingling Gate' pub up past 'Westerhope'. The Jingling Gate was and still is a lovely country pub but at this time it had attracted a lot of rowdies for some reason. The din from upstairs, shouting, foot stamping etc, wasn't helping my headache and my conductor wouldn't go up to tell them to be quiet'. I couldn't blame him, it sounded like absolute bedlam up there. Near the bottom of Stamfordham Road I heard about six blokes come stumbling down the stairs behind me. They were shouting and swearing but at least they were getting off the bus I told myself. I could hear one of them talking to his pal conspiratorially. "Toot his f---ing horn Ginger", he said to his carrot headed crony.

At first, Ginger wisely refused muttering that he didn't want to but his protagonist kept up the pressure. He was saying, "Go on Ginger, it'll be a laugh". Ginger conceded and told his mates to be quiet. I have no idea why the sudden silence would help him in his quest. Perhaps he thought that the tranquillity would lull me into some sort of a stupor, he obviously did because as I drove along his hand began to slowly reach across the steering wheel. Yes, the horn push was located on a stork sticking out from the steering column on the opposite side to where he was standing. I couldn't believe how daft it all was, he must have thought that I was as drunk as he was. Slowly his arm moved across in front of my chest until his ginger head began to appear. The concentration on his vacuous face and in his bloodshot eyes would have inspired an Olympic athlete. When his nose came

341

within range I stuck a nut on it, (head-butted it). This was not the most advisable thing to do while driving a bus but it had seemed like a good idea at the time.

Ginger screamed and fell backwards into his pals just as I was stopping the bus and opening the doors. I was expecting to have to get up and try to eject them if I could but luck was with me and they all fell out of the bus and onto the grass verge. I closed the doors and drove away to the sound of verbal abuse of a very explicit nature. My action was not only a dangerous and uncivilised it also made my headache worse. On the plus side though, it was the only time in my life that I have successfully nutted somebody. I would feel sorry for ginger but if someone is daft enough to be coerced into doing something that they don't want to do by a halfwit, they deserve a sore nose.

✶✶✶✶✶✶

A more light-hearted tale now I think. For the first month or two I didn't have my own route or regular conductor and I worked on a week-to-week basis. It was interesting changing routes and conductors every week but it had its drawbacks. Every time I was given one of the several routes that had to cross the Tyne into Gateshead I didn't have a clue where I was. I had never had reason to go to Gateshead and that side of the river was like another country to me. When I was driving an old type of bus one of the passengers would have to stand behind my cab and direct me through the little sliding window. It always seemed that I was doing as much reversing as I was going forward. In an Atlantian bus my cab was open to the passengers and everybody would shout directions, not always the same ones unfortunately and debates would often occur while I parked at the side of the road. The housing estates were just a labyrinth of unfamiliar streets and I had to try and pick out landmarks to help me get my bearings for future reference.

✶✶✶✶✶✶

One of my temporary conductor's was a little plump girl with a pretty face, I think her name was 'Irene', she was only about four feet eight inches tall (142cm) and she couldn't reach the bell pushes in the roof of the old buses. I wasn't allowed to drive off until I was given two dings of the bell to say that everybody was safely on board. I would be waiting for ages every time we stopped. Eventually I looked back through the little window and saw the problem she was standing in the middle of the bus jumping up and down trying to reach the bell. Eventually one of the passengers got up and rang it for her. I climbed out of the drivers cab, walked to the back of the bus and climbed aboard. I approached her without speaking then I took a pencil out of her uniform pocket and demonstrated how to push the bell with it. She gave me a big smile and the passengers all cheered as I went back to my cab. I never had to wait for a bell from her again. She openly had a crush on me and told everyone that she was trying to become my regular conductress because she thought I was lovely, (Yes it can be a burden). One night we were having our ten-minute break at a remote terminus in 'Bill Quay', Gateshead, and sitting on the side seats at the back of the bus. She told me that she was desperate for a wee but that there were no toilets any where near by. The old terraced houses of Bill Quay were being demolished and there were no people living in the area so I told her that it was almost dark and she should just go behind one of the piles of rubble. Reluctantly she agreed and picked her way through the debris to secrete herself behind a pile of bricks. She came back and sat opposite me sheepishly in the bus. This was when my dubious sense of humour reared its ugly head I'm afraid. "It must have been darker than I thought" I said. "Why do you say that", she replied. "Because you have piddled on your own boots", I told her. She looked down and true enough she had splashed her boots. Far from thinking that it was amusing she immediately burst into tears and sobbed her little heart out. I tried my best to appease her and I apologised for my crass sense of humour. She told me between sobs that she would have thought it was funny too if it hadn't been me that had seen it. I managed to make her smile when I told her that I was always piddling on my own shoes and other peoples when I was in a public toilet. We were late leaving the terminus by the time she had composed herself but I felt too guilty to hurry her. It didn't put Irene off me and she still openly doted on me, I even pointed out that I was a newly and happily married man but she said that she was happy just to be near me, (You couldn't fault her impeccably good taste). She never went upstairs on the bus and when we reached a terminus she would stand at the bottom of the stairs taking the fares off people hurrying to disembark. She would be taking money, giving them their change and reeling off penny tickets for everybody regardless of the actual price of each journey. So, if the fare cost one shilling (12 old pence) she would take the shilling and give them a penny ticket, they would then drop the penny ticket into the used ticket bin without looking at it in their haste to get off. It was a clever scam and Irene was eleven pence (or whatever) richer. She must have made quite a bit of money for herself in this way but I have no doubt that she would have been caught eventually. She wanted to go halves with me but I refused pointing out that someone was bound to notice how many penny tickets she was using.

She never got caught during the six months or so that I knew her, so whoever was in charge of the distribution of tickets must not have been very observant. My moral high ground did not stop me from letting her buy my tea and bacon sandwiches every day out of her felonious takings because that would have been a bit churlish.

⋆⋆⋆⋆⋆⋆

I did get my own route and my own conductor after a while, the route was number 12 known as the 'Millvain' and went between the 'Stack hotel' in Walker and 'Two Ball Lonnen' in the west end of Newcastle. My conductor was a lad the same age as me called Jimmy McMullen and we became pals immediately. He was great with the older passengers unlike some of the conductors and we used to take requests for songs from them. 'The Searchers' and 'The Hollies' were popular groups at the time so we used to sing their songs a lot. Jimmy was taking driving lessons and saving up for a car so I was able to give him advice on how not to behave on his test. One morning we started work at 6am on overtime to do the shipyard workers special. The roads were almost empty of traffic and I asked him if he wanted to have a drive of my Leyland Atlantian bus. His eyes almost popped out, and he thought that I was joking. I assured him that I wasn't as long as he did everything exactly as I told him and when I told him. He was a bit reluctant until I explained that the bus was semi-automatic so he didn't have to think about the clutch and I would be standing right beside him. He climbed in behind the wheel and he followed my instructions like he had promised as he drove along 'Scrogg Road' past Walker Park. When we were approaching our left turn onto 'Wharrier Street' I explained that the front wheels on an Atlantian were six feet behind the driver so he would have to drive as though he was going past the turn and then when I gave him the word he could sweep it into the left hand turn. I gave him the signal and he took the turn perfectly onto Wharrier and I got him to pull over to the kerb and stop before we got to our pick up point for the workmen. After this I could do no wrong in Jimmy's eyes and we had some good fun together. When it snowed, if we had no passengers onboard I would warn him to hold on to something and put the bus into a skid and he was convinced that I must be the best driver in the world. We all know of course that you don't have to be good to be irresponsible, just immature. On another occasion we were parked on 'Hunters Road' at 'Spital Tongues' Newcastle. Jimmy was sitting on the engine cover next to the drivers cab changing the destination signs on the front of the old Leyland bus. I started the bus and moved off with Jimmy clinging to my open window and the little handle for changing the signs. I took him along to the next bus stop before I let him get off, as before there were no passengers on the bus. He had been terrified but he had enjoyed the thrill of the ride. What is it that makes young people do such stupid things, or for that matter, when do men ever actually grow up.

✷✷✷✷✷✷

NEWCASTLE CORPORATION TRANSPORT COMPANY

A 1950 'A.E.C. REGENT III'

THIS IS THE MODEL THAT I PASSED MY PUBLIC SERVICE VEHICLE DRIVING TEST IN.

I LOVED DRIVING THE BUSES
BUT THE WAGES WERE RUBBISH

A 1961 'LEYLAND ATLANTIAN.'

THESE BUSES CAME INTO SERVICE
DURING MY TIME AS A BUS DRIVER.

CHAPTER 30

My son 'Graeme William'

In the mean time, my brother Alan had joined the Army emergency reserves (AER) and was a driver with the Royal Electrical Mechanical Engineers, (REME).

He and my brother Bob had both been in the regular Army as drivers in the Royal Army Service Corps, (RASC) earlier in their lives. I had missed the National Service call up because of my engineering apprenticeship. By the time I had qualified as a marine engine fitter the compulsory call up had been stopped. The reserves were a bit like the Territorial Army (TA) in as much as they were part time soldiers trained as a secondary defence in a crisis situation. The difference was that the TA had local drill halls that they attended as often as they wanted to with a minimum number of drills per year. They did two weeks military training per year always with their own drill hall group of men. Most blokes joined the TA and used it like a social club because the intoxicating beverages were sold at NAAFI prices, (navy, army & air force inst.).

The AER on the other hand had a compulsory two-week training period and two weekend training periods per year. Recruits were from all over the UK and they only met each other at these camps. Each camp would be in a different part of Britain and they always trained with regular soldiers. In an emergency situation the AER would be called up first and then if necessary the TA. I don't think there is an AER now but the TA are much better trained and I know individuals who have been called up from the TA into active service in the middle-east conflicts.

Alan talked my brother Bob and me into joining with him so that we could all go together to the camps. The incentives were the £50 per year bounty and full army pay plus travel expenses. Our employers were obliged to pay us our basic wages for the time we were away on top of this, by order of the Government. The £50 bounty was five weeks wages to me so it was quite substantial. The army wages were about the same as I was getting as a bus driver so all together I would be quid's in. The icing on the cake for me was the fact that I would get to play with real guns and drive huge trucks and armoured vehicles. What boy could resist I ask you?

Margaret didn't want me to join knowing that I would be away for two weeks but she could see how excited I was and like the Angel she is she conceded to my wishes. I didn't know at the time but something was going to happen because of me joining up that I would bitterly regret for the rest of my life. Every time that I think of this event it makes me feel ill and sad. My dates for my first two weeks annual army camp came and they were just before Margaret was due to have our first baby. The consensus of opinion was that I would be back home in plenty of time before she was due. As you have already guessed, things didn't go to plan. After I had been away for a week we were bivouacked in some woods near to Dover on the south east coast of Kent. I remember that it was raining heavily and we were all laughing at a Scottish lad because he had left his boots outside of his tent and they were full of water. A Sergeant told me to report to the Majors tent because he had a message for me. I turned to jelly and an icy hand clutched at my guts as Alan and Bob came with me to see the CO. When we reached his tent he was standing in the rain grinning from ear to ear, which eased my trepidation somewhat. "I am delighted to tell you craftsman Blevins that your wife gave birth to a 6lbs 7oz boy on Saturday morning at 3-05 am" (14th July 1961). I was stunned by his early arrival and delirious with joy. "Your wife and son are both well and healthy, congratulations", the CO continued. Alan and Bob were already running about telling all of the lads the great news.

After I had been carried shoulder high around the tents and had been promised drinks from everybody I went back to see the CO. I asked him if I could go home and he told me that he could organise a travel warrant to be sent for me and transport to take me to Dover railway station for the next day. He told me that because I had not completed my two weeks training I would have to do another two weeks at a later date attached to another unit. His advice was that I had already missed the birth and I only had a few days to go so I should just stay and get it over with. My brothers were of the same mind and pointed out that Margaret was in safe hands living with her mam and dad and she wouldn't want me going away again later in the year. Sadly, I accepted this well meant advice and I have never forgiven myself believing that I took the easy option. I should have been at her side in the hospital even if it had only been for a couple of days.

I can't remember much about the rest of the camp because I was walking about like a zombie. I even lost my rifle in the woods and the sergeant told me that if I didn't find it I would have to face a court martial. I searched high and low and all of the lads helped me. The Scotsman with the soggy boots decided to act on a hunch he had and looked in the sergeant's tent, sure enough it was under his sleeping bag. When we confronted him about it he said that he had seen me lean it against a tree while I had a pee. He thought it would teach me a lesson if he took it because I was walking about in a dream. I was going to kick the crap out of him but the other lads stopped me and told him what a bastard he was. Everybody gave him the cold shoulder for the rest of the camp and we didn't see him again at any of our camps.

True to their word when we got back to our base the lads took me to Aldershot NAAFI club to wet my son's head. I don't know why but I decided to drink 'Cointreau' the orange liqueur, I had never had it before but I liked the taste. At 40% proof and after twelve glasses, Graeme's head was well and truly wetted.

✦ ✦ ✦ ✦ ✦ ✦

When I got home mam and dad Magee were sitting in the living room smiling and pointing to the bedroom door. I put my kitbag down and with butterflies in my stomach I entered the bedroom. Margaret was sitting on the bed with one hand on the cot rail and the other on her lap it's like a snapshot in my mind. I know that it's mushy but when our eyes met I felt that I was complete again. I've noticed ever since that moment that whenever we have been apart I can feel myself being restored when she looks into my eyes. I am aware that this sounds a bit 'Mills and Boon' or 'Barbara Cartland' but it's how I feel I swear to you. It is obvious that I am just a big girls blouse really.

She rose from the bed like a heavenly apparition and came into my arms and I ached with love for her as I did my best to devour her lovely face. (I told you it was worthy of a Mills and Boon paperback). When we had sated our immediate pent up needs we prised our lips apart and she led me to the cot. I looked down and saw for the first time the incredible gift that she had given me. I know that all parents are inclined to wax lyrical about their progeny. Never the less, it is no exaggeration to say that the fruits of my loins combined with Margaret's flawless incubations have all turned out to be breathtakingly beautiful. This smiling little creature that we were to name 'Graeme William' was to be the first of our three children.

I have decided at this point that when I have documented the births of our other two children 'Martin' and 'Kim' I will stop writing this book. I have made this decision on the off chance that they may decide to chronicle their own lives. I don't want my memories of this time to influence their own recollections. What I have written about my early life is exactly the way I remember it, I wouldn't have wanted it any other way. I can only hope that the image they have of me, or any influence I may have had on them over the years was a positive one.

Yes, we were now a family and happily ensconced (for the most part) with my in-laws. I say 'for the most part' because as I have told you Mary and I tended to rub each other up the wrong way from time to time. Her being a matriarchal firebrand and me being a tactless twerp, there was always going to be discord. Being forty years her junior and living in her home, you would have thought I would have had the sense to bow to her seniority and button my lip.

* * * * * *

This next bit may not get past the censorship after Margaret's scrutiny but it is too good an anecdote to leave out so I will chance it.

We decided that one child would suffice us for the foreseeable future and that we should consider contraception. The 'Pill' had not been invented back then so the only options were 'inter-uterus devices', 'Dutch caps' and condoms. We tried the Dutch cap, which resembled a wire rimmed bathing hat for a 'Barbie Doll' but it took ages to prepare and the mood had left us by the time it was ready. The inter-uterus device was an intrusive procedure that involved having a small piece of wire inserted into the neck of the uterus. This was a non-starter for Margaret because she had no desire to become a repository for scrap metal and I had visions of being hooked like a salmon. So, it was time for me to man up and get involved with the use of condoms. I won't go into details about the farcical fitting procedure, let me just say that it was my first time and I had never been very good at repairing punctures. Tenacity won the day and I succeeded in the end but neither of us was happy with the results and it didn't take long for us both to realise it. How can I put this in a delicate way, do you know the sensation you get when your foot goes to sleep? Well that is what it felt like for me 'down there' it was what I could imagine it would feel like to pick your nose while wearing a 'Marigold' washing up glove. I had the distinct impression that I could hear someone spasmodically rubbing a finger up and down a wet window. I removed the offending latex item and flung it over my shoulder with contempt. From that moment on, we have relied on the 'Pope' and the Catholic Church's favourite method of birth control, 'Coitus-Interruptus'. A euphemism for this method could be that you could liken it to, leaping from a moving train before it reaches the station. If you would like to know how successful this method of contraception is just ask any father of ten in Ireland.

The following morning the bedroom door opened, there was a pause and then my ma-in-law called in a louder voice than normal, "YOUR BREAKFAST IS READY". The door then slammed shut and we were left wondering what the problem was, we didn't have to wonder for long. When I got out of bed I saw the condom hanging over the mirror of the dressing table. As you opened the bedroom door your eyes were always immediately drawn to the mirror, as no doubt Mary's were, especially with its new adornment. Margaret was appalled by this prospect and didn't want to leave the bedroom. It took ages to get her to face the frosty reception that we knew we were about to receive. Nothing was said but there was a lot of crashing down of cups and teapots going on. I don't think that this incident placed me in a very good light in Mary's eyes I was obviously some sort of animal. I don't know if she told Harry (Patrick Henry) my father-in-law about this bestial behaviour but I have no doubt that he would have found it hilarious as he kept a straight face while placating her.

✶✶✶✶✶✶

Another funny but hair-raising incident happened between Mary and myself when Graeme was about a year old. Margaret and I had gone out somewhere while Mary had been babysitting for us. Margaret asked Graeme if he had been a good boy for his Nanna because he could be a bit of a live wire at times. Mary replied for him, saying, "No, he's been a real handful, I'm worn out". Graeme was standing beside me so I bent down and said, "Have you been naughty then" and smacked his bum gently through two inches of terry towelling nappy and plastic pants.

I swear to God that it was just a playful tap but when Mary saw this she metamorphosed from a diminutive housewife into the 'Incredible Hulk'. She screamed, "DON'T YOU DARE HIT THAT BAIRN". Then she grabbed the bread knife and lunged at me across the table in a straight-armed thrust designed to carve me a new belly button. Harry grabbed her by the waist and with the table between us I was able to avoid her manic swordplay. If she had been wearing a Mexican hat she could have been mistaken for 'Zorro', she was certainly trying to carve 'M' for Mary on my chest. Harry managed to lift her bodily out of my way to facilitate my escape into the bedroom. Hanging there in his arms slashing at me with the bread knife it looked like a demented ventriloquist act. The knife didn't smash through the bedroom door like a horror movie and Mary finally calmed down and accepted that it was only a playful tap that I had given her little angel.

You may think that I am demonising Mary in the same way that some stand-up comedians do with their mother-in-law's, this could not be further from the truth. Mary was a hard working, straight talking, honest, loyal, and fearless woman. I should know, I am married to her clone. Mary wasn't demonstrative in giving her affection the way that my family were but you could feel the fierce love emanating from her. As with Margaret, you knew that she would fight a lion with her bare hands to protect her loved ones. All of the women in my life are the type that you could imagine holding the old homestead together in the wild west of America. My granny Clarkson, my mother, my mother-in-law, and my wife Margaret have all been strong women in spite of the fact that they have all been vertically challenged. I have had the best of both worlds because I had the pleasure of teaching Margaret how to be more demonstrative and she took to it whole-heartedly I'm happy to say.

I will tell you a little story about Graeme when he was about twelve years old that always gives me pleasure. On open day his teacher told us that she was worried about him because he always seemed to be with the girls in the playground. I was a somewhat taken aback and asked, "Do you mean that you think he could have homosexual leanings"? She began to laugh and said, "No, the exact opposite, the girls are all infatuated with him and he seems to revel in it". I gave a sigh of relief and said, "Well you don't have to worry about him anymore, he just takes after me and he will just have to live with the adulation". Margaret just shook her head and smiled and we all had a laugh.

MY MOTHER-IN-LAW
A FEISTY LITTLE WOMAN

MARY ANN MAGEE

I MARRIED HER CLONE

I CAN ATTEST TO MARY'S FEROCITY WITH A BLADE.
`OH! YES.`

ROYAL ELECTRICAL + MECHANICAL ENGINEERS
CRAFTSMAN 1st CLASS. BLEVINS. W. 23885298

1962

'ME' LEARNING TO SHOOT.
(WHY SHOULD BRITAIN TREMBLE)

'DAD' MAGEE,
SISTER-IN-LAW 'ENA'
'ME' RESTRAINING 'MARY'
SISTER-IN-LAW 'CONNIE'

I WAS REASONABLY
SAFE IF I AVOIDED
DIRECT EYE CONTACT.

CHAPTER 31

Buses, bullets and bombs

I was still driving on the buses when an event took place that most people from that era find is indelibly imprinted on their minds. The kind in which you always remember where you were and what you were doing when you became aware of it. Margaret and I had been to the cinema with my pal Arthur Hall and his wife Maureen. We were walking down home in the dark. I noticed that there were a lot of people standing in their doorways talking to their neighbours. This seemed odd to me because it was a cold November evening and quite late. When we got into the house, Mary was crying and she told us that the American President 'John. F. Kennedy' had been assassinated, (22 November 1963). Margaret started to cry too as we watched the non-stop TV coverage of the shooting. I remember having this icy feeling of impending doom sweeping over me.

You may wonder why the murder of a foreign political leader should cause such consternation and emotion among us. The fact is that we were in the middle of the so-called 'cold war' between the USSR and the Western Alliance. America was almost always having a war of words with the Russians. There had been a couple of tense stand off's between them and President Kennedy had always called their bluff. Now that he was dead a nuclear holocaust seemed imminent. After all, we had nuclear missiles and we knew that we would be targeted first by the Russians. Apparently, it would only have taken three hydrogen bombs to turn our beautiful British Isles into a radioactive cinder.

Common sense must have prevailed thank God because we are still here more than fifty years later. It all seems like a script for a disaster movie now but I can assure you that the fear was upon us and it was tangible. Let us hope that the troubles in the Middle East don't prove to be our undoing

✱✱✱✱✱✱

I will now relate my last two memories of my time as a bus driver. I had been up to the depot on my day off to collect my wages from the office and I was on my way home on a bus. I had no sooner sat down on the side seat just off the exit platform than I began to get an awful pain in my left side. It seemed to come in agonizing pulses and was increasing in intensity. By the time I reached the Newcastle and Wallsend boundary I was doubled up with pain. Mobile phones were only found in science fiction novels back then and buses didn't have two-way radios like they do today. I decided that my best course of action would be to get off the bus and seek help. I staggered into a corner shop and pleaded with the female shopkeeper to phone for an ambulance for me. She took one look at my pathetic appearance as I stood there clutching my side, stooped over and looking up at her. I must have looked a second rate stand in for 'Lawrence Olivier' in his portrayal of 'Richard the 3ʳᵈ'. "I'm sorry but I'm not allowed to make phone calls on behalf of the public" she said. I explained in a faltering voice that I was in unspeakable agony and in need of medical assistance. To which she replied, "If you go up the street there is a public phone box and if you dial 999 you can get the emergency services free of charge". I could see that this paragon of mercy was not going to be swayed, so I vacated the shop. As I left, I told her how proud she should be for her steadfast devotion to duty in the face of another human beings suffering. (OK, so I may not have been so eloquent).

I found the phone box and managed to make the call, it cost me nothing just as the saintly lady had said. As I sat on the pavement in semi-delirium I no doubt reflected that I hadn't thanked her for her concern for my fiscal welfare. I don't know if there were any other people about but I know that nobody asked me if I was OK as I sat there. Perhaps they thought that I was just a young daytime drunk and they didn't want the hassle. I prefer to think that there was nobody about otherwise it doesn't speak too well for my townsfolk does it. The Ambulance came in about fifteen minutes and took me to the 'Royal Victoria Hospital' in Newcastle. I was given an X-Ray and was told that I had a couple of calcium stones moving about inside my left kidney (Renal Colic). This is what was causing me such acute pain and they would have to be removed. The doctor gave me an injection of morphine and I have to say that it put the smile back on my face. I have never had much sympathy with drug addicts and perhaps dismissively write them off as self-harming hedonists who the rest of us have to pick up the pieces for. I can however understand how it could happen to someone with an addictive nature by accident. I had several brushes with Renal Colic and three operations, so morphine became part of my life when I was in my twenties and thirties. I can see how it could be easy to succumb to temptation if you were that way inclined. The way that I felt when I was on morphine was indeed sublime and I think that this is what stopped me from getting hooked on it. I don't like the idea of not being in full control of my faculties and no matter how nice it feels it's not for me.

I had the operation to remove the stones and when I woke up the nurse gave me a small bottle containing two little stones. She told me that there had been three but one of them had been sent for analysis. They were only about one millimetre in diameter and jagged like bits of pumice stone. It wasn't hard to see how they hurt like hell as they made their way through my kidney. The good news was that they had reached my urethra and were able to be removed with an instrument up my penis. The bad news was that when the painkiller wore off, it felt like I had been kicked in the guts by a mule. I asked the nurse why I was still in so much pain when they hadn't even had to cut me. She smiled and said, "Just a minute, I have something to show you". At this she went away and returned with a tray containing some medical instruments. She pointed at something that looked as thick as a fountain pen and said, "That is what the doctor had to push up your 'Willy' so that he could remove the stones". I found it incredulous and thanked God that I had been comatose at the time. I can only assume that the doctor in question never had any difficulty getting the hosepipe onto his garden tap.

I found that if I just tolerated the pain during the day I could save a couple of my painkillers and take them at bedtime. This way I could guarantee a blissful and pain free nights sleep. As I have said, over the next few years Renal Colic raised its ugly head on a number of occasions and I was obliged to have a couple of more invasive operations. I employed the same tactics of saving up painkillers so that I could get some pain free sleep. I now realise how stupid and dangerous this practice was and I would strongly advise against it. After a few years my body must have stopped producing too much calcium (the cause of Renal Colic) and I have not been bothered by it since my early thirties. I still have the little bottle with the two stones in it up in the attic somewhere.

✦✦✦✦✦✦

A sad thing happened during my last week as a bus driver. I was driving up Barrack Road in Newcastle when a little dog ran out in front of me and I ran over it. Jumping out of my driver's cab I ran to see how it was, it was screaming pitifully. I was horrified to see that the left hand front wheel had completely flattened the dog's hindquarters from its waist back over. The hideous site of this and the awful screaming was gut-wrenching. I couldn't understand how it was still conscious with half of its body just unrecognisable mush. I think that it was a 'Jack Russel' terrier and they are known to be a tough little animal. People were shouting that someone should call the RSPCA to come and put it to sleep. I knew that this would take ages and I just couldn't bear the thought of it suffering the way it was. I jumped back into the driving seat and drove the bus forward until its double back wheels went over the poor little creature. The screaming stopped.

Women were telling me what a monster I was and at the time I felt like one. The men were trying to explain to them that it was an act of mercy but they were having trouble getting their heads around that concept. I don't regret my course of action and I know that I would do it again if it were called for. I know that this recollection from my past was not pleasant as anecdotes go but the trauma of the incident has stayed with me for fifty years so I felt that it was worth recording.

CHAPTER 32

George Angus & Co. Ltd.

I was nearing the end of my bus driving days now because my brother Bob was working in the press-shop at George Angus & Co. He heard that his Foreman was looking for an engineering fitter to work in his Die fitting department. He mentioned to the Foreman, 'Sid Dixon', that his young brother (me) was a fitter and looking for a job. Sid told him that If I came to the factory the next day and told the security who I was he would give me an interview. True to his word, Sid came as soon as the security man called him and took me along to his office in the press shop. The first thing he said to me was, "Don't worry about the noise, you get used to it". I found this amusing because I had just been thinking how quiet it was, it was obvious that Sid had never worked in a shipyard environment. I had a good interview and Sid offered me the job there and then, I was to start as soon as I had worked my two weeks notice with Newcastle Corporation Transport. I like to think that my success had something to do with the fact that Sid had told me that he had known my mam when she worked there and saying what a lovely woman she was.

I must say that I was a bit worried about being accepted by the other fitters in the department. I had it in my head for some season that being a fitter in a factory must be more complex and that coming from the shipyards would put me at a disadvantage. Reading this now makes me cringe, I have no idea where these insecurities came from apart from the fact that I was still young and wet behind the ears. Anyway, it came to pass that I would become ensconced as a 'Die Fitter' in the press-shop of Geo, Angus & Co, in Wallsend. The job entailed the building and repair of die boxes and the setting up of hydraulic presses ranging from 10 tons, up to 750 tons for the manufacture of oil seals, O-rings, gaskets and diaphragms. These were all made from a synthetic rubber patented by George Angus who had a small factory in Walker, Newcastle making leather washers for water taps. Britain was having trouble getting natural rubber during world war two until this synthetic stuff was created. It catapulted the little Tyneside factory into international fame almost overnight providing the armed forces with vital oil seals. Sid the Foreman introduced me to the other five fitters in the department and showed me to a vacant workbench.

As I did earlier in this chronicle I will describe my new workmates using only first names to save any embarrassment to anyone. They were all forty-ish at the time and as far as I know they have all gone to the great press-shop in the sky now. I base these encapsulations on my observations over the sixteen years that I worked with them. In no particular order they were, Stan, Bob, Fred, George and Freddy.

Stan was a nice bloke who had served in the 'Royal Engineers' during world war two. He was a bit rough around the edges and always said what he thought, which is why I suppose that I liked Stan. He left a couple of years after I started to become a racing 'Bookie'. On my first day when we sat down for our morning tea break I had forgotten to take a cup in with me. Stan offered to lend me a spare cup that he kept in his locker. I thanked him and he produced a white porcelain pint pot that he had been given when he was in the army, it was stamped WD 1941. I made a pot of tea and sat down to drink it but I missed the bench somehow and dropped the pot. It smashed into a hundred pieces flooding the floor with my tea. I was mortified and stuttered how sorry I was to Stan as he stared in disbelief. "I carried that bloody thing right through world war two and you have managed to do what the Germans couldn't in your first five minutes". I promised to get him another pot but he just laughed and shook his head. I realised that it wasn't the best start I could have made and I vowed to myself that I would replace it with something special.

That lunchtime I got the bus home and luckily my ma-in-law Mary was out. I looked in her cabinet and found a lovely old 'George V' souvenir mug. "That should be just the job", I thought and rushed back to work. Stan was delighted when I gave it to him and said that he would have to remember never to lend it to me. Strangely Mary never missed the mug, I suppose that it had been among the other souvenir mugs for years and she had just stopped noticing it, (I know you would have forgiven me Mary).

✶✶✶✶✶✶

Bob was a smooth character who had an eye for the ladies and there were plenty of them in the factory for his perusal. He was an intelligent bloke and interesting to talk to but when he was talking to one of the women it became uncomfortable. He would begin with playful banter but it would degenerate into something a bit more lascivious. A lot of the girls were able to put him in his place but some just looked embarrassed and walked away. I pointed this out to him a few times but Bob was such a chauvinist he just couldn't see the error of his ways. His abysmal, or even creepy chat up lines must have worked at least once though as he was a married man.

I had only worked there for a couple of months when I was compelled to rebuke him. He had been talking in a derogatory manner about an older woman that worked in the next department to ours. Apparently it was her birthday and the other girls had bought her a bunch of flowers but Bob was saying in a petty voice that it was just because she was the cousin of one of the Foremen. My response may have been due to the fact that the woman reminded me of my mother. I said something along the lines of, "If you can't think of something nice to say, why don't you keep your hole shut, you baldy bastard". This last bit was doubly effective because I still had all of my own hair at the time. Bob went red and stormed off without even a goodbye. Stan said, "Well, that's it, he will never speak to you again". Apparently Bob and Stan had had an argument once and Bob hadn't spoken a word to him for two years. I said that I would try to live with the disappointment and we all had a good laugh. Stan was correct Bob did stop talking to me, even though I deliberately kept on talking to him as though there was nothing wrong. He would just turn his head away and pretend that I wasn't there. It was hilarious at first but after a few weeks the childishness began to get me down. I have always been of the opinion that it's better to talk through your differences with someone than to bottle them up and allow them to fester.

I decided to confront him and offer him an olive branch after all I was the youngest and my remarks had been a trifle uncomplimentary. I waited for him to go to the toilets so that there wouldn't be an audience. As we washed our hands I told him that I was sorry for my outburst (I didn't mention the baldy bit) and explained about the woman resembling my mother. He turned to me and I could see the relief on his face at me breaking the deadlock. He explained that he had been badmouthing the lady in question because she was the cousin of a Foreman that he hated. The logic in this second hand abuse escaped me but I decided that it wasn't worth pursuing. There was no contrition in his explanation though, which rankled a bit. His next line, although it amused me almost scuppered the peace talks, "You know Bill, you did take liberties talking to me the way you did". To which I replied "Think yourself lucky Bob, I almost smacked you in the mouth". He looked a bit shocked at this and I thought I had blown it. After a few seconds reflection I began to laugh, patting him on the back as though it was a joke. He paused and then started laughing himself in a nervous 'Thank God for that' sort of way. I can't remember Bob actually doing any work at all and as he was the shop steward for the union he just booked his time down to attending meetings. He was also the factory 'Bookie' so he had the rest of his time taken up by people coming to place bets on the horses. I have no idea how he got away with it, unless he held some dirty secret on someone high up in management.

We never fell out again over the next sixteen years and we rubbed along quite affably but I have no doubt that my card had been marked in Bob's eyes. I very much doubt that he could have been persuaded to pee on me if I had been on fire.

✶✶✶✶✶✶

Fred was one of those people who you don't think you are going to like but who grow on you. I could tell that he thought I was just a young greenhorn at twenty-two years old and I thought that he was a bighead, as did all of the blokes that worked with him. He would expound on a multitude of subjects and I soon realised that far from being a big head he was a well-read man. I always enjoyed our debates and I think that he realised that I wasn't just a greenhorn and that I actually had one or two brain cells in working order. He had been a 'plant fitter' (earthmoving equipment, bulldozers that sort of thing) before he came to Angus's so he was a well-experienced tradesman. I would say that he was probably the most capable man in the department. His grasp of engineering and his innovative ability vastly surpassed the fitters who had served their apprenticeships with George Angus & Co. As did mine believe it or not, I soon realised that my earlier fears of not coming up to scratch because I was from the shipyards were totally unfounded. Over the years, apart from a few exceptions, the only truly versatile fitters I have worked with have come from heavy engineering backgrounds. I think that is why Fred eventually took to me and we became firm friends.

✶✶✶✶✶✶

George was a big, handsome, gentle, naïve man that I liked immediately. I have never met a man so open, friendly, trusting and honest before or since. He served his apprenticeship in an engineering firm called 'Donkins' on Shields road in Newcastle. They built the steering gear for Tugs and Trawlers, or any small vessels in fact. Sometimes I would tell him about going on sea trials with HMS Lion and other ships. And he would tell me of going on trials up the River Mersey or the Thames in Tugs or he would be in a Trawler going up the Firth of Forth or the River Severn.

He was as strong as an Ox with forearms like my thighs and hands the size of shovels. All of the women young and old loved him and he would flirt with them all. Not in a licentious way like Bob but in a warm tongue in cheek way that brightened their day. He didn't like driving cars very much and to be honest, he was a dreadful driver. I was in his car with him several times and I think my finger indentations were a permanent feature in his dashboard. He and his wife would get a picnic together and head out in the car every Sunday. They never got further than the second lay-by up from the Coast Road on the northbound carriageway of the A19 road. This lay-by is only about two miles from their home but as George told me, it is quite high up and you can see green fields. Anyway, this was as far as he wanted to drive and so they would sit there for a couple of hours and have their picnic. I swear to you that this is a true story and George told me that they hardly ever spoke on these occasions. They would just sit with their Thermos flask of tea and their box of sandwiches and look at the fields. This little tableau took place most Sundays and sometimes in the evenings on warm summer nights. It's lovely if you think of it through rose coloured glasses.

At some point in George's career he had been trained as a locksmith and I never saw a lock that he couldn't pick with a couple of bits of wire. People would come from all over the factory to see him because they had lost their keys. After he had opened the locks to their toolboxes or gained access to their lockers, he would then make them a new key by hand. I was fascinated by his skill but he would never teach me, no matter how much I grovelled to him. It wasn't because he thought I might use the skill feloniously, I think that it was because he loved his unique status in the factory. I thought of George a few months ago because I lost the key to my garden shed and as usual I couldn't find the spare key either. It was an expensive lock because I have all of my tools in the shed. In the end, I had to borrow an angle grinder and extension lead from my neighbour to grind through the hardened steel lock. It cost me a fortune to replace and needless to say, I found the spare key for the original lock a couple of days later. George would have opened it in seconds and I had seen him do it with the same make of lock.

✶✶✶✶✶✶

Freddy (not the earlier 'Fred') was a really strange bloke and hard to categorise. He was the one who took me under his wing when I started and showed me most of what I needed to know over the next few weeks with regards to die fitting. He may have been asked to do so by the Foreman or he may have just taken it upon himself, either way, I couldn't have asked for a better mentor. He had served his time with George Angus & Co and had been a die fitter for over twenty years this was much longer than the other four fitters. It wasn't exactly brain surgery but Freddy knew all that there was to know about the job and he had infinite patience. All of the years that I knew Freddy he never lost his calm or got annoyed with anyone or anything. He always had a detached contemplative aura about him and would help anyone without complaint. He may sound saintly to most people but there was something about Freddy that spooked me.

I was passing his workbench one day when I noticed that he was looking closely at a knife that he had been cutting some rubber with. He called me over and said, "Bill, do you think that you would rather stab someone or shoot him?" I was taken aback by the question but I replied, "Do you mean in a life or death situation, like in a war or something". "No", he said in his calm matter of fact way, "I mean if you just wanted to kill someone would you rather stab or shoot him"? I remember that it gave me a chill to look at his serene thoughtful expression as he fondled the knife. I said, "To be honest Freddy, I would rather just not have the urge to do either".

Another time I noticed that he seemed to be playing with something on his workbench. Curiosity got the better of me and I went to see what his source of amusement was. To my horror, he had poured some release oil over a spider and every time the poor creature tried to crawl out he pushed it back in with his pencil. During this grotesque pastime he was smiling gleefully. I was disgusted and I reached over and crushed the poor suffering arachnid with my thumb. Freddy looked up at me and said, "Why did you do that". I replied, "If you have to ask, its psychiatric treatment that you need Freddy".

Every Friday night Freddy would go to the 'Stoll' cinema on Westgate Road in Newcastle on his own. The Stoll specialised in soft-core porn movies from Europe with subtitles for those who actually cared what was being said. Yes, Freddy was a fully paid up member of the raincoat brigade. These films were pretty lurid for the times with plenty of heaving naked bosoms, glazed lust filled eyes and full pouting lips, (who needed the distraction of subtitles). By today's lax standards they would probably meet the criteria for children's television. In those days these films were all the titillation that was available and Freddy was an unashamed devotee of them. Far from keeping his 'penchant' quiet, Freddy was always asking one of us if we would like to join him in his sordid hobby.

I know that I have painted a less than flattering picture of Freddy but as I have also said, he was always helpful to everyone, a hard worker and always friendly, just a bit of a weirdo with a strange outlook. He was a 'Freemason' and during the government of the malevolent Mrs Thatcher I prevailed upon Freddy to propose me for membership into his lodge. It was hypocritical in the extreme for me to do this because I hated the idea of someone being able to use the membership of a club for their own advantage. The facts were that my children were all going to be looking for work in the next couple of years and getting a job was becoming almost impossible for young people. I have never frowned on nepotism within the family because it is only human to look after your own. If someone got a job or was promoted because they were related to the Boss, it wouldn't ruffle my feathers in the slightest, it is what I would expect. However, I do hate the old boy network, when wearing your old school, regiment or club tie opens doors for you. I admit that I was willing to hedge my bets a bit and only use the 'Masons' in the pursuit of jobs for my children. The ethicality of this concept is quite frankly open to scrutiny. As it happens, I never had to sully my questionable ethics by using my membership in the Freemasons to secure jobs for my children. The truth is, I resigned from the Masons before my eldest son Graeme left school because it just wasn't for me. Would I have used the Masons for the advantage of my children? The answer is, yes of course I would. "So much for my moral fibre", I hear you say. Well, "Too much fibre in your diet gives you the shits", that's what I say.

I found the ceremony boring after seeing it a few times, although the social side was quite pleasant. It's not the secret society that people think it is, in fact you can find out all about it in your local library if you so wish. They are givers to many charities and do a lot of good work behind the scenes. There are many members that like to keep their membership a secret I have to say and these are the ones who use it for their own advancement. I knew many people who gained promotion in this way though some of them possessed an IQ that was not much higher than their collar size.

I found that the membership who came from all walks of life were always friendly and even fraternal to me and I never detected any duplicity from anyone. The trouble was, it really bothered me listening to the after dinner conversations of my Masonic brothers. They would be promising to put a good word in, or to give a glowing reference to someone with regards to somebody that they had never met. I know that I have just admitted that I would have accepted favours on behalf of my children if I had been offered them. At least I chose the moral high ground and resigned before I was tempted, that must count as a 'Brownie' point. The final straw came when I was sharing a table with a bunch of policemen, (There are a great number of policemen in the Freemasons). I was having a pleasant chat to a bloke sitting opposite me who was in fact an ex-policeman himself. The other coppers produced a couple of bottles of whisky and offered us both a drink. We both thanked them but refused the drink explaining that we were both driving. After a while one of them came up behind the ex-copper, he was obviously a bit drunk and tried to pour some whisky into his glass. The ex-copper put his hand over the glass and told him firmly that he didn't want any. The copper with the bottle looked annoyed and said, "You don't have to worry about drink-driving because Harry and Dave are patrolling the Coast Road tonight and they both know us all". When I heard him make this confession I couldn't hold my tongue and told him and his drunken pals what I thought of them. The idea of policemen getting drunk and then driving their cars home with impunity because their pals were in the patrol cars really stuck in my throat. After I had given them my critical assessment of their lack of responsible behaviour you could have cut the atmosphere with a knife. I decided then that this would be my last Masonic meeting and it was.

✯✯✯✯✯✯

CHAPTER 33

My first car

My wage packet at George Angus & Co was a joyous thing to behold. Until now I had only been earning £11 per week in the shipyards and £10 per week as a bus driver. We won't count the couple of weeks blood money I earned digging the Tyne Tunnel it was too short and too grim. Now as a die fitter I was earning £22 per week, twice as much as I was used to getting. I had sold my motorbike and now that I was a family man I decided to buy my first car. I was in a wire fenced compound known as 'Northern Motors' at the top of Byker High Street, behind the 'Blacks Regal' cinema. I got my eye on a grey 1954 'Rover 90' and fell in love with it. It was almost ten years old and had 95000 miles on the clock. The Rover 90 was a prestige car in its day and as I sat behind the huge steering wheel, sniffing the leather upholstery and looking at the burnished Walnut facia it felt like it. OK, the carpets were a bit threadbare and the rubber tread on the brake and clutch pedals was wafer thin but the car had me smitten. I think that I paid £140 for it in monthly instalments over the next year. It had a 2200cc six-cylinder engine and a Rover patent free wheel attachment on the four-speed gearbox. Once you had driven off, you didn't have to use the clutch any more to change gear, only when you were coming to a stop. Every time you took your foot off the accelerator the car freewheeled. The idea was that the car would be more economical due to not having the compression of the engine slowing you down. It meant of course that when you were going down a hill, the car would go too fast because of the lack of engine drag and you had to use excessive braking. This resulted in me having to change my worn out brake shoes more often than was normal. It was also dangerous because when you braked in an emergency you had the full inertia of the cars weight without the engines compression to help you to stop. The free wheel attachment was made illegal I believe and Rover stopped fitting them in their later models. I don't think that it helped with the economy either because my car only did about 14 mpg around the doors and 18mpg on a long run. It was an old car and it did weigh one and a half tons after all. The tank held 14 gallons (63 ltrs).

I remember that the top of the red leather front bench seat was cracked and worn. It was about four-inches wide and ran between two lengths of piping between the front and back of the seats. Margaret got some red velvet from somewhere and she painstakingly sewed a four-inch strip of it from one side of the car to the other between the piping. It looked really opulent and professional she could have been an upholsterer.

I had to carry a gallon can of engine oil in the boot of the car because the piston rings were worn and she burnt oil at an alarming rate. I had to top up the engine every 100 miles or so or the red warning light came on. I also had to keep six spare spark plugs in the car at all times because the ones in the engine kept oiling up and the car would break down. I even bought a portable sandblasting machine that plugged into the cigarette lighter socket for roadside breakdowns. I lost count of the times that I had to take out the plugs and sandblast them at the side of the road and it wasn't always at a convenient place or time. That is until I saw an advert in a magazine for a revolutionary new sparkplug called the 'Spitfire Jet Igniter'. It had no visible electrodes just a domed end with three holes from which flames shot out. The advert claimed that they never oiled up and in fact the dirtier they got the more efficient they became. They were quite expensive compared to the 'Champion' plugs that I was using at the time but if their claims proved to be true it would be worth it. I was getting a bit sick of roadside maintenance and the only other alterative was to fit a new set of piston rings to the engine. I didn't have the equipment to lift the engine out and it sounded a bit daunting to do it while it was still in the car.

I sent for six of these miraculous plugs and fitted them into my Rover. I couldn't believe the difference they made immediately to the performance it was like a sports car, faster and smoother. I drove the Rover for another three years and I swear to you that it never broke down and I never had to change the plugs again. I still had to top up the engine oil regularly, so it was obviously still burning oil but it never again oiled up the plugs, amazing. I have never seen the 'Spitfire' plugs advertised since that time, so I assume that one of the big sparkplug companies bought them out and mothballed the patent. If you were a component manufacturer you wouldn't want something being made that would last indefinitely would you?

The 'good' things about my Rover were the armchair comfort and spaciousness that it provided. It really was a luxury vehicle and you travelled in almost total silence. Quite often when I was waiting at traffic lights I would have to look at the instrument panel to check that the engine was running. There was a secret draw in the boot that held an array of original Rover tools.

The 'bad' things were the comparatively small boot space that was really tiny. Then there was the spare wheel that was held in an open steel frame and exposed to the elements underneath the rear of the car. It had to be lowered by the use of a winding handle inside the boot. You then had to lift the huge spare wheel that was covered in road filth out of its cradle, subsequently, so was I when I had to change a wheel while on my way to a wedding during a downpour. Also, due to the cars considerable weight and the old fashioned cross-ply tyres she would metamorphose into a sledge at the first signs of frost. You could turn the wheels from left to right and the Rover would travel in a straight line regardless. This penchant that she had for linear motion prompted slow and careful driving from me in adverse conditions I'm glad to say. For all of the cars foibles and insatiable thirst for petrol, I will always have a soft spot for my inimitable 'Rover 90'

******

CHAPTER 34

My son Martin

Margaret had expressed her desire to have another baby and I was only too happy to contribute to its production. I had been having plenty of rehearsals for this eventuality and a live performance appealed to my creative nature, (rather an apt word wouldn't you say, 'creative'). I am certain that the way I threw myself into the roll I would have been critically acclaimed and once again our genes were intertwined, (No, our genes, not our jeans). Although come to think of it, our jeans may have became a bit entangled at times.

The result was possibly the best looking baby that the world has ever seen and he was born at 2-45pm on Sunday 18 October 1964, weighing 7 lbs. I feel that I must hasten to add that all of our children and subsequent grandchildren have all been world-class beauties. Martin, as we decided to call him, was indeed almost too bonny to be a boy. We used to get sick of people saying what a pretty girl he was so we had to start clothing him from head to toe in blue to give them a clue. His features were perfectly symmetrical and still are. He had a lovely head of platinum blonde curly hair that added to the confusion. His hair has darkened to a mid-brown and he has lost his curls over the years. He is 48 years old as I write this, he's over 6 feet tall (1-83 metres) and he is ludicrously handsome.

You will remember that I completely missed Graeme's birth because I was away in the army. Well, although I was with Margaret when she went into the 'Green' maternity hospital to have Martin, I still wasn't there for his arrival. This is because fathers were not allowed into the delivery room in those days. I had to wait until he had been cleaned up and placed into his mother's arms before I could go in. This was less traumatic and more sanitised for the poor stressed out fathers. I have to say that I am envious of the fathers of today that can be with their wives right through the birth. Martin was only about two years old when I sold my old Rover and I asked him once if he remembered my first car. I knew that he would know what it looked like from photographs but uncannily he could remember standing up in the front of the car (no seat belts in those days) and described the interior of the Rover to me. Just like me when I remembered being in my dad's arms and looking up at the searchlights and tracer shells during World War two.

He was always an even-tempered toddler and curious about everything around him. Where Graeme had to be amused all of the time or he would get stroppy, Martin would amuse himself by taking his toys to bits and trying to put them back together. I was told that I was the same myself as a small child, a sink full of water and a couple of wooden clothes pegs and I was set up for the day. Martin's curiosity did cause a bit of chaos I have to admit. On one occasion he squeezed behind the TV, braced himself against the wall and pushed the television over. The TV was smashed but luckily it was insured and Martin now knew what they looked like when they were horizontal. Another time he was curious about something on the top shelf in the china cabinet. The cabinet was about three feet high and one foot deep and it stood on four six-inch legs. It had two full sized glass doors and two glass display shelves, on which Margaret kept her best china tea set, ornaments, wine glasses etc, beautifully set out. The doors were set back and it formed a small ledge along the bottom. Martin was able to get his little foot onto the ledge and heave himself up until he had both feet on. The cabinet toppled over on top of him with a heart stopping crash of breaking glass. We were almost too afraid to lift it up in case we found him mutilated. By a miracle the doors hadn't broken and the noise of breaking glass had been the contents rearranging their molecular construction. Yes, toughened glass is a lifesaver and Martin was completely unharmed when it could have been a catastrophe.

I must tell you this story before I move on. When Martin was thirteen or fourteen years old, he brought home an old wreck of a 'Honda' 50cc step-through motorcycle. It looked as though it belonged on a scrap heap, the wiring harness had been pulled out and was in a clump, like a half eaten spaghetti Bolognese. I don't know where he got it but I'm sure they were glad to be rid of it. Margaret wanted him to take it straight down to the dump but he begged us to let him try to fix it. It was a lovely sunny day so I just laughed and opened the garage doors to give him access to my tools. I had previously owned a Honda 70cc step-through and I still had the workshop manual for it. He took the book outside with him and I admired his youthful optimism as he set about his seemingly impossible task. He was out there all day, only coming in for his meals and I realised that he had inherited my dad's patience I have often wished that I had too. After tea, Margaret and I were sitting watching the TV when there was the distinctive sound of a Honda step-through. We looked at each other in total disbelief, got up and rushed to the back door. Martin was riding his Honda up and down the drive grinning from ear to ear. I couldn't believe that he had done it I was so proud that I could have cried. He rode the bike on the field beside our house between Henley Gardens and the A19 road for months and eventually he threw it into a pond somewhere.

✶✶✶✶✶✶

COOLING HIS
FEET, IN THE
BACK YARD OF
61 GERALD ST.,
WALLSEND.

GRAEME AGED 2 YRS. 1964.

GRAEME WITH
HIS MOTHER AND
WELL HIDDEN
BROTHER MARTIN.
STEPPING STONES
OVER THE 'WANSBECK'
AT 'MORPETH.'

MARTIN SAFELY INSIDE
HIS MOTHER WITH GRAEME

'ME' WITH SON GRAEME
AND OUR FIRST CAR.
(1954 'ROVER 90') 1964.

'ME' WITH MY
'SCAMEL' TRUCK.
STILL DEFENDING
QUEEN AND COUNTRY.

And so, life went on as we adapted to having two little lads and still living with Margaret's parents. There was a point system for the allocation of council houses and by having Martin it meant that we would move up the list and be a step closer to acquiring our own rented home. This was due to our being considered as living in overcrowded conditions. Margaret, myself, Graeme and Martin all slept in the small back bedroom there was no bathroom or hot water and an outside lavatory. This was situated down the back stairs and across the yard. Bath time for the boys was in the old Belfast sink in the scullery. They did use the half size tin bath in the back yard now and then but not to get washed in like my two brothers and I did in Union Street. It was more recreational and they only used it to have a splash about in when it was really hot.

CHAPTER 35

67 Tarrington Close

We were favourably assessed and offered a council flat in 'Willington Square' a small housing estate in East Wallsend. I say flat but each home had two floors so they would be better described as maisonettes. You entered each dwelling off a balcony into a quite spacious entrance hall on the left of which was a door into a good-sized kitchen. If you went straight ahead it led you through a door into a huge living room that had a large south facing window. To the right of the front door in the hall was a flight of stairs that led you up to the second floor. Upstairs there was a large bedroom facing south and a smaller bedroom facing north, plus a decent sized bathroom/toilet. Number 67 occupied floors eight and nine of a fourteen-storey building. I think that this is why we had jumped up the waiting list for a house. Nobody had fancied the idea of living in one of these newfangled tower blocks that had sprang up. There were a group of three of these monolithic structures standing together like a row of giant gravestones. 'Tiverton Close' was to the east, 'Tarrington Close' in the middle and 'Taunton Close' to the west. They overlooked the Coast Road and the factory of George Angus & Co., Ltd. This was very convenient when you consider that I was working there. My sister Hilda lived above us on the tenth floor, my brother Bob lived in the four story flats next to Tiverton close and my brother Alan lived on Henley Gardens that was only about half a mile away. Alma, Alan and Bob all worked in George Angus & Co, along with me so we were still a very close-knit family.

I soon realised that this avian existence was not ideal for the bringing up of children. They would play with the other children that lived on our floor and would gather in the lift space and stairwells. Or they would ride their scooters or tricycles along the balcony that ran the full span of the building. The balcony ran past the front door of every home on each floor and it was about 4 feet wide (122cm) with a reinforced glass balustrade 4 feet high running the full length. Our children were not allowed to go down to the bottom to play among the lines of garages. It would have taken us too long to reach them from the eighth floor if they needed us. I have no idea what I thought my parents could have done to help me, when I could have been anywhere in Northumberland at that age. Perhaps that is why we tied the apron strings so tightly with knowing what I was like as a child. I have no doubt that my children have their own vivid memories of this elevated existence the good and the bad, they are all just pieces in their own unique, ever-changing, magic, jigsaw puzzle.

I have to say that the views were wonderful back and front. The living room and the big bedroom looked south over the Tyne valley and into County Durham (as it was called then). The kitchen, bathroom and small bedroom looked north to the fields of Northumberland and the distant Cheviot Hills. If you looked east when standing on the balcony you could clearly see the North Sea with St Mary's lighthouse on the coastline. Margaret and I found it hard to get to sleep when we first moved in because it was too quiet for us up there. We had lived our lives with the shipyards on our doorsteps and the din of the riveting and caulking machines and the clamour of shouting workmen went on 24 hours a day. The lack of noise kept us awake at night for quite some time until we got used to it. If there was a high wind you could feel the building sway when you were lying in your bed, it must have been amazing if you were sleeping on the 14th floor. There were two lifts in the building but they were forever breaking down. When both of them were out of order we had sixteen flights of stairs to climb. Margaret had the worst of it, because she would have bags of shopping to carry and two lively little boys to usher. She would have to leave the big 'Silver Cross' pram in the stairwell until I came home from work'. We got rid of the big Silver Cross pram and bought a pushchair to make it easier. It only served to make it easier for me because Margaret chose to haul the pushchair full of shopping up the sixteen flights of stairs while ushering the kids ahead of her. As I have said before she is a pocket-sized dynamo who would put the vast majority of men (including me) to shame. We lived in the maisonette for three years and we were very happy, even with its dodgy lifts.

CHAPTER 36

My daughter Kim

Margaret had given up work with the birth of our first son Graeme. I was proud of the fact that she hadn't needed to go back to work since that time. I still had vivid memories of my mam toiling in a factory for 54 hours per week including alternate nightshifts.

I was away for my two weeks army training at 'Borden' in 'Hampshire' when towards the end of my training I received a letter from Margaret proudly telling me that she had procured herself a job in the pay department of 'British Ropes'. They had taken over the old 'Haggies' Rope Factory in 'Willington Quay' Wallsend. I was furious at this unexpected announcement we hadn't even spoken about her returning to work. I felt that it undermined my ability as a husband and provider and I was still livid when I arrived home late on the Friday night. Under normal circumstances I would have dropped my kitbag and pounced on Margaret in the hallway. Before I got my greatcoat off we would have been lying up the stairs renewing our friendship shall we say. On this occasion I petulantly brushed her aside without a word or a kiss. I sat on the living room sofa with a pathetic 'how could you do this to me' look on my face. Margaret was looking hurt and bewildered as I churlishly berated her, "How could you get a job without talking to me first and making it look as though I can't provide for us", (Yes, this is how daft I was).

She began to cry and kept asking me how I could be so horrible to her. I had never made her cry before and it was like a knife in my heart. I quickly lost my childish illusion of holding the moral high ground and adopted the more accurate thoughtless bastard persona. I explained to her that I believed that I had to be the breadwinner in the family and that she should never have to go out to work. She in turn explained that she needed to go out to work to keep her brain from atrophying. I found this concept strange because if someone had told me that I didn't need to go out to work ever again I would have been a happy young man. No doubt I would have became an old man with a fossilized walnut for a brain today and there are some that might say that I did anyway. Needless to say my contrition was absolute and I grovelled my way back into her affections and this time we made it past the staircase.

Margaret loved her new job working in the pay department, calculating the wages of the men from their worksheets. She dealt with enquiries and made up the pay packets to be distributed to the workforce. Her sister Connie was looking after Graeme and Martin so she was completely relaxed about their welfare. This contented state of affairs only lasted for about three months before she discovered that she was pregnant again. I was in the doghouse because she was convinced that I had impregnated her deliberately to stop her from working. I swore (and indeed still swear) that this was not the case although I can see why she would have come to this conclusion.

Because we both disliked the mechanics of contraception as I have stated earlier, we relied solely on what I will entitle the '3 ITY' and '1 ETY' form of birth control.

Sensitiv(ITY). = Knowing when the event is about to take place.

Controllabil(ITY). = Being able to delay the event.

Agil(ITY). = Being able to outpace the event.

Sobri(ETY). = Don't drink and drive, so to speak.

Call it what you like, coitus interruptus, paying the full fare but getting off before the terminus, it is by no stretch of the imagination a foolproof method and so if I needed a defence I could plead temporary insanity.

So, Kim my darling daughter, if you are reading this, you were in fact an accidental conception but a happy one for us. You are in good company because both your mother and I are the youngest children of large families. Both of our mothers were over 40 years old when we were born so you would have to be daft to think that we were planned. I was aware that Margaret was happier and had more to talk about in the evenings since she had started work again and I was happy for her. If getting her pregnant was deliberate then it must have been on a subliminal level of consciousness. I have been under suspicion of sabotage and wilful distribution of rampant spermatozoa for many years but forgiven due to the end results, a daughter that we both wanted.

Kim was born in the 'Willington Quay' maternity hospital, Wallsend. Wednesday 24th May 1967 at 4-45am and weighing 9lbs-1oz. Now this is a large baby by anyone's standards and guaranteed to make a superhero's eyes water. Margaret is only 4feet 11inches (1-5 meters) so perhaps it was a good thing that I wasn't allowed in at the birth, they would probably have been stepping over my recumbent form. I can imagine a scene with Margaret in two halves and a smaller Margaret being lifted out like one of those Russian dolls. (Good plot for a story that).

There were no mobile phones and very few telephones in working class houses in those days so the first I new about it was when I called in to see her at 7am on my way to work. She was sitting up with a cup of tea and looking radiant only two hours after what must have been an ordeal for her. My beautiful daughter Kim was lying in her crib next to her beautiful mother. She had a full head of black hair to begin with but it turned blonde to match her two brothers very quickly. None of our children ever kept us awake all night like the offspring of some of our friends and they were always really contented. We had the occasional bad night if they were teething but very rarely.

Kim was a lovely bright little girl and I suppose you could say a daddy's girl.

This is of course before puberty set in and I was outranked by spotty little gobshites, (OK, a touch of karma I suppose). They knew more about life and the universe than I could ever hope to glean in a thousand lifetimes. This was in spite of the fact that most of them would have had difficulty tying their own shoelaces. The rosy mist would eventually clear and she would see through their façade and dump them, only to meet another spotty little gobshite. Ask any father of a teenage girl and you will hear the same plaintive story. Once a girl acquires her menstrual cycle her common sense promptly rides off on it. A strategy that I honed for the protection of my girl was for me to find a chink in the armour of these young Lothario's and pick at it until she noticed the flaw. One time that I remember was with a lad that had failed to impress me for some reason or another and I asked him if he had any hobbies. He said that he had an air rifle and that he liked shooting. I was delighted with the prospects in this piece of information, if he just shot at targets it would be of no use to me but if he preferred to shoot at living creatures then I knew that his days were numbered. Kim, like all of our family love animals and anyone who would kill an animal solely for sport and not to eat it are deemed as beneath human contempt. So, I pressed on with my cordial enquiries asking him what sort of things he shot at. He was only too pleased to tell me what inspired his manly pursuit, mice, rats, rabbits, birds. It would seem that there was no end to the savage creatures that dwelt in our midst and he had slain or at least maimed his share of them. To the unknowing eye, Kim's facial expression hardly changed but I knew that his bridges had been well and truly burned. I asked her a few days later what had happened to the great white hunter and she just said that he had been binned as soon as they left our house, 'RESULT'.

I will now give you a couple of little anecdotes involving Kim that always amuse me. I had collected Martin and Kim from the 'Denbigh Avenue Primary' school in Wallsend. As I walked home holding each of their hands, Kim (six years old) was chattering away excitedly about being in the egg and spoon race in the school playground. She was telling me how fast she had ran and how she had won the race. Martin (eight and a half years old) looked around me at his sister and said, "No you didn't". Kim said, even louder, "YES I DID". Martin calmly informed her that she had dropped her egg in the middle of the race, so her win didn't count. She was silent for a few seconds and then she said, "Oh, well fuck you then".

I was gobsmacked and Martins eyes were out on stalks as he held his free hand over his mouth. I asked her where she had learnt a word like that and she said that she couldn't remember. I told her that it was a very rude word and that she wasn't to say it again. She looked up at me like an Angel and said, "All right daddy I won't". We walked home in silence while I struggled to stifle a laugh. I was secretly quite impressed by the fact that she had used the profanity in the correct context. It wasn't surprising I suppose, from being a baby she had always been good with talking and understanding English and now it would seem that she was becoming fluent in the Anglo Saxon version.

On another occasion when she was about twelve years old, we were all sitting down at the table for our tea. She informed me that she was learning about sex at school now. "That's nice", I ventured hesitantly. "We learned about menstruation today", she volunteered. I had no desire to pursue this worthy topic but felt obliged to smile and look interested. As I had expected, Kim expounded on the gynaecological workings of the female body. Her brothers were looking a bit queasy but I have to admit that I was becoming a wiser man with regards to these inner mysteries. She was quiet for a while and then she said, "Next week we are going to learn all about contraception". An icy hand gripped my heart as she turned her innocent little face (or so I thought) towards me. "Do you know what contraception is then dad"? She asked me sweetly. I had always vowed to answer my children's questions about sexual matters as honestly as I could because

I had been as green as grass in that department until I was in my mid-teens. So I replied, "Well sweetheart, contraception is something that a man and a woman who love each other have to use so that they don't have any more babies until they are ready". She thought for a moment and then said, "Oh, you mean like 'Blobs' that sort of thing", (Blobs being a slang word for condoms). Graeme spit a mouthful of food all over the table, Martin once again clamped a hand over his mouth and Margaret looked stunned. Resignedly I just said, "Yes Kim, like Blobs". I hadn't known what a Blob was until I was about sixteen so she had shown me once again her grasp of the English language, this time it was the colloquial variation.

CHAPTER 37

Kendal Gardens

Well, there you have it, I told you in Chapter 30 that when I had documented the births of our three children I would bring this chronicle to a close and I gave you my reasons for this decision.

So at the end of this time capsule I am in 1967, aged 26years, with a perfect wife and our full complement of perfect children. I have a well paid job that I love going to in the mornings. Mrs Thatcher (Hoick, Spit,) has not yet stirred from her demonic pit, OH! JOY. This would have been my final paragraph if Margaret had not told me that I should at least carry on writing until we have moved house again. This is fair I suppose when you consider that we were going to be in this house for 44 years up to the point in time that I am writing this, (And many more to come I hope).

By having Kim, we were now eligible to apply for a three bedroom council house. I duly applied but was told that it would be quite a while because the list was a long one. The girl in the council office told me that my best course of action was to try and arrange an exchange with someone. I was telling my sister Hilda who lived on the 10th floor about our hopes to arrange an exchange and she got excited. Hilda was now divorced and remarried to a nice bloke called Ronnie Plumb. Her brother-in-law, a bachelor called Andy Plumb had wanted an exchange into Tarrington Close to be near his brother. Unfortunately although Andy's house was lovely and in a nice area it still only had two bedrooms. I went back to the council housing office to ask if it would be possible to swap anyway so that my children would have more freedom to play outside. The girl in the office told us that there was someone in a three-bedroom house who wanted to downsize but would not move into our 14-story block. So she suggested that we should organise a three-way swap. This would entail the person in the three-bedroom house moving into Andy's, us moving into the three-bedroom house and Andy moving into our Maisonette.

To our joy, they put us in touch with a woman in Kendal gardens, High Howdon, Wallsend. She was happy after inspecting Andy's house and the complicated three-way exchange was organized. As you can imagine it had to be timed perfectly so that we all had access with our furniture. A few days before the move the woman asked me for some money because she reckoned that her gas-cooker was in better condition than the one at Andy's house. I don't remember how much it was that she asked for but I had no intentions of giving it to her. I told her that the council supplied all of the gas-cookers and that if she had any complaints she should take it up with them. The transformation was quite scary as she slowly changed from being a mild mannered woman into a venomous old witch. She snarled at me, "Well if that's the case, the exchange is off". Then she slammed the door in my face.

I went straight over to the housing office to explain the situation and the housing officer went ballistic. He told me that this was the third time that she had done this and that she was not going to get away with it again. I don't know what he did or said to her but Andy and I got word to say that the move was still on. I don't know whether it was some sort of scam she had been trying to pull or just a ploy when she had changed her mind. Regardless, the change in her demeanour was an unpleasant thing to have witnessed. I remember thinking that I wouldn't want to live next door to her. Happily the exchange went off without a hitch and I never had the need to encounter the old harpy ever again. She did have the last laugh though and I will explain how she achieved this.

All council houses that were built during the period when these houses were built were fitted with a unique set of electric wall sockets. They were unique because you could only purchase the plugs for your various electric appliances from the town hall or council offices. Normal plugs at the time were exactly the same as they are today, with three flat pins and an internal fuse. These plugs had three round pins and the fuse screwed into the plug to become the 'live' pin. Tenants of these council houses were obliged to leave all of their plugs behind when they vacated a property. As you may have guessed, she had taken them all away with her plus every light bulb in the house. To make it worse, it was the weekend and the town hall and council office was closed so I was unable to buy any. I had to dash around to my brother Alan and my sisters Joan and Alma's houses to borrow a few off each of them because they lived in the same type of houses. This met with our immediate needs and at least we could make ourselves a cup of tea. I could have reported her spiteful behaviour to the housing officer but I was just happy to have made the swap at last. I was also quite amused by her childish but highly successful revenge for not being allowed to have her own way. I soon acquired a full compliment of plugs and bulbs to satisfy our needs and we began our new life in our new home. A home I have to say, that we have been happy in for half a century. Apart that is for the first week or so.

✿ ✿ ✿ ✿ ✿ ✿

Margaret and I had the large front bedroom, Kim was to have the small front bedroom and Graeme and Martin the medium sized back bedroom. Unfortunately, for the first couple of weeks the two boys also shared their room with a malignant presence of some kind. I am not joking and Margaret would confirm the validity of this because she shared the experience, this really was scary stuff.

Every night the two boys would start screaming as though on cue at exactly 10pm. As we ran up the stairs we could see them through the open bedroom door illuminated by the stair-head light. They would both be sitting up in their beds staring and pointing at the dark wall behind the bedroom door out of our line of sight. As we rushed into the room switching on the light they would stop screaming and lie down sleeping peacefully. They never mentioned it the following day and were never too scared to go to bed. It was very uncanny and unsettling for us and we found ourselves waiting every night at 10pm for it to begin. They were both too young and not good enough actors to have conceived such a complicated practical joke. Besides that there were no timepieces of any kind in their room to give them their cue to begin. Remember that I had been raised in a haunted house and this was not benign as 'Charlie' had been. This unhappy occurrence continued for over a week at 10pm every night like clockwork. At last I decided to have a showdown with this entity even though it scared me more than I admitted.

I went up to the room while the boys were screaming and pointing at the wall but I didn't put the light on and as I entered I could feel a cold chill in the air. There was definitely an angry presence there and in response, my own fears turned into rage against this invasive obscenity. As I stood between my screaming sons in the dark chilled air I said loudly, "IF YOU DON'T LEAVE THIS HOUSE, I WILL DAMN YOUR SOUL TO THE DEEPEST PITS OF HELL".

I swear to God that this is a true event and that the malignancy vanished in an instant. My children were never disturbed again and as far as I know they don't recall any of it. Reading this may in fact be the first that they have heard of our shared phenomenon. From that moment on, the house became a warm and welcoming place and remains so to this day. In my mind, I have always suspected the former resident of still harbouring a grudge and projecting her spite filled thoughts. I have read that poltergeists are possibly the manifestations of disturbed human minds.

⚹⚹⚹⚹⚹⚹

UR CHILDREN ON SAFARI IN THE BACK GARDEN

KIM (AGE 1.)
MARTIN (AGED 4.)   1968.
GRAEME (AGED 6.)

BACK
GARDEN
AT
KENDAL
GARDENS

AS THE GARDEN IS NOW. A BIT MORE CIVILISED.

'MY WORLD', MARGARET + M
KIM, MARTIN, GRAEME.
1968.

I LOVE THIS PHOTOGRAPH

And so I have reached my (then) age of 27 years old in this journal. I have related my childhood, my adolescence, my courtship, my apprenticeship, my wedding and the birth of my three children. Also, I have taken up residence in what is most likely to be my last home. Now, almost three quarters of a century after my first memory of searchlight's and tracer shells in the sky as my dad held me in his arms, I will bring this opus to its conclusion. Remember that what I have documented here has only been approximately one third of my life. The other two thirds have been incredible I can promise you. Far from settling down to live out our lives in harmonious domestic bliss, we have been fortunate enough to circumnavigate the earth several times. Apart from Europe and most of the Mediterranean Islands, we have driven across Texas in the good old USA, from Houston to San Antonio to visit the 'Alamo'. We have dined with the 'Amish' people (Pennsylvania Dutch) not far from Philadelphia. We have ridden the subway in New York and gazed in awe from the top of the Empire State Building. I have used the toilets in the iconic Capital Building in Washington DC. Not just for number one's let me add, yes, for number two's, how many among you can make that claim? (HA! I thought as much). Every time I see the building in films or on TV I am compelled to declare that I have defecated in it to anyone who will listen, as though it gives me some sort of celebrity status. After having been subjected to the 'Haka' war dance and chant, we have been feasted by Maori tribesmen and travelled from one end of New Zealand to the other. We have walked the hills of South Korea. We have sailed the harbour of Sydney. We have wandered the streets of Shanghai and walked the huge city walls of 'Xi an' where we visited the Terracotta Soldiers in the amazing country of China. We have sailed down the River Nile in Egypt and flown in a hot air Balloon over the 'Valley of the Kings'. I have peed off high objects in most of these exotic locations and best of all I have made love to my woman on every Continent apart from the 'Antarctic' and 'South America', (There may still be time). So you see that there is plenty of material to write several more books if I could be bothered.

I will probably continue to write some anecdotes of my life in a non-chronological way just as they come to me. Perhaps I will try my hand at some short fictional stories and poems for my own amusement and possibly yours.

THANK YOU FOR YOUR TENACITY.

XXX

X

EPILOGUE

I will now encapsulate my life for those who are less disposed to reading.

Childhood

I can only describe my childhood as idyllic my every moment was filled with love and security. My mother and father were and still are iconic in my eyes as parents. My family were an eclectic mix of eccentrics but wonderful to be a part of. If I was able to change the past, it would be to have my parent's lot in life be a bit easier. They had a hard life raising six children with little or no money and no handouts from a welfare system because there was no welfare system back then. I was blissfully unaware of any hardship or the fact that they sometimes didn't eat so that the rest of us could. God, I love them.

Schooldays

I used to think that I hated school but now like most people I realise what a great time it was. I wish now that I had studied more because I know that I have always been an under-achiever. As my old teacher 'Fred Airey' told me, I have a lazy brain. As that nautical hero 'Popeye' used to say, "I am what I am and that's all what I am".

Teenage Years

A wonderful awakening of the body and then the brain tries to catch up.

Apprenticeship

One long playtime but taking in just enough engineering tuition to turn me into a passable mechanical fitter/machinist.

Courtship

Absolute bliss, as you would expect.

Marriage

This was my best decision by far. I realised early on that there was no place that I wanted to be where Margaret was not. She awakened me with our first kiss and in my seventies she can still awaken me.

Early Parenthood

I basked in the adulation of our beautiful children

Adult Parenthood

It can be fleeting and emotional with periods of sunshine. Witnessing the change from adulation to toleration can be a bit sad especially when you have had to witness it happening three times but perhaps I'm just too sensitive for my own good. Margaret still looks at me with adulation from time to time and this restores me.

SEVENTEEN

SEVENTY

MARTIN
6.

KIM
3.

GRAEME
8.

KIM, MARTIN, GRAEME,
44.   47.   49.

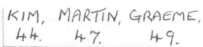

THE RESULTS.

403

IT'S NOT THE FIRST
TIME THAT MARGARET
HAS BEEN LIFTED UP
BY A BAG OF HOT AIR
SHE SAYS.

BALLOON RIDE OVER THE
'VALLEY OF THE KINGS.'

MARGARET POSING WITH TWO OLD RELICS.

'DONALD' MY LAST PROPER MOTORBIKE
750 cc SHAFT DRIVEN 'KAWASAKI' SPECTRE
BUILT 1982. REGISTRATION N°, EPT407X.

MY ARTHRITIC KNEES
FORCED ME TO SELL
'DONALD' WHEN I WAS
72 YEARS OLD.

'DONALD' + ME
ONE LAST RIDE. (NO HELMET, STILL NAUGHTY).

405

MY SUBSTITUTE AFTER 'DONALD'
200ᶜᶜ PIAGIO 'VESPA' G.T.
REGISTRATION Nº., NKO3XDS

IT WAS A LOVELY NIPPY
LITTLE BIKE BUT NOT
'DONALD' AND MARGARET
DIDN'T LIKE THE SMALL
WHEELS.

SELF APPRAISAL

Having read through this book I am aware that I am not as nice a person as I thought I was. Not many of us would come out smelling of roses after a lifetime I suppose that is if we are honest with ourselves. I don't think that I am a bad person compared to many others that I have known but there is room for improvement I have to say. I know that I have a sarcastic sense of humour that is often seen as very amusing, at other times though it can be very cutting. I apologise to anyone that has been stung unwittingly by my dubious wit. I say unwittingly, because I have been known to use my sardonic humour as a weapon of derision when I have wanted to. So, what I may have thought was light-hearted witty banter, could have been misconstrued as an insult by someone with an innocent outlook. You walk a thin line when you engage in sarcasm and that is the truth.

I don't think that I am spiteful or envious and I hate duplicity. If I have a grievance I am inclined to air it at once and attempt to sort things out. This straight talking is not popular and I have lost count of the times when it would have been wiser just to bite my tongue. I hope that I have not hurt too many people over the years without just cause.

I try to be considerate and respectful to everyone, whatever their social background is, or their colour, culture, religion or sexual orientation as long as this respect is reciprocated. (I am still adverse to people with conservative leanings but I tolerate them because I know that I am the better human being after all). Believe it or not, I have been led to believe by some people, that I may be opinionated.

SUMMARY

Remember that our 'Self' is made up of the sum of our genetic memories and our own personal memories this means that each of us is a unique creature.

Therefore, I am the only 'me' that has ever existed and this makes me happy. I don't know if I will depart this life in excruciating pain or in rapturous peace but I am thankful for my time in the Sun.

MY OWN FINAL WORDS.
"I HAVE KNOWN SUCH EXQUISITE MOMENTS"

'THE END'
'Or is it?'

POST SCRIPT

I finished this chronicle a couple of years ago and I have been persuaded now to have it made into a book. Having my ego stroked like that at the age of seventy five is somewhat pleasant I must admit and the idea of having my story in print appeals to my vanity.

I feel that it is necessary to bring a few things up to date just because I think that I should. Firstly, all of my siblings, Joan, Hilda, Alma, Alan and Bob have now passed on and I am the last of the brood of Hilda May and Archie Blevins. I am not sad because I know that I was privileged to be a part of this family and that it will go on.

Margaret and I alone have contributed our own children, 'Graeme-William', 'Martin' and 'Kim'. They in turn have contributed our grandchildren, (Lewis-William and Sean-Graeme), (Robert-Liam and Kate-Willow), (Ethan). I think that the gene pool is well stocked. Keep up the good work children, you are my immortality.

Lightning Source UK Ltd.
Milton Keynes UK
UKHW02f1144130318
319349UK00009B/328/P